GARRISONS
AND
GOVERNMENT

Chandler Publications in
POLITICAL SCIENCE
VICTOR JONES, *Editor*

GARRISONS
AND
GOVERNMENT

Politics and the Military
in New States

Edited by

Wilson C. McWilliams

OBERLIN COLLEGE

CHANDLER PUBLISHING COMPANY
124 Spear Street, San Francisco, California 94105

CONTENTS

SUMMATION

PREFACE

*When Joab and all the army that was with him came, it
was told Joab, "Abner the son of Ner came to the king,
and he has let him go, and he has gone in peace." Then
Joab went to the king and said, "What have you done?
Behold, Abner came to you; why is it that you have sent
him away, so that he is gone? You know that Abner the
son of Ner came to deceive you, and to know your going
out and your coming in, and to know all that you are
doing."— II Samuel 3: 23–25*

The relations between the state and the military form part
of a skein which is bound up in the fabric of human history. Since
the beginning of the tale, states have put arms in the hands of
men; generals have counseled kings; statesmen have sought to
entwine armies with the cords of law. (*Deuteronomy* 20 contains
a code for the organization of the army and the conduct of war.)
Yet, like all perennialities, there is a pulse in the study of those
relations, surging when the salience of armies in politics is high
and receding as it declines. In the nineteenth century, the voice
of scholarship sunk to a whisper; it has become increasingly
thunderous since 1914.

Too many studies, however, share that defect to which
Tacitus pointed in *The Histories:* The military is often hidden
from public scrutiny, leaving students without adequate information and popular commentators with few alternatives between
panegyrics and paranoid suspicion. As the Roman knew, in such
situations it is easy to identify and discount the adulator, but the
equally uncritical assailant may seem to possess independence
and objectivity.

The Second World War stimulated efforts at a more genuine

vii

understanding of military organizations, typified by Samuel Stouffer and his associates' massive *The American Soldier* and by the continuing studies of Morris Janowitz. Yet, the greater number of such studies have been isolated by the walls of specialization, lacking in comparative analysis in relation to other disciplines, to other states, and especially to other periods of history. Many have been wanting in theoretical focus and concern. Fortunately, students have had before them Hans Speier's magisterial example, and political scientists like Samuel Huntington and David Rapoport have ably followed it. Inevitably, of course, their work—like this book—can be only a small beginning in the examination of a field which begins with Cain and which has no ending short of man himself. Still, slight beginnings and even darkened understandings may be of help to our vision in a world of which we know little. It is in that spirit that this collection has been prepared.

Its genesis may most immediately be traced to the Conference on the Military in the Developing Nations, held at Oberlin College under the auspices of the student International Affairs Committee in the spring of 1965. But it would be possible to trace the causes of this book further back along a chain of events, in which the most important might be the reflections that grew out of my own military service.

Like David Rapoport, I was struck by the fact that the United States Army, far from being the most "un-American" of institutions, could only have been invented by Americans. If a book like this one may properly have a dedication, it would have to be offered to those comrades-in-arms who taught me part of the meaning of the honored phrase, *Ich hatt' einen Kameraden:* Robert Graham, who saw the army with the eyes of an artist; my commanders, Wallace M. Hanes, Eldred Weber, Edgar Fenstemacher, Glyn Pohl, Angus Mundy, and Fritoso Lopez; and the officers and men of the 11th Airborne Division, 1955–1957.

That list, though extensive, leaves too many unnamed among creditors whose due can never be repaid. John Gitlitz and George Lewis made valuable research contributions to the Introduction, and the members of the International Affairs Committee, Oberlin College, contributed much time, enthusiasm, and suggestion to the manuscript. Dennis Hale, Mitchell Cohen, and Jonathan Eisen provided the sympathetic assistance of critics and friends. Finally, I owe much to John D. Lewis, Ewart K. Lewis, George A. Lanyi, John H. Schaar, Norman Jacobson, and Ernst B. Haas for their constant inspiration as teachers and as scholars.

GARRISONS
AND
GOVERNMENT

Introduction

Historical Views of the Military in Politics

The study of politics embraces all the organizations and collectivities by which men have sought to realize and to defend the good life. Simply because armed forces are among those organizations, they are worthy of attention, both in themselves and as parts of larger societies and polities. The vocabulary of politics and the vocabulary of the military overlap, and the common terms are of critical importance to both: power, force, authority, patriotism, discipline, loyalty, honor, duty, order.

Although that catalogue of stern words suggests some of the dramatic relation between the military and politics, it is too prosaic to capture that relationship entirely. The annals of political history, contemporary and past, are punctuated by military events. Few would deny that military organizations have played a prominent role in that history; fewer still would neglect the importance of war, insurrection, and revolution in the shaping of politics.

To be sure, the majority of modern social scientists have tended to see the military as only a reflection of deeper and more fundamental processes in society and politics—a dramatic and flashy reflection, surely, but for that reason likely to mislead the uninitiated. Even these social scientists have normally conceded that the trained observer could profitably examine military institutions for clues and indications as to the nature of the "basic" forces at work.[1]

To an older tradition in political science, however, the role of the military in politics was by no means so dependent or passive. Aristotle, for example, credited military organization

---

[1] For an example, see Friedrich Engels, "The Armies of Europe," *Putnam's, 6* (1855), 193–206.

with an important, though not exclusive, influence on the form of government prevailing in a particular state.[2]

Other political scientists regarded even such a concession as too limited and as bespeaking only naïveté. "History teaches," wrote Gaetano Mosca, "that the class that bears the lance or holds the musket regularly forces its rule upon the class that handles the spade or pushes the shuttle." [3] To such theorists, it appeared that men might seduce those who controlled force through the temptations of wealth, the yearning for admiration and affection, or the exaltation of religious faith and moral idealism; but in any contest, it was force that prevailed.[4] It was not necessary to deny the existence of moral courage among men or the appeal, for some, of virtue for itself. It was necessary only to contend that such motives were, for most men, weak ones. Few could meet the standard of Epictetus, who announced that a tyrant would be unable to enslave him, being able only to cut off his head.[5] Politics, this school contended, is shaped by the average rather than the exceptional man, and for most, force is the *ultima ratio,* the last argument and arbiter, if not the first basis or highest hope, of political action. As Machiavelli wrote:

Thus it comes about that all armed prophets have conquered and unarmed ones failed; for . . . the character of peoples varies and it is easy to persuade them of a thing but difficult to keep them in that persuasion. And so it is necessary to so order things that when they no longer believe, they can be made to believe by force.[6]

Whether they regarded the military as an independent or dependent variable (or as both in any concrete situation), political scientists have conceded the importance of the military as an area of study. Most, moreover, have caught some glimpse of the

[2] Aristotle, *Politics,* Sir Ernest Barker, ed. (Oxford: Clarendon Press, 1952) , Book IV, Chaps. 3, 13; Book VI, Chap. 7.

[3] Gaetano Mosca, *The Ruling Class* (New York: McGraw-Hill, 1939) , p. 228. The statement, taken out of context, is an oversimplification of Mosca's thesis.

[4] S. Andrzejewski, *Military Organization and Society* (London: Routledge and Kegan Paul, 1954) , pp. 26–28.

[5] Epictetus, *Discourses,* T. N. Higginson, trans. (New York: Walter Black, 1944) , Book I, Chap. 19; Book IV, Chap. 1.

[6] Machiavelli, *The Prince* (New York: Modern Library, 1950; orig. pub. 1532) , Chap. 6, p. 22. See also Machiavelli's *Discourses on the First Ten Books of Livy* in the same publication (orig. pub. 1531) , Book I, Chap. 27.

grandeur and the horror that have made armies and soldiers the subject of the tales and songs of agony and glory, of heroism and futility. The tales and songs reflect an interest in the military that is as old—or older—than politics, a human perenniality which helps explain the fact that the study of the relations of politics and the military is as old as political science itself.

Antiquity admired the strong of arm and the steadfast in battle, but the classic hero was far from a "military man." He fought individual combats, a solitary warrior reveling in his own strength. Herakles was closer than many imagine to the barroom tough who can "lick any man in the house." [7] In fact, one can easily conceive of the first military forces as a union of weaker or more pacific men formed in order to constrain the hero. The idea of an army involves some reference to discipline, and discipline in turn implies organization for a purpose, a challenge not to men in general but to particular men at particular times. Yet, that does not tell us what purpose or goals a military will or should seek.

When Plato examined the nature of courage, he rejected the idea that the hero who "knows no fear" has true courage. To be deemed courageous, a man must *know* fear but face it nonetheless as a "lesser evil." Further, to be deemed truly courageous, a man must know the greater evil and the greater good. The highest courage, for Plato, included a knowledge of the good itself and hence a knowledge of all the other virtues and "goods" of men. No man possesses such knowledge, and the highest form of courage among men lies in facing one's ignorance, in realizing that until knowledge is gained, all the vaunted courage and virtue may, in the event, prove to be no more than sham.[8]

---

[7] Hans Speier, *The Social Order and the Risks of War* (New York: George Stewart, 1952) , pp. 112–128.

[8] *Laches*, W. R. M. Lamb, trans. (Loeb Classical Library; Cambridge, Mass.: Harvard University Press, 1946) , *passim*. Nicias, who makes the Socratic argument that courage is knowledge, ties this knowledge to the ability to foresee the future. Yet Nicias, the Athenian commander at Syracuse, was proverbial for his hesitation and indecisiveness; a man who would know everything—and especially, everything about the future—before acting can hardly be said to have courage. Laches, his counterpart, is said to be like Lamachos, Nicias's co-commander at Syracuse. Lamachos's courage, however, was of the unreflecting variety that caused him to perish in the battle, so that whatever balance he may have provided for Nicias was lost.

That seemingly academic discussion forms the basis of a coherent philosophy of armies and of war. War is not the noblest pursuit of man or even the most courageous. At best, it is a necessary deviation from what is truly the bravest of human endeavors. Plato defended a "professional" army in *The Republic,* but with arguments that were double-edged. Guardians had the virtue of being kindly to friends and savage to enemies, but that virtue is said to be the quality of dogs and not of men. Indeed, the virtue of the Guardian is identical to the "helping one's friends and hurting one's enemies" which already, early in the dialogue, has been proved to be unjust.[9] Perhaps military training may serve as a stage in the education of the young; war can be justified only as a melancholy necessity bound up with the nature of things.

It also follows that rulers must seek to make their soldiers as just men as circumstances permit (else the rulers would themselves be unjust). Hence, war must be fought, not to harm the enemies, but only to dissuade them from their injustice in attacking the state. This policy requires restraint and also some grounding in the principles of true courage. Consequently, it follows that soldiers should be as few and as highly trained as necessity permits, for any dilution of quality weakens the constraints on injustice.[10]

This doctrine of war and arms influenced the development of the doctrine of just war *(justum bellum)* and that of the Christian and secular theories which derive their premises from it.

The philosophy of Thomas Hobbes differed greatly from that of Plato, but Hobbes yielded nothing in his detestation of war. Nevertheless, Hobbes observed: "Covenants, without the sword, are but words." He was far from disparaging the importance of covenants, which he regarded as the foundation of all justice. Rather, he was insisting that a covenant is vulnerable to foreign or to private violence if it lacks the force of the public sword. Covenants were the result of shared ends among citizens:

[9] *The Republic,* Benjamin Jowett, trans. (New York and Boston: Books, Inc., 1943), Book II, pp. 373–376; Book V, pp. 468–471.

[10] Plato suggested, obviously, that such a dilution would take place, possibly because of military necessity; hence this suggestion that monarchy degenerates into timocracy.

desire for survival, security, and protection against arbitrariness. A covenant whose members will not take the sword is no covenant at all, for each member must realize that his escape from the state of war is bound up with his unity with his fellows. Hobbes denied that the citizen had surrendered to the state the right to defend his life, and it would be hard to justify offensive war on the basis of such a doctrine. Yet Hobbes clearly felt that the individual had some duty to defend the state; to refuse to do so would be equivalent to preferring despotism or the state of war to the rule of reason.[11]

Hobbes, Plato, and a host of other theorists contended, in short, that the army could claim no higher station than that of servant to the community in those cases where human folly, pride, and ambition outweighed the claims of understanding and the appeals of reason. A soldier's sacrifices might be deserving of honor, not because of the intrinsic worth of military valor, but because of the value of the community and the institutions for which the sacrifice was made.

Neither Plato nor Hobbes was part of the long tradition of theorists who argued that a citizen militia was the highest form of military organization.[12] Plato conceded that in an instance of extreme necessity and peril it might be proper to arm the citizenry, but this was clearly an exceptional and negative case.[13] Others, who viewed the Roman Republic through the glasses of nostalgia, were inclined to make a more positive argument, seeing in the decline of military virtue among the people the *fons et origo* of military defeat and despotism alike.[14]

Yet militia forces had proved inadequate when troops were required to remain in arms for extended periods or to serve on frontiers far from their civilian homes. Equally, it failed when military art demanded extended training or technical skill. The

[11] *Leviathan*, Michael Oakeshott, ed. (Oxford: Blackwell, 1946; orig. pub. 1651) , Chaps. 14, 17.

[12] For a Thomistic example of this tradition, see Aegidius Romanus, *De Regimine Principum* (Rome, 1482; orig. pub. 1285) , Book IV, Chaps. 10, 11, 25.

[13] *The Laws*, R. G. Bury, trans. (Loeb Classical Library; Cambridge, Mass.: Harvard University Press, 1952) , Book VII, p. 814; Book VIII, p. 830. Aristotle, *Politics*, Book II, Chap. 5, pp. 1264–1265.

[14] C. C. Bayley, *War and Society in Renaissance Florence* (Toronto: University of Toronto Press, 1961) .

militia model could apply only to a small, defensive city which,
by the grace of fortune, was assailed neither by persistent nor by
better armed foes. Friedrich Engels was to share the admiration
of the Renaissance for the militia, seeing in the tribal armies of
the ʿGermans a kind of primitive democracy. (Indeed, many of
the utopian hopes of Marxism are based on the belief that such a
posse comitatus can again come to substitute for the standing
forces of "the state.") Ultimately, Engels realized that changes in
the economy and in social organization had made the militia
system militarily unviable.[15]

Machiavelli's argument may seem only another of the naïve
rhetorical appeals for a restored militia in which many Renaissance authors indulged themselves. One central problem of *The
Prince* was the inability of the petty princes and small states of
Italy to defeat large, well-armed invaders like France and Spain.
Machiavelli argued that war is a concern not of mercenaries, but
of rulers and of peoples. The great state requires a prince to give
unified and effective command to its armies, and in an important
sense war is his *only* concern. If the prince is to have a good
army, he must recruit it from his own subjects. Such recruitment
demands a great deal of public support for the prince and
necessitates some elements of republican or democratic government. That conclusion may seem pleasant to the modern eye, but
the argument which reaches it presumes that war is the chief
concern and purpose of the state, not merely a sad necessity. The
state, to the Machiavellian, should write its laws so as to secure
good arms rather than strive to find good arms to defend laws
judged valuable on their own account.

This doctrine reflected an outlook which Machiavelli shared
with many of his contemporaries. Nature was regarded as alien
and hostile to man, governed by blind and indifferent forces. It
was man's best part to pit his own will and force against nature,
to combat what otherwise was his fate and destiny. Man might
help compensate for his weakness in force by the firmness of his
will. The very indifference of nature, moreover, made it possible
that her forces might be understood, mastered, and turned to

[15] Friedrich Engels, *The Origin of the Family, Private Property and the
State* (Chicago: C. Kerr, 1902), pp. 183–190. Machiavelli, *Discourses,* Book III,
Chap. 24.

man's uses, becoming tools in the struggle with nature. It was, as Felix Gilbert argues, a cult of force—an image which saw life as war, and excellence in struggle as human virtue.[16]

Nature was not limited to the inanimate and animal spheres. Man was himself a part of nature, and the struggle to master nature was partly a struggle against one's fellows and against oneself, pitting the weapons of cunning, will, and force against man's yearning for comfort and repose.

This doctrine, which gained wide currency, was bound to call forth opposition. While it is easy to overestimate the differences between Kant and Machiavelli, the former did draw a sharp line between the human and the nonhuman elements of nature with his assertion that man must not be used as a means. Man was still to try for mastery over nature, but he should treat his fellows in terms of the "law of freedom" and act in terms of a universal law applying to all men rather than according to his individual will. Ethics demanded that force and coercion be restricted and abandoned, if possible, in favor of a morality of individual freedom and voluntary cooperation.[17]

Such teachings, characteristic of the Enlightenment, were the origin of two critical concepts which have colored much of subsequent thought about the relations of army and state (often in very misleading ways). First, they suggested an antithesis between *morality,* conceived in terms of freedom, and *power,* especially in its military forms. Second, when tied to the theory of historical progress, they suggested that man was moving from a "military" phase of society to an "industrial" one based on "productive" cooperation, motivated by individual "interests," and guided by the "invisible hand" of the market or the laws of historical "evolution." [18]

[16] Felix Gilbert, *Machiavelli and Guicciardini* (Princeton, N.J.: Princeton University Press, 1965) , pp. 130–139, 179, 197. Machiavelli, *The Prince,* Chaps. 12–14; *Discourses,* Book II. Introduction.

[17] This position may be taken to represent the major influences of the Kantian tradition on subsequent thinkers. Kant himself was too sophisticated to ignore the difficulties associated with carrying such ideas into practice, and assigned an important place to the "cunning" by which nature in history produced peace through conflict.

[18] Herbert Spencer, *Principles of Sociology* (New York: Appleton, 1898) , II, 568–642. William Graham Sumner, *War and Other Essays* (New Haven, Conn.: Yale University Press, 1911) , pp. 3–42.

The Machiavellian view never died entirely, and the disillusionment with early efforts to put Enlightenment doctrine into practice called forth a new analysis which partly incorporated it. For Hegel, freedom was the goal of human development. Yet the ultimate reality of spiritual freedom was foreclosed to living men by their tendency to pursue the limited, private gratification of their senses and to seek security for their lives and property. The political community, the state, was the highest form of freedom man could safely attain; a unified world would only abet his tendency to relax into an illusory search for material security. War, though evil, was not *absolute* evil, for it shattered illusions of security and drove men to seek the more universal, more disinterested, and hence freer support of communion with their fellow citizens.

Theorists influenced by Hegel came to credit war with even more positive qualities. Von Clausewitz cautioned against the risks of war, but saw war as morally neutral, a "continuation of policy by other means." The historian von Treitschke carried the adulation of war to its extreme, arguing that it was the "health of the state" (as opposed to a rather extreme cure for disease, as Hegel had implied). For von Treitschke, the army was the school of political virtue and, far from being the servant of the state, should be regarded as its mentor and the epitome of its ideals.[19]

Such extremes only confirmed the adherents of Enlightenment doctrines, or the liberalism which descended from them, in their conviction of a permanent conflict between the soldier and civilization. The two views have persisted, comparatively unchanged, to the present day; Rapoport terms them the "liberal" and the "technocratic" approaches to the military.[20] The first continues to see soldiers as violent, autocratic, and the vestige of a barbaric age. It continues to hope that progress will gradually

[19] Heinrich von Treitschke, *Lectures on Politics*, A. L. Gowans, trans. (New York: Frederick Stokes, n.d.) , pp. 99–109. Karl von Clausewitz, *War, Politics and Power*, E. M. Collins, trans. (Chicago: Regnery, 1962) , pp. 63–87.

[20] David C. Rapoport, "Military and Civil Societies: The Contemporary Significance of a Traditional Subject in Political Theory," *Political Studies, 12* (1964) , 178–201. For a contemporary example of the liberal school, see A. M. Rose, "The Social Structure of the Army," *American Journal of Sociology, 51* (1946) , 361–364.

eliminate the military altogether. Yet it fears that if war and peace appeal to antithetical personalities and if the most civilized state is the most peaceful, then civilized states cannot effectively fight wars and run the constant danger of conquest by the barbarian. The Nazis, who merely reversed the values of liberalism, held exactly this view: that the decadent West could easily be overcome by the "healthy barbarism" of the Third Reich. The event proved otherwise; as de Tocqueville had predicted, democracy is slow to go to war and ineffective in the first clashes but gains strength as war goes on, while her foes decline. Modern war no longer allows democracies a cushion of time, and the fears of the liberal have hardly disappeared.

The technocratic school, however, sees the army as sharply distinct from the passionate *Landsknecht* or the classical hero. The army is viewed as the supreme example of rationalized organization, substituting training and scientific organization for natural courage and serving as a supple instrument in the hands of the statesman. Critics of the military may also adopt this position, centering on the typical rigidities of bureaucratic hierarchy. "The army game," for example, refers to an uninspired effort to solve problems "by the book." Yet this school neglects the nature of the "moral factors" and the need for them which von Clausewitz saw as elements of strength, especially the "military virtue" required by a professional army.

Some evidence may be found to support both positions, but because the two are radically contradictory, evidence for one tends to refute the other. Technocrats may take comfort in Samuel Huntington's finding that American officers regard war as uncertain and seek to avoid it save as a last resort.[21] Civilians with strong emotional or ideological commitments may be more militant than the military, for professionals—whatever their own commitments—may be aware of technical difficulties or military perils to which others are blind. At the same time, the image of the soldier as a rigid and unimaginative bureaucrat is contra-

---

[21] Samuel P. Huntington, *The Soldier and the State* (Cambridge, Mass.: Harvard University Press, 1957) ; particular systems of training may produce the warrior-berserker attitude, however. See my review of Jules Roy, *The Battle of Dienbienphu*, in *Commonweal, 82* (April 16, 1965) , 119–120.

dicted by at least one study which found that, in attitudes toward
risk taking, military personnel resembled college students oriented toward theory and aesthetics more than those who are
pragmatic "high need achievers." [22]

Perhaps the simplest criticism of both positions is that neither takes account of the complex nature that is man's, the
interplay of reason and emotion, of external events and internal
ideas—including ideas of morality, loyalty, and obligation. Even
the prudence which Huntington discovered in soldiers is suspect.
General Ludwig Beck's forecasts of disaster for Hitler's prewar
maneuvers were uniformly in error: his prudence may well have
been based on a *desire* for a Nazi defeat rather than on a rational
calculation.[23] Moreover, the friends of professional soldiers tend
to be exclusively drawn from their fellow professionals; war
threatens their circle of affections far more than it does that of
citizen soldiers or reservists. A general who feels intense affection
for his troops may feel the same exaggerated prudence that led
General McClellan to imagine massive Confederate armies which
prevented him from taking aggressive action.[24] Machiavelli, after
all, attacked mercenaries because they were unwilling to risk
their lives in battle; citizen soldiers, he considered, would be
more ferocious. The technician's caution may be only the surface
and "manly" expression of a deeper and more human reserva-
tion.[25]

Both liberal and technocratic schools tend to divide life into
neat compartments: war and peace, force and freedom, reason
and emotion, state and society. They deny that man is a political

---

[22] A. P. Scodel, P. Ratoosh, and J. S. Menas, "Some Personality Correlates
of Decision-Making under Conditions of Risk," *Behavioral Science, 4* (1959),
19–28. It may be surprising to some that General Grant once desired to be a
professor of mathematics, as reported in Bruce Catton, *U. S. Grant and the
American Military Tradition* (New York: Grosset and Dunlap, 1954).

[23] For the relations of Beck and the Nazi regime, see Walter Goerlitz,
History of the German General Staff (New York: Praeger, 1953); and J. W.
Wheeler-Bennett, *Nemesis of Power* (New York: St. Martin's, 1954).

[24] McClellan's popularity with his troops, and vice versa, was proverbial;
see Bruce Catton, *Mr. Lincoln's Army* (New York: Doubleday, 1951).

[25] Samuel A. Stouffer, *et al., The American Soldier* (New York: Wiley,
1965), II, 130–149.

animal; for politics must take cognizance of the need for force to maintain freedom, the need of emotion to support reason, the seeds of war that lie dormant in peace, and the yearning for peace that arises amid war.[26] Politics, in short, cannot neglect empirical men in favor of the frail barriers of philosophic concepts which would consign parts of man's spirit to distinct historical "epochs," nor, in consequence, can it relegate war to the "irrational" side of man's life. In the political world, force may serve a purpose—albeit a negative one—and form an essential defense of civilization. It would be a strange naïveté which contended that progress would have been advanced by acquiescence in the conquests of the Nazi regime.

Armies are neither so passive in the hands of the state, nor are they organized in such functionally rational terms, as the technocratic school believes. Hegel and von Clausewitz knew they spoke of an ideal, and expected existing armies to deviate from it. Armies may, in fact, refuse flatly to obey civil authority; they may resist certain policies; they may demand that their views be considered or their interests protected. Prussian officers swore "unlimited obedience" to their king (*keine rechtlichen Grenzen*), but he was far too wise to interfere with the right of the officer corps to elect its own members. The style, structure, and policies of an army are deeply influenced by the culture in which it has developed. Autocratic leadership can hardly be expected to succeed among troops drawn from a democratic culture like that of the United States: one study indicates that military experience actually stiffens the resistance of military personnel to authoritarianism and to styles of leadership based on it.[27]

[26] Sigmund Freud, *Civilization and its Discontents* (London: Hogarth, 1955; orig. pub. 1929). Harold Lasswell, *World Politics and Personal Insecurity* (New York: McGraw-Hill, 1935).

[27] Stouffer, *et al., op. cit.,* I, 379–380. Hannan Selvin, *The Effects of Leadership* (New York: Free Press, 1960). T. H. McCormack, "Military Experience and Attitudes toward Authority," *American Journal of Sociology, 62* (1957), 428–490. E. G. French and R. P. Ernest, "The Relationship between Authoritarianism and the Acceptance of Military Ideology," *Journal of Personality, 24* (1955), 181–191.

The mercenary forces and professional standing armies of the early modern era were hardly models of military efficiency. Personnel, normally recruited from the lowest elements of society, could be made to fight only through pecuniary hopes or a brutalizing discipline. Either made such forces inflexible in the field, unable to withstand serious defeat or hardship, and vulnerable when pitted against armies endowed with a sense of zeal or less alienated from the societies they defended. The exceptions to this rule arose through the loyalty of armies to their commanders, but such loyalty could be perilous for the state. Indeed, most monarchs preferred armies which could be controlled through the maxim *divide et impera.*

The victories which the great mercenary Wallenstein was able to gain with his large and unified army were not sufficiently valuable to the Holy Roman Emperor to make him run the risk to imperial control posed by Wallenstein himself. Even when armies became more "nationalized" and were used by absolute monarchs to unify their respective states, the monarchs were forced to purchase the loyalty of the entrenched classes by conceding the exclusive leadership of the military to the aristocracy or the upper echelons of the middle class. Such a concession obviously worked to secure the social position of such classes and to exempt them from bearing a proportionate share of the burdens of the state, which tended to fall on the peasantry. Yet with all their inefficiencies and the restrictions which they placed on the state, the mercenary and professional armies were ideal instruments for states which feared popular insurrection or the resistance of hostile nobles, provinces, or religious groups as much or more than they feared defeat in war. The mercenary and professional armies were, in other words, the result of the limitations on the authority of governments. It might have flattered an eighteenth-century monarch to be called an enlightened despot, but the epithet signalized, on one hand, that he no longer ruled in terms of traditional law and, on the other, that he was unwilling to allow the community at large to judge whether he was truly enlightened or not.[28]

[28] Alfred Vagts, *A History of Militarism* (New York: Norton, 1937).

S. B. McKinley observed that the democratic era was connected to a change in military technology which made the infantry predominant on the field of battle.[29] Certainly, that change was important in enabling popular rebellions to defeat their former overlords who had once overawed them with mounted and armored forces. McKinley neglected the fact that the infantry was dominant on the battlefield long before the democratic revolutions took place. A possible explanation was provided by Walter Millis, who observed that only in the American Revolution did a standing army encounter, for the first time, an armed people versed in the use of weapons.[30] Yet Millis's argument fails to account for revolutions among peoples not so versed or armed. Both explanations neglect the influence of authority and idea. The democratic revolutions demanded a people who were able to organize; they demanded a conviction that the people were the rightful sovereigns of the state. The first demanded improved communications; the second, a new doctrine of the relationship between the individual and society.[31] States which could prevent either from developing or restrict such developments sharply (Tsarist Russia being the obvious example) were able to survive despite the military changes associated with the democratic era.

The absence of any one-to-one ratio between military technique and political institutions was also clear in the case of the mass armies introduced by the French Revolution. It might seem to a von Scharnhorst that military reform was impossible without political transformation. More "genuine" Prussians were doubtful and, one suspects, uncertain whether military efficiency was worth the price if von Scharnhorst were right. In fact, although the "massification of war" required public support and loyalty, it also required an elite capable of coordinating and managing the

---

[29] S. B. McKinley, *Democracy and Military Power* (New York: Vanguard, 1934). See also Gerhard Ritter, *Die Neugestaltung Europas im 16. Jahrhundert* (Berlin: V. des Druckhauses Tempelhof, 1950), pp. 19–28.

[30] Walter Millis, *Arms and Men* (New York: New American Library, 1956), pp. 11–63.

[31] *Ibid.*, pp. 64–271. Vagts, *op. cit.*, Chaps. 4, 5.

greatly expanded forces and the resources necessary to supply them. Personnel and commanders became, in many respects, less essential to the army than was its general staff.[32]

Indeed, it became increasingly clear that weapons like the machine gun, and later the tank, were quite capable of defeating mass armies and that such weapons required considerable training and skill. In other words, it became apparent that no revolution could succeed in a modern, industrial state while the army of that state remained intact. Only a military *coup* or the defeat of the army by a foreign foe made revolution possible.[33] Weapons of mass destruction could be wielded effectively by the few against the most inspired, but worse armed, resistance of the many.

Dark forebodings oppressed more than one democratic theorist when he examined these developments. Elite rule and totalitarianism seemed the most likely prognosis for the future. Even on these terms, it is important to note that it is not *military* rule which is the specific object of fear. Civilian life has become more "militarized" and military life more "civilianized." The first is characterized by more organization, discipline, and hierarchy; the second, by greater concern with technology, scientific research, sociology, and economics. However grim such tendencies may be, they do not portend military rule. Rather, they suggest a growing interdependence between the civilian and the military sector, in which the danger is not rule by generals, but the "garrison state," a political order which takes military power as its highest goal and value. Such a state is Machiavelli's ideal realized in fact; it is the inversion of von Clausewitz's conviction that the army must always be subordinate to civilian policy. Nor

---

[32] Prussian and German officers commented, for example, that Lee and Napoleon could never have achieved victories in the newer form of war, and were inclined to blame the defeat of both on their inability to handle staff problems or delegated authority. On the relation between von Scharnhorst and traditional leaders, see Goerlitz, *op. cit.*, Chap. 2, and Heinz Karst, *Das Bild des Soldaten* (Boppard a. Rhein: Harald Boldt, 1964).

[33] Katharine Chorley, *Armies and the Art of Revolution* (London: Faber and Faber, 1943). Chalmers Johnson, *Revolution and the Social System* (Stanford, Calif.: Hoover Institution, 1964), p. 16.

is there an absence of indications that the garrison state may be coming into reality.[34]

In another sense, the garrison state has a very "civilian" aim: a desperate desire for security in a world which seems alien, incomprehensible, and possibly hostile. That yearning may have been confined to a comparative few in Machiavelli's day; today, it has become ubiquitous in a universe dominated by change, and a change which has escaped the comfortable optimism of the "idea of progress." [35] Change and risk are only more fearsome because of the success of civil society in providing men with prosperity, for men have more to lose and hence more to fear.

In a world of mass organizations, pervaded by the atmosphere of change and insecurity, much that was basic to democratic thought has been called into question. The initiative in policy has shifted decisively away from the public and from private groups. War and foreign policy may seem to typify that shift; the army or the CIA may appear as its most demonic illustration.[36] The process is more general than any example, the result of the dynamics of a world more closely tied by the bonds of material interdependence, yet still divided by the walls of loyalty, value, and affection which unite some men and separate them from others.

In our times, our own weakness and ignorance as individuals are driven home sharply. Others we have never seen and whose minds are a closed book make decisions which are vital to our lives. There is no private universe into which we can retreat, and if we seek to do so, we find only loneliness and isolation. The desire for community and fraternity may be deeply buried in the soul, but its fires never burn brighter than when men find them-

[34] Harold Lasswell, "The Garrison State," *American Journal of Sociology*, *46* (1941), 455–468. G. M. Lyons, "The New Civil-Military Relations," *American Political Science Review, 55* (1961), 53–63. Morris Janowitz, "Military Elites and the Study of War," *Journal of Conflict Resolution, 1* (1957), 9–18.

[35] Speier, *loc. cit.* George A. Lanyi and Wilson C. McWilliams, *Crisis and Continuity in World Politics* (New York: Random House, 1966), pp. 107–111.

[36] David Esmond, "Community and Its Nemesis: The New Left and International Politics," *The Activist* (Oberlin, Ohio), *6*, No. 1 (1965), 17–18. W. T. R. Fox, "Representation and Efficiency: Dual Problem of Civil-Military Relations," *Political Science Quarterly, 76* (1961), 354–366.

selves bereft in an impersonal world. Here Hegel provides a warning, for he was aware that such tensions in the spirit of man may be resolved by an external threat which appears accidental but is actually the result of the internal dynamics of the psyche. Faced with a greater fear, men may discount their fear of their fellows and may express the desire for affection and communality which they would otherwise conceal.

The fraternity of battle is as old as man, though it takes on a new form in a new age. And the futility of that fraternity is as old as human folly, for the brotherhood which battle permits is purchased only at the price of the likelihood of death for the brethren thus gained. Fraternity is indeed too sweet to endure without once it has been known; yet once known and lost, we may fear to risk the loss again.[37] The deeper isolation which that fact threatens is only strengthened by the fact that the fraternity of battle may imprison us behind the walls of guilt. Communion between minds does not eliminate separation in flesh, and if a comrade dies, the emotions of the flesh leap in momentary delight at one's own survival—a delight which will always stand as a reminder of the imperfections of men.[38] Communion and fraternity may be essential to man, but the wisest of soldiers have always known that these qualities could not be found in the bond of battle, which is based on fear of the foe and on the yearning to survive.

The threat of war or the garrison state is menacing indeed. The democratic era, the material environment which was favorable to democracy, has passed. Its passing need not mean the end of democracy; it merely shifts the emphasis from external fact to internal fact, from the empirical world to the moral idea. If we seek to strengthen democracy in its hold on civilian and soldier alike, we must be aware that ideas assailed by the environment will not prevail forever. Yet men are in some degree masters of

[37] R. Sobel, "The Old Sergeant Syndrome," *Psychiatry, 10* (1947), 315–321. E. A. Weinstein, "The Function of Interpersonal Relations in the Neuroses of Combat," *Psychiatry, 10* (1947), 307–314. Stouffer, *et al., op. cit.,* II, 80, 99–100, 104.

[38] St. Augustine, *Confessions* John K. Ryan, trans. (New York: Doubleday, 1960), Book IV, Chaps. 5, 6. R. R. Grinker and J. P. Spiegel, *Men Under Stress* (Philadelphia: Blakiston, 1945).

events; they can seek to restrain those forces which menace democracy and perhaps to create an environment which will nurture what is best in men and states.

Functions of the Military in New States

In the industrial states, democratic or not, military organizations are unlikely to play a dominant or directive role in politics. Some of the reasons for this will be discussed subsequently, but for present purposes it is enough merely to call attention to two major reasons: the increasing complexity and number of skills required for governing society, and the existence of organized opinion supporting the established political system and culture.

The developing states face an infinitely more difficult task than that of preserving such a state of affairs: they are concerned with creating a state. The developing *states* are, in fact, engaged in the work of "developing nations," of forging the institutions and attitudes conducive to "modernity," as defined in the image of the industrial nations. They lack the economic and social organizations which tie men together across the barriers of face-to-face society in anything but the most rudimentary sense. Their peoples, largely traditional in outlook and doctrine, are often unable and almost always unwilling to understand or to make the sacrifices necessary for such modernization.[39]

Such facts have made rule by an elite, endowed with the vision and the skills necessary for political creativity, seem mandatory to many such states. Lacking the resources—especially given the requirements of development—to provide material rewards for obedience, such elites have been forced to rely either on the nonmaterial rewards of political idealism or on the negative sanctions of threat and force, whether such threats are thought to originate outside the state or within it. The weakness of idealistic appeals over the long term has directed more and more attention to those negative sanctions, and hence to the military and the police. This development only follows the logic that Machiavelli had prescribed for the founders of new states. Speaking of the tyrant Hiero of Syracuse, he observed:

[39] Lucian W. Pye, *Aspects of Political Development* (Boston and Toronto: Little, Brown, 1966), Chaps. 1, 2, 5, 6.

He abolished the old militia and raised a new one; abandoned his old friendships and formed others; and as thus he had friends and soldiers of his own choosing, he was able to build . . . securely, so that while he had great trouble in acquiring his position he had little trouble in maintaining it.[40]

Many observers have gone further, arguing not only that the military is an essential support to any regime in a new state but that it is an ideal organization for governing such a state.[41] These claims, advanced by more than one military regime and supported by many distinguished social scientists, rest on two principal arguments: (1) that the military is best suited to undertake economic and social reform and modernization, and (2) that the army provides an excellent vehicle for assimilating disadvantaged or newly mobilized groups and for developing national political integration. While not necessarily denying these assertions, critics have been prone to argue that military rule is likely to result in a pervasive militarism which, in addition to its intrinsic defects, may actually retard development. All three arguments deserve further examination.

The Military and Modernization

Those who contend that the military can best undertake the tasks of modernization typically argue that military organizations, or at least their leaders, have acquired two essential skills: technical knowledge, and the habits of discipline and modern organization. In addition, the military may be able to overcome traditionalistic or partisan resistance to projects for development with a maximum of efficiency and a minimum of compromise.[42]

During World War II, it was found that American soldiers were likely to feel greater discontent with their jobs and with the army if they were highly educated. Stouffer and his associates

[40] Machiavelli, *The Prince*, Chap. 6, p. 23.

[41] Pye, *op. cit.*, Chap. 9. John J. Johnson, ed., *The Role of the Military in Underdeveloped Countries* (Princeton, N.J.: Princeton University Press, 1962).

[42] E. A. Shils, in John J. Johnson, *op. cit.*, pp. 7–68. Edwin Lieuwen, "The Military: A Revolutionary Force," *Annals, 334* (1961), 30–40. Pye, *loc. cit.* F. R. von der Mehden and C. W. Anderson, "Political Action by the Military in Developing Areas," *Social Research, 28* (1961), 459–479.

hypothesized that this discontent resulted from a loss in status relative to civilian life.[43] In developing states, that relation may well be reversed: educated men may find themselves subject to better educated superiors and may be given more status in the army than would be possible in the civilian economy. If that resulted in a comparatively high degree of job satisfaction and contentment with the army, we might also presume that the relatively high *esprit* and commitment of educated American soldiers, reflective of their commitment to civilian society, might be lacking in new states. Soldiers might well be prone to discontent with governments dominated by the less educated and be inclined to view the army as an ideal vehicle for reform.

That very hypothetical conformation of the modernization thesis rests, however, on the proposition that in a given state the army provides a more satisfying environment for the educated than does civilian society. In particular cases the opposite situation may obtain. In more than one European army the military was a means whereby *less* educated groups were able to maintain their traditional status relative to civilian society.[44]

The entire argument rests on the proposition that military groups have more "modern" attitudes and are more "advanced" than are civilian elements. Certainly, this has been true in highly traditional states, where entrenched elites have been able to restrict social and economic changes in civilian society *if* these entrenched groups have *not* been able to impose similar constraints on military change. That condition has existed in many Middle Eastern states, close to the centers of world politics and conflict, where military modernization was the price of the survival of the state. It has been less evident in Latin America, where external pressures for military change have been almost nonexistent, or in Africa, where modern armies, created by colonial powers, have been little more advanced than civilian groups.

To be sure, the military may be useful in breaking up traditional resistance in alliance with civilian groups, as seems to

[43] Stouffer, *et al.*, *op. cit.*, I, 82–104.
[44] Hans Rosenberg, *Bureaucracy, Aristocracy and Autocracy: The Prussian Experience, 1660–1815* (Boston: Beacon, 1966), pp. 59–60, 129, 138–139, 144 n. 8.

have been the case in Prime Minister Obote's *coup* in Uganda (or, with less civilian participation, in Nigeria), or in displacing a rigid and semitotalitarian regime, as in Ghana. Eliminating such resistance, however, is not equivalent to ruling after change has been imposed. The best argument for military rule in such situations may be that although the military is not the *ideal* elite to direct policy, it may be an improvement over some groups and may be able to rule in a stable manner.[45] This argument is possible only where the military *refuses* to accept the leadership of civilians—a very dubious blessing indeed.

The evidence indicates, in fact, that military organizations are very rarely innovators, and that at best they follow changes initiated in other states or other sectors of society—a fact which applies to social and organizational change, as well as to technical change. Especially if the military organizations are isolated from external pressures for change, they tend to become bastions of organizational conservatism.[46] All organizations, of course, show some tendency to defend established routines, techniques, and patterns of authority. The military, precisely because it is able to rule by force, is far more able to perpetuate such patterns than are civilian organizations, which are more subject to internal challenges.[47] It is important to realize, moreover, that the major internal challenge to a military regime comes from guerrilla war, a form of combat which places emphasis on traditional military skills far more than on highly technical and modern modes of war.

In fact, apparent zeal for modernization on the part of military organizations in new states may only illustrate a passion for *control,* in which organization and routine replace politics

[45] Guy J. Pauker, "Southeast Asia as a Problem Area in the Next Decade," *World Politics, 11* (1959), 325–345, terms military intervention a "preventive alternative."

[46] W. Kaempffert, "War and Technology," *American Journal of Sociology, 46* (1941), 431–434. John U. Nef, *War and Human Progress* (Cambridge, Mass.: Harvard University Press, 1950).

[47] Daniel Lerner and Richard Robinson, "Swords into Ploughshares: The Turkish Army as a Modernizing Force," *World Politics, 13* (1961), 28–29. E. L. Katzenbach, "The Horse Cavalry in the Twentieth Century: A Study in Public Response," in *Public Policy* (Cambridge, Mass.: Harvard School of Public Administration, 1958), pp. 120–149.

and personality.[48] By providing a secure environment, such stabilization may encourage civilian innovations and protect the fruits of productive effort and labor. Even when military rule initially serves to liberate civilian efforts from traditionalistic restraints or from a quasi-anarchical politics, it may subsequently come to act as a barrier to change in the effort to protect itself or its established patterns of organization. Karl Marx wrote of the regime of Napoleon III:

[The] culmination of the "Napoleonic idea" is the preponderance of the army. The army was the *point d'honneur* of the small-holding peasants; it was they themselves transformed into heroes, defending their new possessions against the outer world, glorifying their newly-won nationhood . . . But . . . the army itself is no longer the flower of peasant youth; it is the swamp flower of the peasant lumpenproletariat . . . It now performs its deeds of valor by hounding the peasants . . . by doing police duty . . . [The] empire was necessary to free the French nation from the weight of tradition . . . With the progressive undermining of small-holding property the state structure erected upon it collapses. The centralization of the state that modern society requires arises only on the ruins of the military bureaucratic governmental machinery which was forged in opposition to feudalism.[49]

Assimilation and National Integration

Armed forces have played a major role in the development of nationalism, and it is not surprising that there are hopes for similar results in the new states. Men who wear the uniform of a national government are identified with that government by those who see them; it is not surprising if they come to identify the prestige of the national government with their own dignity. Moreover, discredited individuals and groups which suffer from disadvantage or prejudice have more than once found an opportunity to rise in status by displaying courage in the service of the

[48] Morris Janowitz, "Changing Patterns of Organizational Authority: The Military Establishment," *Administrative Science Quarterly, 3* (1959), 473–493. Rosenberg, *op. cit.* Kurt Lang, "Technology and Career Management in the Military Establishment," in M. Janowitz, ed., *The New Military* (New York: Russell Sage), 1964.

[49] Karl Marx, "The Eighteenth Brumaire of Louis Bonaparte," in L. Feuer, ed., *Marx and Engels* (Garden City, N.Y.: Doubleday, 1959), pp. 344–345.

state, winning an acknowledgment of "full citizenship" from the society at large. "The uniform," Marx wrote, was "the state dress" of the peasantry, and "war their poetry." [50]

Military forces may also create the basis of nationality by teaching the national language to minority groups (in new states these "minorities" are often the overwhelming majority) or by educating them in modern skills and in the political culture of the society (or, more often in new states, of the dominant groups in the political process).[51]

There tends to be a major conflict between the image of the military as the spearhead of modernization and the image of the armed forces as a vehicle for national integration. "Modernization" tends to emphasize the control of the public by a comparatively small military; "integration" involves masses and presumes meeting their demands for reward and status, at least to some degree. Bodin observed long ago:

> If the lower classes are once armed and are not constantly employed against the enemy, there is no doubt that sooner or later they will try to, and succeed in, changing the form of government to secure a share for themselves . . . If only the ruling class is armed, one day it will be defeated in the field . . .[52]

For purposes of greater control, a military high command may prefer not to teach its troops the national language, electing to keep them organized in separate and often hostile ethnic units. This segregation is, of course, inefficient in military terms but may seem preferable if the threat of war is small and the army is conceived of as an instrument of domestic rule. (Austria-Hun-

[50] *Ibid.* See also Shils, *loc. cit.* M. Khadduri, "The Role of the Military in Middle Eastern Politics," *American Political Science Review, 47* (1953), 511–524. Andrzejewski, *op. cit.* R. D. Challener, *The French Theory of the Nation in Arms, 1866–1939* (New York: Columbia University Press, 1959). D. T. Cornish, *The Sable Arm: Negro Troops in the Union Army* (New York: Norton, 1966). M. D. Foot, *Men in Uniform* (London Institute for Strategic Studies, 1961).

[51] H. Wool, "The Armed Services as a Training Institution," in E. Ginzberg, ed., *The Nation's Children* (New York: Columbia University Press, 1959), II, 158–185. H. Daalder, *The Role of the Military in the Emerging Countries* (The Hague: Mouton, 1962). Pye, *op. cit.*

[52] Jean Bodin, *Six Books of the Commonwealth*, M. J. Tooley, ed. (Oxford: Blackwell, n.d.; orig. pub. 1576), Book V, Chap. 5, p. 170.

gary, for example, followed this policy even though she was an international great power.) It is even more likely that a government—and especially a military regime—will seek to restrict the officer corps to persons of certain loyalty, whether that loyalty is determined ethnically or ideologically. (Military schools and tests ostensibly applying the merit principle can easily be bent to the purposes of such a policy.[53])

These restraints are more likely where the prestige of the military is high and where military careers appeal to groups already high in status. Obviously, in such situations, the military tends to parallel the existing status system rather than acting as a vehicle for assimilation or upward mobility. In fact, such a result might be expected to be one of the long-term constraints associated with a military regime (unless the prestige of government is low relative to civilian and private pursuits). High status and advantages tend naturally to stimulate efforts to defend military prerogatives against interlopers and even to pass them on to one's heirs.[54]

The maximum effectiveness of the military as a vehicle for the integration of previously excluded groups is likely to be found where the prestige of the military is low relative to the highest civilian status groups, but high relative to the status of the excluded groups themselves. While American Negroes were unhappy in the army during World War II, their discontent centered on instances of discrimination and on the existing pattern of segregation in military units. Since discrimination was also encountered in civilian life, Negroes tended to feel far less discontent with the army as such than did Caucasians. Far from representing a decline in status, the army was actually an improvement for many Negroes (this was especially true, obviously, for Southern Negroes). Thus, Negroes tended to feel a far greater

[53] K. Demeter, *Das deutsche Heer und seine Offiziere* (Berlin: von Reimar Hobbing, 1935).

[54] F. C. Endres, "Soziologische Struktur und ihr entsprechende Ideologien des deutschen Offizierskorps von dem Weltkrieg," *Archiv für Sozialwissenschaft, 58* (1927), 282–319. H. Nuber, *Wahl des Offizierberufs* (Berlin: K. Vowinckel, 1935). Cf. R. J. Smith and C. E. Ramsey, "Attitudes of Japanese High School Seniors toward the Military," *Public Opinion Quarterly, 26* (1962), 249–253.

unit pride and a greater sense that their service was worthwhile than did Caucasians.[55]

The experience of the American army also served to indicate the tension between the aims of integration on one hand and modernization and control on the other. In the eyes of the more fortunate, prejudice tends to magnify discreditable incidents involving lower status groups; hope tends to magnify achievements when the case is reversed. Negro soldiers showed a much higher expectation of improved status as a result of military service than was justified by changes in the attitudes of Caucasians. Even apart from war conditions, lower status groups are likely to feel that their services have been unjustly slighted by the privileged and by the government. (Negroes showed a higher cynicism and suspicion of war aims than did Caucasians.) [56] Such groups may be tempted to take matters into their own hands, especially if they comprise a large portion of the armed forces and are able to organize and to find sympathetic leadership.

The lower the prestige of the army, the more marked these tendencies are likely to be; for the lower military prestige, the lower the estimation of the value of military service on the part of civilian society. Moreover, the lower the prestige of the army, the more likely that officers and other leadership groups will themselves feel unjustly treated and will seek to appeal to the grievances of lower ranks. The errors of Professor Spiro (see pp. 264–272) in forecasting the political future of African armies rest on a foundation of sound observation; yet the fact that armies have low prestige leads to different results than he imagined (for example, there was never a military seizure of power in Prussia or in the Second German Empire). When military service is sufficiently rewarding in itself, there is a far smaller likelihood that soldiers will seek to add the laurels of the forum to those of the field.

Bodin suggested that the tension between national integra-

[55] Stouffer, et al., op. cit., I, 502–503, 536–537, 542–543, 564, 583. See also Foot, op. cit. R. J. Dwyer, "The Negro in the Army: His Changing Role and Status," Sociology and Social Research, 38 (1953), 103–112. R. K. Davenport, "The Negro in the Army," Social Issues, 3 (1947), 32–39.

[56] Stouffer, et al., op. cit., I, 508, 514–515, 536–537, 583; II, 618–620. Cornish, op. cit.

tion and governmental control might be resolved if lower-class armies were kept "constantly at war." That possibility is discussed more fully in a later section. For the moment, it is enough to observe that this suggestion only indicates that efforts to achieve national integration through the military tend to slide over into "integral nationalism" of a quasi-totalitarian variety.[57] Military education and techniques for influencing opinion are typically shaped by the desire to achieve control; at best, they skate on a thin layer of ice between education and manipulation.[58] This fine line calls attention to the perils of militarism perceived by the critics of military rule in the new states.

Armies need not be supportive of integral nationalism, however. They can be supportive of political pluralism, and often they are. This result is likely if the military recruits most of its personnel from minority social strata or from ethnic groups which operate at a disadvantage in the normal political process. European aristocracies found in the army a defense of their traditional status; a like situation has existed in more than one new state. The Kenyan army has drawn its personnel largely from non-Kikuyu elements, for example. In fact, armies formed by colonial powers are likely to mirror this image: many were recruited from minority groups thought to be suspicious of "nationalist" movements among dominent ethnic communities. For the most part, such protection for minority groups is likely to involve some threat to the pace of development; recruitment is likely to appeal to traditional groups, which value warrior virtues more highly than they do civilian skills or trade. This is not always the case: the fact that the Nigerian army drew more officers from the relatively advanced and progressive Eastern Region and fewer from the North may have had some important bearing on the first military seizure of power.[59] This example

[57] E. M. Lemert, "Social Participation and Totalitarian War," *American Sociological Review*, 8 (1943), 531–536. J. Benoist-Mechin, *L'Histoire de l'Armée depuis l'armistice* (Paris: A. Michel, 1936).

[58] T. T. Patterson, *Morale in War and Work: An Experiment in the Management of Men* (London: Parrish, 1955). P. M. Linebarger, *Psychological War* (New York: Duell, Sloan and Pearce, 1960).

[59] William F. Gutteridge, *Armed Forces in New States* (London: Oxford University Press, 1962), pp. 46–47, 80–81.

of Nigeria only reaffirms the earlier proposition that armies may
serve as a spur to modernization in those states where they are
drawn from the more advanced elements of society. It is, of
course, precisely in these situations where national integration is
minimal: an "advanced" minority uses a monopoly of military
power to achieve rapid development despite the objections of
traditionalists and others.

Militarism and Political Development

"As the twig is bent," says the proverb, "so is the tree
inclined." Political culture in new states is still amorphous and
unformed; small events and slight pressures may have a greater
effect on its patterns and directions than do great crises in states
whose political culture is highly organized and held by the great
majority of the population. A major criticism of military rule, or
military dominance in the political process, is based on the effects
it is thought to produce in the political culture being shaped
among emerging peoples.

As has already been suggested, criticism may be made of the
effects of military rule on the merely technical aspects of economic and social development. At the very least, military rule is
likely to involve an excessive diversion of resources from the
civilian economy into military expenditure. Technical defects
may be the least of the shortcomings of military rule, however.

In the normal conflicts between "experts" and public, magnified in new states by the process of development, military
regimes are likely to resort to force earlier as a technique for
resolution than are civilian governments. Indeed, they may resort
to force irrationally—in situations where persuasion would serve
as well.[60]

Even the efficiency of this process is doubtful, for it may
produce on the part of a resentful public a sullen and passive
compliance which achieves less than might have been gained by
an initial period of persuasion that won public commitment and
confidence. Worse, the appeal to force may establish a pattern of
political change achieved by military violence, which undermines
that most fundamental of the justifications for military rule: the

---

[60] Daalder, *op. cit.*, pp. 21–22.

need for stability.[61] Force and violence have a more compelling logic than has trust. A man can surround himself with enemies if he continually asserts that he is so ringed and acts accordingly; protestations of trust and affection do not necessarily produce the same result. Machiavelli realized part of the logic of violence when he observed:

[It] is much safer to be feared than loved, if one of the two has to be wanting . . . for love is held by a chain of obligations which, men being selfish, is broken whenever it serves their purposes . . .[62]

But he who appeals to force is likely not only to find himself alone when fortune frowns, but to establish a principle that might makes right, which leads in directions he may not have imagined. Marx noted:

The French bourgeoisie . . . apotheosized the sword; the sword rules it. It destroyed the revolutionary press; its own press has been destroyed. . . . It supplanted juries by military commissions; its juries are supplanted by military commissions . . . It repressed every stirring in society by means of the state power; every stirring of its society is repressed by means of the state power . . .[63]

The danger is extreme in new states. Apart from the menace of *coups* by factions within its own ranks, it must be remembered that in most new states the armed forces are not a vast apparatus able to impose control at will. They are a very small, though organized segment of an equally small modern sector of society. Organization enables them to act, and their size is sufficient to control the modern sector of the state. However, small size renders them vulnerable to guerrilla insurrections, especially since modern communications have made it possible to coordinate the actions of widely dispersed groups.[64] Indeed, the revolution of

[61] M. Handman, "Bureaucratic Culture Pattern and Revolution," *American Journal of Sociology, 39* (1933) , 301–313. E. Lieuwen, *Arms and Politics in Latin America* (New York: Praeger, 1961) . T. Wyckoff, "The Role of the Military in Latin American Politics," *Western Political Quarterly, 13* (1960) , 745–765.

[62] *The Prince,* Chap. 17, p. 61.

[63] Marx, *op. cit.,* p. 334.

[64] Brian Crozier, *The Rebels: A Study of Post-War Insurrections* (London: Chatto and Windus, 1960) . F. C. Osanka, ed., *Modern Guerrilla War* (New York: Free Press, 1962) . S. P. Huntington, "Patterns of Violence in

communications has transported and continues to transport a vast new audience into awareness of the decisions and policies of central governments; the increasing number of mobilized persons must be an important element in the calculus of any political regime, and, as Chalmers Johnson indicates (see pp. 80–98), an especially important element if it would avoid the perils of guerrilla combat.

Experience with military government has suggested that rule by the armed forces can serve as a preparation for democracy and for civilian rule, but only if the military regime has (1) comparative freedom from pressures to act "efficiently" in terms of quick economic or technical "progress," and (2) a clear commitment and knowledge of the means to civilianization or democratization as an eventual goal. The second condition is more possible in new states than is the first, but neither is highly probable. Even in the best of circumstances, it is hard to argue that military dominance in politics is an *ideal* basis for the development of a political culture.[65]

Democratic armies have existed and continue to exist, but they have been most often associated with values learned before military service, especially among enlisted men. In new states, there are no such preexisting *public* values: they can be hoped for only among particular groups in the modern sector which may provide the material for the officer class if not for the army at large. Yet rule based on appeals to force may have negative effects on even the most fervent of democratic convictions, and a commitment to yield power as soon as conditions permit is likely to be modified by a tendency to see the "permission" of circumstances as indefinitely delayed if power conveys advantages to its holder.

The experience of Prussia is a clear indication of the perils of "modernization" achieved through reliance on a politicized military. As was the case in many states on the Continent, the

World Politics," in Huntington, ed., *Changing Patterns of Military Politics* (New York: Free Press, 1962). L. W. Pye, *Guerrilla Communism in Malaya* (Princeton, N.J.: Princeton University Press, 1956).

[65] A. Vagts, "Military Command and Military Government," *Political Science Quarterly, 59* (1944), 248–263. J. Gimbel, *German Community under American Occupation* (Stanford, Calif.: Stanford University Press, 1961). H. C. Dillard, "Power and Persuasion," *Yale Review, 42* (1952), 212–225.

army proved a useful instrument in overcoming the resistance of the traditional nobility to centralization and to the modernization of the administrative apparatus of the Prussian state. As prescribed by the most optimistic proponents of military rule in new states, the Prussian princes, especially Frederick William I, recruited their administrative cadres among technicians trained by the army.

As Hans Rosenberg has demonstrated, such militarily trained administrators brought their military attitudes into civilian life. Their very successes encouraged the development of militarism, the belief in prosperity achieved by compulsion and in the less functional primacy accorded to the demands of the military—demands which a comparatively poor and developing economy could ill afford. More serious was the value placed on obedience in contrast to discussion and citizen participation. The pattern of passivity and submission encouraged, on one hand, a lack of commitment and willingness to defend the state (*Zivilcourage*) among most citizens, and a savage and irresponsible resentment among others who had broken the bonds of habit and fear which served to repress that resentment among their fellows.

The specific situation of Prussia as a developing state was more responsible for these effects than was the upper-class pattern of recruitment in the Prussian officer corps. As Rosenberg put it:

In the poor and backward Prussian state the impatient . . . royal leaders, apt to overtax the strength of their subjects, did not rest content with the mere improvement of discipline and efficiency. They aimed at superdiscipline, superconformity, superefficiency . . . Loyalty, therefore, they confounded with unquestioning submission to the service code and unconditional subservience to the machine of compulsion . . .[66]

Kinds of Armies in New States

Military and civilian societies are interdependent, and the relations between them are complex. Moreover, every military organization has about it something unique, which derives from the peculiarities of its structure and traditions, its heroes and

[66] Rosenberg, *op. cit.*, p. 90; see also pp. 17, 35–38, 40, 64, 142, 166, 207–208.

tales of glory. Finally, there is something individual in the reaction of each soldier to all of these experiences and relationships. To the participant, and often to the military historian, these unique aspects may bulk large, and any effort to understand a particular military organization must give them due attention. As always in the affairs of men, certain general patterns or "types" of civilian-military relations may be distinguished, which may be useful for purposes of analysis.

The Noninstitutional Army

An army may have no relation to the organized patterns of daily life and politics. In the "liberal state," for example, the army was almost completely removed from the normal centers of civilian attention and was regarded as something to be reduced, if possible, to the vanishing point. Many Americans, at one time or another, have held such views, and the attitude has sometimes characterized our society as a whole. Obviously, this pattern of relations is restricted to societies which have antimilitary values or which devote their attention almost exclusively to nonmilitary goals. (The two are not identical: westward expansion in America was hardly "military," but it was certainly "militant" in style and value.) Noninstitutional armies have also been characteristic of many traditional societies. The tribe which sends its young men out each spring as raiders may have no established military organization at all. Bands form on the basis of *ad hoc* choices and individual allegiance; discipline is nonexistent; war has a "function" only insofar as it allows the expression of desires normally excluded from community life.[67] The chivalric armies were only a slightly more formal variety of this ancient pattern, which Hans Speier calls "agonistic war," in which considerations of proper "warlike" conduct regulate war almost without reference to civilian life or governmental policy.

The Vanguard Army

An army may also be regarded as almost the sole institution of the state; the nation at large is conceived as a backward form of

[67] Fred Gearing, *Priests and Warriors*, Memoir 93, American Anthropological Association, *64* (1962) , 47–54. Speier, *op. cit.,* pp. 223–229.

the army which it will eventually come to resemble. The image of the army as a vanguard may, but need not, involve the ideal of a "nation in arms." Quite as often, the vanguard is based on the image of the army as an elite, more devoted and better equipped to pursue those values which are thought to be the appropriate goals of the community. This elitist image has become the dominant one, as few men are willing to make the sacrifices demanded by a "nation in arms." [68] This image has, of course, been characteristic of many of the military regimes in the non-Western world: Turkey, Egypt, the Sudan, and Pakistan, to name only a few. It is typical, and possibly accurate, in those states to which the "modernization" hypothesis applies (that is, in archaic and feudal states which have survived into the modern period) if those states have been located close to the centers of world politics and conflict.

Obviously, the term "vanguard" suggests an analogy to Lenin's "vanguard party," which was to lead the proletariat. Given the dominantly economic basis of all development, including military development, the army is, in normal circumstances, a less desirable vanguard than is the party. Lenin's model seems better adapted to states which are politically "retarded" but which are "advanced" in some sections of their economic organization, while the army vanguard is appropriate only to states backward in both respects. Indeed, the success of a vanguard army demands that it transfer authority to civilian leaders. Yet the habit of conceiving the army as the custodian of the state's highest values is hard to shake, especially when authority is transferred to civilians only ill-accustomed to political responsibility. Despite the clarity of Ataturk's vision, Turkey has never made such a transfer secure.[69] The idealized image of the *guerrillero* has been too essential to the ideology of the Cuban revolu-

[68] David Rapoport, "A Comparative Theory of Political and Military Types," in Huntington, ed., *op. cit.*, pp. 71–100.

[69] Lerner and Robinson, *loc. cit.*, pp. 19–44. E. Ozbudun, *The Role of the Military in the Recent Political Development of Turkey* (Cambridge, Mass.: Harvard University Center for International Affairs, 1965), unpublished study.

tion for Castro's regime to have discarded it.[70] Joffe's study (see pp. 101–129) observes the same phenomenon in Communist China.

The Army as a Guardian "above" Institutions

In two situations the armed forces may conceive of themselves as "above" political institutions, charged with a unique role in supervising and controlling their conduct in the interests of the state. First, a vanguard army may watch the civilian novices to whom it transfers power from an increasingly remote position, yet be ready to intervene if necessary. The Turkish army may be regarded in this light. Second, and more frequently, the army may assume a guardian role where political institutions are unstable, especially if the army has an unbroken existence through several such regimes. "The state" which it serves may seem to the military to be an abstraction, separated from any concrete institutions and certainly from the vagaries of politicians. Peru, in Payne's analysis (see pp. 249–263), emerges as a striking illustration. Yet the status of "guardianship" assumes that the army retain a detached, Olympian perspective, above the day-to-day politics of the titular leaders. Such detachment is hard to maintain. Any civilian regime which attains, or hopes to attain, reasonable permanence and stability is bound to conflict with the pretensions of the army. Moreover, the army's suspicion of the motives and intentions of political leaders tends to become an institutional pattern. This suspicious attitude makes it easy for weaker civilian groups, which suffer defeat in the political process, to appeal to the army to reverse the verdict, normally suggesting that their successful opponents harbor tyrannical or revolutionary intentions. If the army intervenes, however, it loses its detachment: it can only become the instrument of a party or a vanguard army. (The Brazilian army has recently gone through a similar process and confronts similar dilemmas.) Worse, by identifying too closely with one civilian party, the army may offend those of its members who are opposed to that party; it encourages rival parties to build up military factions of their own and to appeal to the ambitions of individuals and cliques within the army. The general result is that the military loses its

[70] Theodore Draper, *Castroism: Theory and Practice* (New York: Praeger, 1965).

cohesion, and the prospect of *coup* or *countercoup*, not that of order and stability, is all that the army is able to provide.

The Institutional Army

Armed forces are fully institutionalized when they are, and regard themselves as, one among a number of political institutions, bound so indissolubly to the political system as a whole as to share a common fate. The military regards itself as one institution among many and as inside the structure of norms and laws which bind all.

The institutional army presumes at least (1) a common standard of authority and political right conduct, accepted by both military and civilian sectors of society, (2) a fairly stable agreement on military policy, which removes any fear that the position of either civilian or military may be undermined, and (3) discipline in the organization of the armed forces. The need for the first is obvious. Of the second, it may be observed that agreement on military policy need not presuppose a large army; indeed, at times, as in the United States, it may exclude that possibility. Such concurrence demands only that the existing military establishment not be revised in ways which officers and men feel likely to endanger them. Discipline is a more debatable necessity. Some have pointed out that rivalry among military groups may strengthen control over the armed forces, for each group will seek to win the approval of authority. Yet the decisions of that authority must be accepted, and it is quite possible to reject individual decisions while accepting—or even vigorously defending—the position of authority as such. Japanese army leaders never denied the authority of the Emperor; discontented officers assumed the right to free the Emperor from the "perverse" councillors who had concealed the "true" state of affairs. Discipline is essential if the decisions of those who occupy positions of authority are to be carried out.

The American army has been almost entirely institutional from its beginning. The prototype of the army, the Continentals, played a major role in the adoption of the Constitution, and devotion to the document has always been strong among the military. Only a conflict of institutions, the Civil War, brought any sizable number of soldiers into conflict with the government, and the Union victory firmly established the authority of national law and the national government, not to mention the national creed.[71] A recent manual for the instruction of newly commissioned officers asserted:

Certainly these things at least are . . . desired in every military officer of the United States:

1. Strong belief in human rights.
2. Respect for the dignity of every other person.
3. The Golden Rule attitude toward one's daily associates.
4. An abiding interest in all aspects of human welfare.
5. A willingness to deal with every man as considerately as if he were a blood relative.[72]

Conflicts may still take place among military factions, especially between those strong in Congress (like the National Guard) and those with greater strength in executive councils, but such conflict is well within the established system of institutions.[73]

The existence of an institutional army does not in the slightest imply the existence of a politically "good" army. The German generals who expressed their enthusiasm for shooting Socialists or Catholics were giving voice to their devotion to the established ways of the Prusso-Germanic state.

Obviously, the collapse of a given institutional system of authority may lead the army to oppose whatever new pattern succeeds it or to stand aloof as "a state within a state" which awaits the opportunity to restore the former state of affairs. The *Reichswehr* after 1919 is an obvious example.[74] It is also true that an institutional system can collapse if discipline is carried to an

[71] Catton, *U. S. Grant and the American Military Tradition, passim.* B. H. Liddell Hart, *Sherman* (New York: Praeger, 1960), esp. pp. 204–205.
[72] *The Armed Forces Officer* (Washington, D.C.: U.S. Department of Defense, 1950), pp. 4–5.
[73] Martha Derthick, "Militia Lobby in the Missile Age: The Politics of the National Guard," in Huntington, ed., *op. cit.,* pp. 190–234. I. G. Newton, "The Negro in the National Guard," *Phylon, 23* (1962), 18–28.
[74] Francis L. Carsten, *Reichswehr und Politik, 1918–1933* (Berlin: Kiepenheuer u. Witsch, 1964). Harold Gordon, *The Reichswehr and the German Republic* (Princeton, N.J.: Princeton University Press, 1957). Wheeler-Bennett, *op. cit.*

extreme. The French Army after the Dreyfus case, for very complicated reasons, came to develop a cult of conformity and a doctrine of obedience to orders (*respondeat superior*) carried to such a mechanical extreme as to substitute discipline for authority: the army lacked any devotion to the values and goals of the state. While many officers supported Vichy for ideological reasons, probably as many or more served that government because an officer was duty-bound to obey without question. De Gaulle, whose theory of the army elevated it to an autonomous status alongside civilian authority in the state, was almost alone in thinking it the duty of the army to defend the values and ideals of the political community as a whole.[75] Institutionalism may also be undermined if other groups violate the "rules of the game," especially if these touch military policy. The complex balance in Indonesia, which Lev describes (see pp. 150–170), was upset when the Communist party—or officers sympathetic to it—attempted to seize control in 1965. Both parties, army and Communist, sought to seize the legitimating figure of President Sukarno, and the precipitate action of the Communists delivered him (at least temporarily) into the hands of the army. Communist charges that their action was intended to forestall an impending army *coup* were hardly without foundation. American experts had long been urging such a course of action. More important than such charges is the fact that neither the Communists nor the army trusted the other to accept the "rules" of the system.

One fact must be emphasized: An institutional army must be willing to defend the institutions of the state even to the point of disobeying orders. Few Americans, for example, would desire an army so subordinate to "civilian control" that it would obey a President who ordered it to disperse Congress or who otherwise exceeded his constitutional authority. However, disobedience is always risky, for it endangers discipline and opens the door to the exercise of independent judgment by other officers and men. Marshal Juin, for example, pointed out that de Gaulle set the

[75] Raoul Girardet, *La Société Militaire dans la France Contemporaine* (Paris: Plon, 1953), esp. p. 318. Charles de Gaulle, *The Edge of the Sword* (New York: Criterion, 1960), pp. 103–128.

precedents for the military revolts of 1958 and 1961. Himself a loyal servant of Vichy, Juin complained that de Gaulle not only disobeyed, but won honor thereby.[76] (The French generals, incidentally, had a constitutional case: Algeria was an "integral part" of France.)

Moreover, political intervention by the military may be part of the *rules* of a system of institutions. War is too important to be left to generals, as Clemenceau remarked. So, similarly, war is too important to be left entirely to civilians, and civilian policy may well have implications for the nation's readiness for war or the likelihood that war will occur. Much military intervention is "concealed" by the fact that it is so institutional that citizens do not recognize it as military intervention at all. Most military forces establish veterans' organizations or military study groups, or engage in public relations; yet such actions are clearly part of any pluralistic system. Conversely, citizens often fear military intervention where none exists at all. Political parties, especially minority parties, may seek to capitalize on the prestige of military leaders in order to win elections. Such candidacies may have nothing to do with the military or its interests: the Democrats were the "antiwar" party when they nominated General McClellan in 1864 and General Hancock in 1880. Similarly, parties may turn to a military leader as a candidate able to unite an otherwise fissiparous coalition, as the German democrats did in supporting Marshal von Hindenburg in 1932, and political organizations may well seek to organize veterans' groups of their own (the G.A.R. was for years the buttress of the G.O.P.). The great number of generals and uniforms in such movements may alarm many, but they have no relation to military intervention per se.

Institutional armies are likely to develop in association with several factors. Rank and caste separate an officer from his men; if such barriers are extreme, it is unlikely that officers will be obeyed in plots against civilian regimes. To be sure, the hope of gain may lead some troops to support a *coup,* or the discipline of fear may cause others to obey; but such weapons are double-edged: the civilian regime may outbid the commander, and the

---

[76] Alphonse Juin, *Trois Siècles d'Obeissance Militaire, 1650–1953* (Paris: Plon, 1964).

fear of disciplinary action will not hold a soldier in the front line of desperate combat. The professional armies of the eighteenth century, for example, were rarely tempted to try to seize political power. However, rank and caste may also alienate younger officers from their superiors, as de Tocqueville foresaw, and noncommissioned officers may become unhappy with their lot. Either may be close enough to enlisted men to incite them to a *coup*. Some profess to find a relationship between such groups and the ideologies of the left. Yet, as Andreski has pointed out, such groups may be "rash" but not always "revolutionary": the young Japanese officers of the interwar period were romantic nationalists, and the leading political figures from NCO ranks have been Sergeant Batista, Sergeant Mussolini, and Corporal Hitler.[77]

The complexity of civilian society also encourages an institutional military. As Germani and Silvert indicate (see pp. 227–248), the majority of military regimes exist in societies of a simple nature, where economic and social life require little central management, technical skill, or expertise. To the extent that these qualities are demanded, the military is dependent on civilians who possess such skills or on officers trained to exercise them. Such training, however, may make officers diverge sharply from traditional "military" models, so that they feel more sympathy for their civilian counterparts than for their fellow soldiers. Some might be tempted in the direction of a military vanguard (as in Egypt); but under normal circumstances, modern societies create a dependent military which cannot rule directly, though one which might seek to displace a particular regime, as the French army did in 1958.

Perhaps the most important factor in developing an institutional army lies in preventing the alienation of military personnel from civilian life. De Tocqueville was acute in supposing that a short term of service for enlisted men would bring the society into the army and would guarantee that troops would not obey orders contrary to their civilian loyalties. The generals who plotted against Hitler found it difficult to find a "general with

---

[77] On rank as a civilizing factor, see Mosca, *The Ruling Class*, Chap. 9. See also S. Andreski, "Conservatism and Radicalism of the Military," *European Journal of Sociology*, 2 (1961), 53–61.

troops" who would resist the Führer; almost all the generals insisted on Hitler's death as a precondition for testing the obedience of their men. Indeed, an institutional army is more likely if the army is large and based on conscription than if it is small and professional. In the first case, the army tends to be merely a stage—and an annoying one at that—in a citizen's life; in the second, it is likely to seem unique, the center of loyalties and affiliations, and possibly more deserving of devotion than is the state itself.

Any other factors which restrict the military to groups alienated or estranged from the population at large may have a similar effect. For example, such alienation and estrangement are encouraged if the army is recruited from the following: minority ethnic groups; isolated, parochial, or disadvantaged classes (such as peasants, who are often a variety of low-cost native mercenaries) ; groups who find in the army escape from dull, repressive, or hopeless environments.[78] Similarly, troops stationed for long periods at foreign bases or isolated posts may develop similar attitudes of alienation from the state.

The effects of war on armies, and the relationship of war to institutionalization, are problematic. This is as it should be: War is somewhat *sui generis* and deserving of a separate discussion of its own.

Armies may expect their enemies from without or from within the boundaries of the state. The classical assumption was that external enemies unify a state while internal enemies divide it. It is hard to deny the second half of the thesis; only if the internal foe were a small, fanatical sect of terrorists would the result be reversed. Facing external foes, however, is no panacea for producing internal unity. A foreign war may be only an extension of conflict inside the state, as, for example, a war waged against another state on ideological grounds to prevent it from acting as a center for subversive agitation. Such a war might exacerbate existing conflicts. The policies pursued by an army or

[78] E. H. Norman, *Soldier and Peasant in Japan* (New York: Institute of Pacific Relations, 1943) . Speier, *op. cit.,* p. 298. V. Isambert-Jamati, "Remarques sur le service militaire," *Revue Française de Sociologie, 2* (1961) , 100–105.

a government during a war may also be inimical to important sections of the domestic community. German annexationism in 1917 alienated many political leaders, and Nazi atrocities offended the sensibilities of more than one German.

In one sense, however, the classical thesis is certainly correct. War opens the road to glory and honor for military personnel in ways which serve the state. That road closed, the ambitions of the military man may well turn toward internal politics.

Even granting this dubious service of war, war raises the possibility of using the army as a political weapon against the state. The battlefield and the front line demand greater horizontal communication between soldiers and units than is necessary in peacetime; normally, under conditions of peace, the most important communication is vertical, down the chain of command. Moreover, the dangers of combat, the sense of mutual dependence, and the lessened efficacy of threats of discipline among men faced by death, all raise the importance of mutual loyalty and camaraderie among military personnel and decrease the importance of formal rank and protocol. The best of peacetime soldiers may be a disaster in war and vice versa. In other words, war unites soldiers to one another and separates them from the community.[79]

Modern war decreases this tendency, for technology plays a greater role, and interpersonal relations a lesser one. The separation between front and rear areas grows indistinct, and with it, the distinction between civilians and soldiers also grows smaller. The bonds of comrades in arms do not develop with their former intensity, and the traditional impact of war on armies is decreased.[80] This fact, incidentally, suggests why armies trained for modern war find themselves at something of a disadvantage in guerrilla war, where the need for "military virtue" is great.

The armies of new states and developing nations, however, are not fully modern, and the wars which they have fought are

[79] E. Shils and M. Janowitz, "Cohesion and Disintegration in the Wehrmacht," *Public Opinion Quarterly, 12* (1948), 280–315. Stouffer, *et al., op. cit.,* I, 364, 366, 382–388; II, 80, 99–100, 104, 118–142. M. D. Feld, "Information and Authority," *American Sociological Review, 24* (1959), 15–22. R. R. Bigler, *Der Einsame Soldat* (Frauenfeld: Huber, 1963).

[80] Speier, *op. cit.,* pp. 253–262.

more likely to resemble the traditional model. The political effects of war will vary greatly depending on whether the result is victory or defeat.

The possibility of defeat is the most important qualification to the theory that war unites a state. Defeat is a severe blow to the *amour propre* of commanders and, to a lesser extent, of enlisted personnel. Both are tempted to lay the blame on scapegoats. Enlisted men may blame their commanders, but they are as likely to lay the blame on the civilian government. Indeed, they are more likely to do so, for such blame does not endanger the loyalties and devotions built up among all ranks during war.

The highest commanders, of course, may find it hard to separate themselves from the blame that attaches to the civilian regime, and such commanders are outside the circle of immediate personal contacts and loyalty. Colonels and battalion officers are more likely to be included and to form the nucleus of revolutionary leadership against a government whose incompetence or malevolence is thought to have "betrayed" its army. Such charges, obviously, are often true as well as psychologically functional; the regime of King Farouk in Egypt or the government of Bolivia during the Chaco War are obvious examples.

If defeat endangers a regime, victory may strengthen it. The success of Blücher in 1815 and of Bismarck after 1848 blunted the criticism of Prussian army reformers, strongest after the defeat at Jena in 1806. British soldiers in 1918 cursed their commanders rather than Lloyd George, while their defeated German counterparts seemed inclined to blame anyone rather than the high command (exceptions, of course, only serve to indicate the rule).[81]

Victory, however, is not always a source of strength. It is especially dangerous when achieved with guerrilla or irregular forces. Fighting under great hardship, such forces are normally sustained only by revolutionary zeal and by individual commitment rather than by discipline. Hence, they tend to be suspicious of compromise; accustomed to opposing officialdom, they are ever ready to scent betrayal in the efforts of a revolutionary regime to stabilize its power. Often romantic, they are impatient with

[81] Barrie Pitt, *1918: The Last Act* (New York: Ballantine, 1962).

arguments which counsel the necessity for delay. The experience of Mexico is illustrative: the task of reducing Pancho Villa or Emiliano Zapata to civilian control could scarcely have been managed without the force of arms. A new government must often turn on its own irregulars; if it is unwilling or unable to do so, it must provide them with a foreign foe against which they can direct their suspicion and hostility. Cuba and China are obvious examples. Some highly disciplined revolutionary forces may be easier to control, but they are always dangerous and never more than in the moment of victory, when their confidence is high and the reason for limiting their demands disappears.[82]

The most powerful argument for military rule in a new state may be that any other regime is likely to be overcome by the revolutionary "forces," armed or unarmed, that surround it. The most powerful argument against a military regime is that those forces are too strong to be contained by any army the new state is able to field. Indeed, it is quite possible that such forces are too strong to be overcome at all.

[82] Johnson, *op. cit.,* pp. 53–57. Cf. Stouffer, *et al., op. cit.,* I, 438, 440. See also my review, "A Throwback to Nineteenth Century Romanticism," *Commonweal, 83* (Oct. 29, 1965) , 128–130.

Part I

Swords and States:

The Classical Problem

The Professional Soldier and the State

<u>1521</u>

NICCOLÒ MACHIAVELLI

[W]ar being an occupation by which a man cannot support himself with honor at all times, it ought not to be followed as a profession by any but princes or commonwealths; if they are wise, they will allow none of their subjects to make it his sole occupation. In fact, no good man ever did, for certainly no one can be called "good" who follows a profession which obliges him to be rapacious, fraudulent, and cruel at all times in order to support himself, as all must be who make a trade of war, whatever their rank. . . . [I]t will not support them in time of peace; hence, they must either strive to prevent peace or take pains during war to provide for themselves after it ends—by whatever means are expedient. Yet neither of these alternatives is consistent with common decency: whoever seeks to amass during a war enough to support himself thereafter must be guilty of robbery, murder, and violence against friend as well as foe, while seeking to prevent a peace demands that commanders engage in low tricks and artifices to deceive their employers.[1] Yet if they fail in these designs and find that they cannot prevent a peace, when their pay is stopped and they can no longer live in their customary luxury, they establish themselves as soldiers of fortune, gather

[1] Observe that Machiavelli objects less to the fact that a commander may seek to prevent peace than to the fact that he must deceive civil authority in so doing.—W. C. McW.

From The Art of War *(1521)* . *This translation by the editor has been adapted from that of Ellis Farneworth (Albany, N.Y.: Henry Southwick, 1815; orig. pub. 1762) , pp. 23–31, 43–46, 54–57. Throughout this selection, the speaker is Fabrizio Colonna, presented in Machiavelli's dialogue as a professional commander and prince of a small territory.*

45

a band of demobilized troops, and do not hesitate to plunder a country without distinction or mercy. . . . In the days of our ancestors, Francisco Sforza, in order to support himself in munificence and splendor . . . , not only betrayed the Milanese, who had been his employers, but deprived them of their liberties and made himself their sovereign. All the rest of our Italian soldiers who made war their profession acted the same part in those days and were no less blameworthy than Sforza (though not all succeeded in their villainies), for their plans and motives were surely as evil as his. . . . [A]ccording to the proverb, war makes thieves and peace hangs them, for those who cannot make a living any other way, when they are disbanded . . . , disdaining the thought of life in poverty and obscurity, are compelled to use means that would normally send them to the gallows.

Caesar and Pompey . . . owed their reputation to their abilities and not to their virtue, but those that lived before that time acquired their glory by being virtuous as well as able men, for the former made war their only occupation while the latter did not. When the Roman Republic was not yet corrupt, no citizen thought of pursuing that profession in peacetime so as to trample on the laws, plunder provinces, turn tyrant, or enslave his country, nor did private soldiers dare to violate their oaths, to enter into factions or cabals . . . or to support tyrannical designs against the commonwealth in order to enable themselves to live by the profession of arms. The commanders, on the contrary, contenting themselves with the honor of a triumph, eagerly returned to their former manner of life, and private soldiers laid down their arms with more enthusiasm after the war than they had taken them up with at its beginning and resumed their peacetime occupations. . . . So that while the republic was well governed . . . there were no soldiers who made war alone their occupation, and consequently, few of them were dissolute or licentious and those few were punished.

Every well-governed state, therefore, should take care that the art of war be practiced in peace only as a training exercise and in time of war only out of necessity, with no reward save that of glory, allowing war to be prosecuted only by the public. . . .

A kingdom that is well governed and constituted ought to be

more fearful of [professional soldiers] than a republic because soldiers are the chief, if not the only, corrupters of princes and tempters to tyranny. No existing monarchy can be evinced as a case to the contrary: there is not one which is well constituted or governed. A well-constituted kingdom gives its prince sovereign power in nothing but the command of its armies. In that one area, in fact, it is necessary that he should have it, for swift decision and action is often necessary and cannot be executed properly unless the supreme command is lodged in one man. In all other matters, however, the prince should not act at all without the advice of his council, and the members of his council should take care to prevent his being surrounded by men who would continually advise him to make war whether necessary or no on the sole grounds that they cannot support themselves in peacetime. . . . [Even] with such kingdoms as we see today . . . those persons are to be feared who make war their only business . . . because a prince must either keep them continually employed in war or in constant pay during time of peace or run the risk that they will strip him of his kingdom, but as no prince can keep them continually engaged in war or in constant pay when it is over, he runs the continual risk of losing his kingdom. While the Romans were still wise and virtuous, they never allowed a citizen to make war his only profession . . . [even though] they were constantly at war. In order to avoid the dangers of such a custom, they changed their forces [for they could not alter the times] . . . for they took only those between eighteen and thirty-five. . . . Augustus, and after him Tiberius, more concerned to increase and stabilize their own power than to promote the public good, began to disarm the Roman people and kept the same armies standing on the frontiers of the empire. Not thinking those forces sufficient to keep the senate and the people in due obedience, they raised other forces, called the Praetorians, which were quartered in the city or near it and which served to bridle the people as well as to guard the emperor. . . . [W]hen the emperors suffered these guards to give up all other occupations, they became insolent and formidable not only to the senate but to the emperors themselves . . . which resulted in the division and ultimately the ruin of the empire. . . . No state . . .

can support itself without an army and if it has no troops of its own, it must pursue the more dangerous course of hiring foreign ones, for these may more easily be corrupted and become the instruments of some powerful citizen who may obtain their assistance to overthrow the established government if he has nothing to oppose him but an unarmed and defenseless multitude. . . . Every state must be more afraid of two enemies than one, . . . while a state which employs only its own troops has only one enemy to fear. . . . I shall lay it down as a general truth that no man ever founded a monarchy or a republic without being certain that the subjects, if armed, would be ready and willing to defend it. . . . [The Venetians], not being possessed of much land territory carried on wars at sea with their own resources, which they did with great spirit. . . . At last, however, being obliged to engage in a land war . . . instead of trusting their own citizens, they hired the Marquis of Mantua. . . . This false step . . . was owing to their belief that they knew how to make sea war, but not on land, and was the result of ill-founded doubt. . . . The Romans, who were most expert in land wars and knew little of naval affairs, being engaged in war with the seafaring Carthaginians, did not hire Greek or Spanish seamen . . . but gave the command to their own land officers, who eventually were able to conquer their enemies' country.

But if the Venetians acted out of the fear that some of their own citizens might seize the government of the state, it was an unreasonable fear, for none of their sea commanders had ever seized a seacoast town, and they could have only less fear of a citizen who commanded an army. Tyranny and usurpation, if they had considered them, are not due to the citizens being armed but to weak and ineffective government; and while a state conducts its government well, it has nothing to fear from arms in the hands of its subjects. . . . [A] state ought by no means to depend on any troops but its own, . . . those cannot be raised in any way which is superior to a trained militia and . . . there is no method which better introduces order and discipline among soldiers. . . .

[I]f a militia is the cause of disorders, such disorders must take place among themselves or with others, but either can be prevented if the militia is not so badly constituted and regulated as to defeat its own end. If it is properly conducted, it obviously suppresses all disturbances among its own constituent parts instead of fomenting them, for they will be obedient to their superiors. If the inhabitants of a country where you raise a militia are so peace-loving and unarmed, or so united among themselves, that they have no factions, a militia may secure them against foreign enemies but will not itself divide them. Men who are well disciplined will be as unwilling to violate the laws when they are armed as when they are not, unless they are corrupted by their commanders. . . . But if the people are warlike and given to faction, a militia is more likely than anything else to reunite them. Though they may have arms and chieftains, these will be of no service to the country as they are, serving only to foment division and animosity where a militia might give them arms that will serve their country and chiefs to suppress, rather than excite, their differences. In a divided country, when any man thinks himself injured, he applies to the head of his faction, who is obliged to assist him in seeking vengeance if he is to keep up his own reputation and interest, instead of discouraging violence. A leader who is appointed by public authority is a very different matter. . . . A militia which is well ordered can extinguish divisions and restore peace; it can render an unarmed, dispirited, and yet united people warlike and courageous without disturbing their union; others who were brave and armed but given to faction may become united, and turn the arms and courage on the enemies of the country rather than on one another. To prevent a militia from injuring others or from overthrowing the laws and liberties of the country, it is necessary to prevent commanders from acquiring too great an authority over enlisted men, for such a development can only be effected by commanders. Authority is either natural or accidental. To guard against the first, it should be provided that an officer should not command men raised in the district where he was born, but only those from places where he lacks natural interest or connections. The other may in great measure be limited by changing the officers and sending them to different posts every year, for a long continuation of command over the same men is likely to create too close a union between them, which may easily work to the disadvantage of the government. . . . [T]he omission of this custom in the Roman Empire . . . was the cause of all the civil wars between the commanders of different armies and the conspiracies formed by those commanders against the emperors. . . . But whether the cause is ignorance or inattention or indolence in mankind, the fact is certain that bad customs are seldom changed whoever leads, whatever examples are presented either to discredit such customs or recommend their opposites.

The Inevitability of Professionalism

1832

KARL VON CLAUSEWITZ

War is a distinct profession, and . . . even if all the male population capable of bearing arms practice this vocation, it always remains distinct and separate from the other occupations which men pursue. The military virtue of an army in the individual [requires that he] be imbued with a feeling and with the spirit of the business; that he rouse, use, and assimilate into his personality the drives appropriate to it; that he penetrate to an understanding of the profession [intellectually] and gain confidence and expertise through practice; that he be completely given up to it; and that his sense of individuality yield to the part which "we" are assigned in war.

Whatever pains are taken to combine the soldier and the citizen in a single individual, whatever may be done to nationalize wars, however much we may imagine that times have changed since the days of the old condottieri, it will never be possible to do away with the individuality of the profession . . . ; [and] those who belong to it . . . will always look upon themselves as a kind of guild. . . . Even with the strongest inclination to look at war from the most exalted viewpoint, it would be wrong to scorn this *esprit de corps,* which . . . should exist more or less in every army. . . .

An army imbued with the true military spirit . . . preserves its formations under the heaviest fire; is never shaken by imaginary fears and in the face of real danger disputes each inch of ground; is proud of its victories [yet] never loses its sense of

Translated by the editor from Vom Kriege, *Book III, Chap. 5 (Berlin, 1832–1834).*

obedience . . . even under the depressing effects of defeat . . .
and is always reminded of its duties and virtues by the short
catechism of a single idea, *the honor of its arms.*

Soldiers may fight bravely . . . and do great things like the
Swiss, the Americans, or the Spaniards without displaying this
military virtue. A commander may be successful at the head of
standing armies, like Eugene or Marlborough, without being
assisted by it. . . .[1] [W]e cannot therefore say that without [mili-
tary virtue] a successful war is impossible. . . . Military virtue in
an army is a specific moral force which may be assumed to be
absent and whose influence may therefore be estimated, like any
other instrument whose power may be calculated. . . .

Military virtue is for the parts what the genius of the general
is for the whole. The general can only guide the whole, not each
part, and where he cannot guide the part, military virtue must
provide the leadership. . . . The natural qualities of a warlike
people may play exactly the same role: bravery, aptitude, powers
of endurance, and enthusiasm.

. . . 1. Military virtue is a quality of standing armies only,
but they require it most. In national uprisings, its place is supplied by natural qualities which develop themselves more rapidly.

2. Standing armies opposed to standing armies can more
easily dispense with it than a standing army opposed to a popular insurrection, for in the [latter] case the troops are more
scattered and the divisions left more to themselves. . . .

The military virtue of an army is one of the most important
moral powers in war, and where it is absent, either its place is
supplied by one of the others, such as great superiority of gener-
alship or popular enthusiasm, or the results will hardly be commensurate with the exertions made. . . .

This spirit can be generated from two sources, and only by
both together: first, a succession of campaigns and victories;

[1] Von Clausewitz here refers to the Swiss in their traditional role as
mercenaries, the Spaniards in their role as guerrillas against Napoleon, and
the Americans in theirs as a militia army. In the War of the Spanish
Succession (1702–1713), Prince Eugene of Savoy and the Duke of Marlborough commanded polyglot coalitions made up in large part of mercenaries
and impressed men.

second, activity by the army carried to its highest pitch. Only by these does a soldier come to know his own powers. The more a general habitually demands from troops, the surer he may be that his demands will be met. The soldier is as proud of overcoming obstacles by labor as of surmounting danger. . . . Once [the spirit] grows into a strong tree, it will stand against the fiercest storms of misfortune and defeat and even against the indolence of peace . . . for several generations, even under generals of mediocre abilities. . . .

With this noble and generous *esprit de corps* of veteran troops . . . we must not compare the vanity and self-esteem of the old-style standing army, held together merely by the glue of regulations and the drill book.[2]

Plodding earnestness and strict discipline may retain military virtue for a time, but they cannot create it. Hence, though they have some value, they must not be overrated. Order, smartness, good will, and a degree of pride . . . are qualities to be prized in an army formed in peacetime, but they are not sufficient. The whole remains monolithic . . . and a single crack will split the whole mass. Above all, the highest spirit in the world is only too quickly reversed, becoming at the first check . . . a . . . *sauve qui peut*. Such an army can achieve only through its leader, and never through itself.

[2] Von Clausewitz here refers to the traditional "standing army" of the eighteenth century, recruited normally by promises of high pay or by guile, from the less desirable elements of society, and held to its duties only by an unbending and sometimes brutal discipline. It was such a Prussian army that Napoleon shattered at the Battle of Jena (1806).

War, the Army, and Political Community

18 >1

G. W. F. HEGEL

There is a kind of subjectivity which dissolves established
life in the political community.[1] . . . The genuine form of subjectivity, however, is the very opposite: that subjectivity which
. . . constitutes . . . the ideal of the whole. . . . In the state at
peace, each group in civic life has its own existence, but this
existence outside and beside one another is possible only as a
result of the idea of the whole. This . . . conception of unity
must also find its own expression.

International sovereignty is such an expression to the extent
that spirit, and [the idea] of the political community as the
concrete expression of spirit, have found their logical expression
in the institutions of the state. But spirit is essentially a universal
identity,[2] which being infinitely free is infinitely negative toward
[that which is not infinitely free] and [hence] has absorbed all
existential differences into itself and is hence exclusive. . . . The
individuality of the political community as an exclusive identity[3] appears as a relation between it and other autonomous

[1] Hegel refers here to radical scepticism and individualism. Traditional
translations use the term "state" rather than "political community." As should
become clear, however, this usage does some violence to Hegel's meaning.

[2] The conventional translation, "being-by-itself," adds nothing in the way
of clarity to Hegel's style, which is far from lucid at its best.

[3] In contrast to "the spirit," the state or political community is limited, in
Hegel's theory, by being involved in the transient and apparent "reality" of
the material world, but is the highest approximation of the spirit possible in
that world.

Translated by the editor from The Philosophy of Right *(1821), Part III,
Sections 320–328.*

states. Since the . . . spirit finds its concrete expression in such political identity, it is that identity which is the first freedom and the highest dignity of a people.

Those who, out of a desire for a larger union which would constitute a larger political community, . . . are willing to abandon their own political identity in order to join with others are ignorant both of the nature of corporate communities and of the pride of a people in its independence. . . .

In reality, the negative relation of the state to itself [4] appears in the relations of *one state to another* as if it were something external. This negative element seems, on the surface, to be an event due to outside causes not necessarily connected to the political community. In fact, however, it is the highest element of the state . . . , the idealization of its own finite materials. It is the aspect of the state in which the political community comes into conflict, armed with absolute power, with all that is particular and individual, such as life, property, and property rights, or even wider circles [of civic life] and makes their relative worthlessness a fact which men's consciousness can perceive clearly.

Indeed, this phase, in which the interest and right of individuals is reduced to unimportance, is at the same time deeply positive, for it forms the basis of the genuine identity [of individuals] as contrasted with that [spurious identity] which is accidental and transient. This relation between the individual and the state and the recognition of it is the highest substantive duty of the individual. Property and life, not to speak of opinions or day-to-day routine, must be sacrificed, if necessary, to preserve the identity, independence, and sovereignty of the political community. . . .

Here lies the ethical element in war. War cannot be regarded as an absolute evil. . . . It is necessary that finite things, such as life and property, be recognized as impermanent and insecure, for chance and accident are inherent in the nature of finitude. In one sense, this necessity appears as a force of nature, for all that is finite is transient and mortal. In ethical life, in the

----

[4] That is, the conflict between the ideal of the state as political community, devoted to the quest for freedom and identity, and those aspects of the life of men and groups which are necessarily particular and divisive, being concerned with material goals and satisfactions.

political community, that power is taken from nature and is elevated into an expression of freedom. . . . What in nature is simply negative becomes, in ethical life, infused with substance and with identity; a thing is not transient merely because it is transient, but because it is willed to be so.

War makes a serious matter out of the pious platitude that earthly things are vain. . . . Moreover, as I have said elsewhere, "finite pursuits are made insecure and the ethical health of peoples is preserved. As the movements of the ocean prevent the corruption which would result from perpetual calm, so a people escape by war from the corruption which would result from perpetual peace.". . . In fact, the organic unity of the political community is established internally by the same ideal which finds expression in war. This is demonstrated by the historical fact that victorious wars have prevented civil strife and strengthened the internal unity and power of the state. So too, those peoples who have been unwilling to establish unified political institutions have been subjugated by others . . . ; their freedom died through their fear of its dying. Moreover, states . . . which are very small . . . have continued to exist merely by virtue of their internal institutions, which would seem, in themselves, to promise neither internal repose nor external security.[5]

In peace, civil life becomes more and more diffuse. Each separate activity becomes more and more parochial and self-interested, and eventually corruption begins. Particularity and division become more and more rigid and ossified. In the end, as in the body when the organs become rigid and the body loses its unity, death ensues. Perpetual peace is sometimes held up as the goal of human progress. Kant, for example, proposed an alliance of princes designed to settle the conflicts of states, and the Holy Alliance was intended to be something of the sort. . . . Yet the political community has identity, and identity contains an implicit negative element. A number of states may make themselves

---

[5] In these last two examples, Hegel refers first to Poland in the eighteenth century, which was partitioned by her neighbors. In the second, he almost certainly refers to Switzerland: the highly decentralized constitution of Switzerland hardly seems, in other words, likely to produce unity or strength in foreign affairs; yet it creates or reflects a united spirit and hence a determination to preserve Swiss independence and Switzerland's way of life.

into . . . a union, but such a union must inevitably create conflict, and hence, an enemy. Peoples are strengthened by war, and nations divided at home may find internal peace through external war. True, war entails insecurity in one's possessions, but this insecurity is precisely what is needed. One may denounce the . . . vanity of worldly things from the pulpit; yet each individual, no matter how much he may be impressed by such eloquence, thinks that he will manage to retain his own possessions. Let insecurity come in the form of cavalry with drawn sabers . . . , and such pietism is transformed and pronounces curses on the invaders. . . .

Citizens have entered into relations with one another by which all sacrifice their particular individuality to that of the state, and hence the sacrifice of such individuality is a public duty. This duty is only one aspect of the ideal in its expression in particular existence, and as such, it becomes a *distinct* relationship to which an appropriate profession,[6] the vocation of courage, is dedicated. . . .

The armed forces of the state are its standing army. The necessity of entrusting the defense of the state to a particular group arises from . . . the same necessity by which each of the other particular interests and activities has its own devotees. There is much unsystematic theorizing about the advantages or disadvantages of a standing army. Mere opinion tends to decide against it because it is easier to see separate aspects of the army than to understand its whole function in the political community. Too, the civilian community is likely to rate particular interests, such as expense and taxation, at too high a level and to see the army not as necessary in its own right but only as a means to the protection of special and private interests. . . .

Conflicts between states may arise out of any specific aspect of their relations. The task of the distinct portion of the community entrusted with its defense is to deal with these. Yet if the state as such is in danger of losing its independence, then it is the duty of all citizens to rally to its defense. . . .

The military profession is . . . assigned the duty . . . of

[6] A better translation might be "station," implying a distinct set of duties to the community.

expressing in action the ideal implicit in the profession; in other words, it must sacrifice itself. Courage is of different kinds. The ferocity of the animal, the bravado of the robber, the bravery due to a sense of honor or chivalry are not courage in the true sense. . . . Only the aim and the content of action gives meaning to the feeling of "fearlessness." Robbers and murderers, having a crime in mind, or adventurers, gratifying their own emotions, risk their lives without fear. The modern world believes, however, that the ideal and the sense of the universal give a higher form to courage. . . . Courage among civilized peoples consists in a readiness to sacrifice oneself for the political community. It is not personal fearlessness which is a virtue but taking part in a collective cause. In India, five hundred men vanquished twenty thousand who were not cowards but lacked the spirit of unity and cooperation.

The nature of courage is found in the . . . end, the freedom of the political community. In realizing this end, courage gives up particular individuality. Hence, in this virtue one finds the most extreme contradictions. In courage there is self-sacrifice which is, however, the expression of freedom; in it, the highest self-control, which is the highest independence, submits to a life of service and to the mechanics of an external system of rules; a total obedience . . . and even the absence of one's own spirit is united with the most total and intense presence of spirit and resolution; and the most hostile and personal action against individuals is joined to indifference, or even kindly feelings toward those one harms.

Democracy and the Army

1835

ALEXIS DE TOCQUEVILLE

. . . When the military spirit leaves a people, the profession of arms is no longer held in honor, and military men fall to the lowest rank among public servants; they are little esteemed and no longer understood. This reverses the tendency of aristocratic ages; the men who enter the army are no longer from the highest, but from the lowest class. Military ambition is expressed only when no other is possible. Hence arises a circle of cause and consequence . . . : the best part of the nation shuns the military profession because that profession is not honored, and the profession is denied honor because the nation no longer follows it.

It is not surprising, then, that democratic armies are often restless, bad-tempered, and dissatisfied with their lot, though their welfare is better provided for and their discipline less severe than in other countries. The soldier feels himself in an inferior position, and wounded pride excites a taste for hostilities that would make his services necessary, or awakes a desire for revolution during which he may hope to win by force of arms the political influence and the personal importance normally denied him. . . .

Moreover, as . . . (to repeat what I have just stated) the wealthiest, best-educated, and ablest men seldom adopt the military profession, the army, taken as a whole, eventually comes to form a small nation by itself, in which the mind is less enlarged and habits are more rude than in the nation at large. Yet this

From Democracy in America (1835). This translation by the editor has been adapted from that of Henry Reeve (New York: Langley, 1840), vol. II, Book III, Chaps. 22, 23, 25, 26, pp. 280–290, 296–303.

small, uncivilized nation has arms in its possession and knows
how to use them . . . ; indeed, the pacific spirit of the community increases the danger to which a democratic people is exposed
from the military and turbulent spirit of the army. There is
nothing so dangerous as an army in an unwarlike nation; the
excessive love for quiet on the part of the community as a whole
always puts the constitution at the mercy of the soldiery.

. . . [I]f democratic nations are naturally prone to peace
. . . , they are constantly drawn to war and revolutions by their
armies. Military revolts, which are almost never to be feared in
aristocracies, are always to be dreaded in democracies. These
perils must be accounted among the most formidable that assail
the destiny [of democracies], and the attention of statesmen
should be persistently applied to find a remedy for them.

When a nation perceives that it is affected internally by the
restless ambition of its army, the first thought which occurs is
that of giving this inconvenient ambition an [external] object by
going to war. . . . War has great advantages, but we must not be
deluded by the belief that it can diminish the danger. . . . That
threat is only suspended by it, to return more fiercely when the
war is over, for armies are always more impatient with peace
after having tasted war. War is a remedy only for a people who
are always thirsting for military glory. . . . [T]he great military
rulers who may rise up in great democratic nations will find it
easier to conquer with their armies than to make their armies live
at peace. . . .

No protracted war can fail to endanger the freedom of a
democratic country. Not that after every victory one need fear
that the victorious generals will seize supreme power by force.
. . . War does not always give democratic communities over to
military rule, but it must invariably and immeasurably increase
the powers of civil government; it must almost inevitably concentrate the direction of all individuals and the management of all
things in the hands of the administration. If it does not lead to
despotism by sudden acts of violence, it prepares men for it
gently by changing their habits. . . .

It is my opinion that a restless and turbulent spirit is inherent in the very nature of democratic armies and beyond hope of cure. Legislators in democracies should not expect to devise any scheme of military organization capable by itself of calming and restraining the military profession. . . .

The remedy for the vices of the army is not to be found in the army itself, but in the country. By nature, democratic nations are afraid of disturbance and despotism; the object is to turn these natural propensities into intelligent, deliberate, and lasting tastes. When men have learned to make a peaceful and profitable use of freedom and have felt its blessings, when they have conceived a manly love of order and have freely submitted themselves to discipline, these same men, if they follow the profession of arms, bring into it unconsciously . . . these same habits and manners. The general spirit of the nation, being infused into the spirit peculiar to the army, tempers the opinions and desires created by military life, or represses them by the might of public opinion. Teach the citizens to be educated, orderly, firm, and free, and the soldiers will be disciplined and obedient.

Any law that, seeking to repress the turbulent spirit of the army, should work to diminish the spirit of freedom in the nation or to overshadow the ideas of law and right would defeat its object; it would do more to favor than to curtail the establishment of a military despotism. . . .

Among the soldiers of a democratic army, some acquire a taste for military life, but the majority, being enlisted against their will . . . , do not consider themselves as seriously engaged in the military profession. . . . They adapt themselves to military life, but their minds are still tied to the interests and obligations which they had in civil life. They do not therefore imbibe the spirit of the army; rather, they infuse the spirit of the community at large into the military. It is through private soldiers especially that it may be possible to infuse into a democratic army the love of freedom and the respect for rights if these ideas have once been successfully inculcated in the public. The reverse happens in aristocracies, where soldiers have nothing in common with their fellow citizens and live among them as strangers. . . . In aristocracies, the officers are the conservative element because

they alone have retained a tight connection with civil society.
. . . In democratic armies, the private soldier stands in this
position for the same cause. . . .

In democratic nations, the man who becomes an officer sev-
ers all ties that bound him to civil life. . . . His true country is
the army, since he owes all he has to the rank he has attained in
it; he therefore follows the fortunes of the army and rises or sinks
with it. . . . [H]e may, perhaps, ardently desire war, or labor to
bring about revolution. . . . There are, nevertheless, some factors which temper this restless and warlike spirit. . . . A man
who, being born in the lower classes . . . , has risen . . . to be
an officer has already taken a prodigious step. . . . The fear of
risking what he has already acquired dampens the desire to gain
what he has not yet obtained. . . . His ambition will be more
and more cooled in proportion to the increasing distinction of
his rank, [which] teaches him that he has more to put in
jeopardy. . . . [T]he least warlike and so the least revolutionary
part of a democratic army will always be its chief commanders.

But these remarks . . . are not applicable to . . . the class
of noncommissioned officers. . . . Like the officers, the noncommissioned officers have broken all the ties which bound them to
civil life; like the officers, they devote themselves permanently to
the service . . . ; but noncommissioned officers are men who
have not yet attained a firm and exalted position. . . . [A] noncommissioned officer is doomed to . . . an obscure, confined,
comfortless, and precarious position. . . . The grade he fills is by
no means irrevocable; he is subject to the arbitrary pleasure of his
commanding officer . . . : a slight fault or a whim may deprive
him in a moment of the rewards of many years of labor. . . . Noncommissioned officers are therefore bent on war . . . ; but if war
be denied them, then they desire revolution . . . to enable them,
aided by the general confusion, to get rid of their superior officers
and take their places. . . .

. . . A democratic nation must despair of obtaining from
soldiers that blind, detailed, submissive, and invariable obedience which an aristocracy may impose. . . . The state of society
does not prepare them for it, and the nation would risk losing its

natural assets if it sought to acquire advantages of this kind. In democratic communities, military discipline ought not to attempt to destroy the free action of the faculties [of the individual]; all that can be done by discipline is to direct it. The obedience thus enforced is less exact, but it is more willing and intelligent . . . ; consequently, it will often become more strict, spontaneously, if danger demands it. The discipline of an aristocratic army is apt to be relaxed in war, because discipline is based on habit, and war disturbs habits. The discipline of a democratic army, on the contrary, is strengthened . . . because every soldier clearly perceives that he must be silent and obedient in order to conquer. . . .

It should never be forgotten by princes and leaders of democratic nations that nothing but the love of freedom can maintain an advantageous contest with the love and habit of physical well-being. . . .

I shall add but a few words on civil wars. . . . Men living in democracies do not naturally have the military spirit; they may acquire it when necessity has forced them to take the field, but to rise up and voluntarily expose themselves to the horrors of war, especially civil war, is a course they are not likely to adopt. None but the most adventurous members of the community consent to run such risks; the bulk of the people will remain motionless.

Even if the public was inclined to act, however, many obstacles would stand in their way, for they can resort to . . . no political powers subordinate to the supreme power of the nation which afford an effective support to resistance against the government.[1]

. . . Those who in such nations seek to carry out a revolution by force of arms must necessarily seek to seize the whole machinery of government as it stands, which can be done better by a *coup d'état* than by war, for as soon as regular war breaks

---

[1] In a footnote, de Tocqueville observes that he is speaking of centralized democratic states, not confederations. Since real power in a confederacy lies with the states, civil wars are only "foreign wars in disguise." The United States, presumably, would have occupied an intermediate position before the Civil War, and increasingly approximated de Tocqueville's model of a democracy thereafter.

out, the party that represents the state is always certain to conquer.

The only case in which a civil war could arise is if the army should divide in two factions: one raising the standard of rebellion, the other remaining true to its allegiance. . . .

Part II

The Military in New Nations:

General Problems

The Military in the Political
Development of New Nations

MORRIS JANOWITZ

New nations are those countries of Africa and Asia which have achieved independence or have been swept into the process of modernization since the end of World War II. These nations face common economic and social problems, and in particular, they face the paramount task of finding a format for civil-military relations appropriate to their social structure. In the process of directing societal change, leaders of new nations have a political choice as to the balance of coercion versus persuasion that will be used. Western scholars have tended to emphasize economic development, social structure, and political institutions during a period in which the military have emerged as a crucial institution and power bloc. The purpose of this discussion is to explore the extent to which the military can effect modernization with minimum resort to force and coercion.

South American countries, as they seek economic development, have many characteristics comparable to the new nations. Even more pointedly, it appears at first glance that these countries are also confronted with similar crises of civil-military relations. But there are fundamental differences. The forms of military intervention represent more than a century of struggle and accommodation, which has produced political institutions different from those found in the new nations. Thus, there is a logic for excluding South American countries from this analysis.

Reprinted by permission from Bulletin of the Atomic Scientists, 20 (*October 1964*), *6–10.*

It appears to be a universal political conception that a new state requires an army. In the course of preparing this study, it was hoped that at least some new nations would make it a national policy not to create an army, or at least de facto to rely on a mobile police force. It turned out that there is no such new nation—even the 200 man army of Togo was capable of political intervention by the use of force. No political leader of a new nation has openly declared that his country can operate as an independent nation without a military establishment. The U.N. has not been able to remove tensions and conflicts about national borders from its agenda, even in Sub-Sahara Africa, where the possibility of such agreements was perhaps greatest. Thus, in exploring the relevance of democratic theory for the politics of new nations, one must take the military, both realistically and theoretically, as a core institution.

The military in new nations can intervene in domestic politics because they control the instruments of violence. The fact that armies have exercised much of their political influence without violent combat or extensive bloodshed should not obscure the significance of force as the basis from which they exercise their political power. Because these military establishments are mainly infantry battalions which can be deployed in urban centers or in rural areas, they have the maximum potential for involvement in domestic politics.

Political Formats

Models for describing the political activities of the military in new nations during the last fifteen years range from performing the minimal governmental functions essential for any nation-state to that of constituting themselves as the exclusive governing political group.

An _authoritarian-personal_ type of civil-military control based on personal and traditional power is found in nations just beginning the process of modernization, such as Ethiopia or Saudi Arabia. This is a format which cannot produce the conditions for modernization, and seems certain to be swept aside by some form of collective leadership—civilian or more likely, military.

Ghana is a case of *authoritarian-mass party* control, as are Mali and Guinea. The civilian political regimes appear to have an organizational capacity to rule and to keep the military confined in its political role. But this approach, because of its ideological assumptions and coercive practices, fails to articulate with the objectives of a tutelary democracy.

. . . India and Malaya represent *democratic-competitive* control by civilian leadership. This leadership is indeed fragile and subject to extreme internal and external pressure. Nevertheless it exists in enough countries to make it a political reality for new nations.

Although the first three formats differ markedly in the form of internal political control, they have the common feature that the military's involvement in domestic politics is minimal. The officer corps is not involved in domestic partisan politics, but functions as an institution symbolizing the independent and legitimate sovereignty of the new nation.

In Indonesia and Turkey a *civil-military coalition* is found. The civilian leadership remains in power only because of the military's assent, or the military may be forced to establish a caretaker government with a view to returning power to civilian political groups. These alliances and caretaker governments are unstable; they frequently lead to a wider level of involvement, where the military set themselves up as the political ruling group, as has happened in Thailand, Egypt, and the Sudan. The result is a military oligarchy, because, for a limited time at least, the political initiative passes to the military. In these two types the military face the same political task: to create a mass apparatus which makes possible a minimum level of political consensus.

Historical Dimensions

The initial step in an analysis of the military in political development is to examine the historical and economic factors which fashioned the military establishments. Three cultural-geographic areas, South and Southeast Asia, the Middle East and North Africa, and Sub-Sahara Africa, show marked internal differences, but in each there is a historical unity based on the aftermath of colonial rule.

In South and Southeast Asia, indigenous military institutions—with the exception of those in Thailand—were eliminated, transformed, or replaced by the metropolitan powers. Despite different forms of political rule and economic organization, South and Southeast Asia were the areas of the maximum impact of colonial rule. Although colonial rule rested on military force, colonialism is not a form of direct military government. Japanese occupation in many areas did introduce military intervention in domestic politics for a brief but sometimes decisive period; nevertheless, the nations of this area emerged from a historical tradition of colonial rule and not of military rule. Presently four armies have politically expanded roles, while eight are limited—but in only two is the limitation based on democratic-competitive politics.

In the Middle East and North Africa the indigenous Ottoman traditions were ones of political involvement and political rule by military officers. Moreover, the impact of colonial rule—as compared with Southeast Asia—was less extensive and less direct. Although there was warfare and violence, military institutions were not radically transformed but only gradually adapted and accommodated to the influence of modernization. Even after liberation, the modernization and professionalization of the military in many countries of this area had to confront residues of older officer elements. For the military after national liberation, political involvement was a tradition and not an innovation or exception. Military oligarchies can be found in four of the twelve countries with professional modern armies, civil-military coalitions exist in six nations, and in only two are the military limited to a nonpartisan role.

In Sub-Sahara Africa there is a still different historical tradition. The colonial governments easily destroyed indigenous military institutions and, by contrast with other colonial areas, the area was relatively demilitarized. The metropolitan governments ruled with tiny colonial armed forces and, except for short periods of warfare during the two world wars, the role of the military reflected their limited and primitive resources and the newness of the countries. Yet, even after a short period of independence, military intervention has taken place with explosive speed.

Other Dimensions

The origin of the military is not the only indicator of political roles after independence. Clearly, military formations born in the struggle for national liberation have maintained wide political involvement. While the post-liberation armies are too new to be effective or tested, the ex-colonial armies are divided about equally between those which have remained as instruments of national sovereignty and those which have intervened in domestic politics. The British-trained troops do not possess an overriding built-in resistance to political intervention, as the cases of Pakistan and the Sudan demonstrate. Leaving aside the Sub-Sahara countries because of their recent independence, it appears that the likelihood of political involvement increases after independence—of the countries ruled by the military, all but one have been independent for more than ten years.

Nations with more modern technology are likely to have more efficient military establishments, but there is no relationship between per capita gross national product and the size of the military. The size of the military is less related to economic base than to total population. A military establishment appears indispensable, and even the poorest and smallest countries are involved in developing one. The Libyan army of 4,500, composed almost exclusively of infantry troops, may be compared with the Indian defense force of over 500,000 men with first-line jet planes and naval units. In other words, investment in the military is a fundamental cost which new nations are prepared to invest, whatever their economic ability to pay.

In those nations where the military have had some successful operational experience, especially in suppressing internal insurrections, they have contributed to social cohesion and, in a sense, to the development of an orientation that rises above partisan politics and embodies national ideals. Successful operational experience has made the military more professional, which in turn becomes a further basis for intervention in domestic politics.

Even where armies have limited political roles, they have economic and social functions which influence political change.

BASIC DATA ON ARMED FORCES OF NEW NATIONS

Country	Population	Date of Independence	Civil-Military Model	Political Role	Origin of Armed Forces
China	*600,000,000*	*1949*			*Natl. liberation*
SOUTH AND SOUTHEAST ASIA					
India	402,600,000	1950	Democratic-competitive	Mark of sovereignty	Ex-colonial
Indonesia	90,000,000	1949	Civil-military coalition	Political bloc	National liberation *
Philippines	24,718,000	1946	Democratic-competitive	Mark of sovereignty	Ex-colonial
South Korea	23,848,000	1945	Military oligarchy	Political ruling group	Post-liberation *
Thailand	21,881,000	Non-colonial	Military oligarchy	Political ruling group	Non-colonial
Burma	20,457,000	1948	Military oligarchy	Political ruling group	National liberation
South Vietnam	13,790,000	1954	Authoritarian-personal control	Mark of sovereignty	Ex-colonial †
Afghanistan	13,150,000	Non-colonial	Authoritarian-personal control	Mark of sovereignty	Non-colonial
Ceylon	9,612,000	1948	Democratic-competitive	Mark of sovereignty	Ex-colonial
Nepal	9,044,000	1951	Authoritarian-personal control	Mark of sovereignty	Ex-colonial
Malaya	6,698,000	1957	Democratic-competitive	Mark of sovereignty	Ex-colonial
Cambodia	4,845,000	1953	Authoritarian-personal control	Mark of sovereignty	Ex-colonial
MIDDLE EAST AND NORTH AFRICA					
Pakistan	86,823,000	1950	Military oligarchy	Political ruling group	Ex-colonial
Turkey	26,881,000	Non-colonial	Civil-military coalition	Political bloc	Non-colonial
Egypt	25,365,000	1952	Military oligarchy	Political ruling group	Ex-colonial
Iran	20,457,000	1945	Civil-military coalition	Political bloc	Non-colonial
Morocco	10,550,000	1956	Democratic-competitive ‡	Mark of sovereignty	Ex-colonial §
Algeria	10,930,000	1962	Civil-military coalition	Political bloc	National liberation
Iraq	6,952,000	1934	Military oligarchy	Political ruling group	Ex-colonial
Saudi Arabia	6,000,000 est.	Non-colonial	Authoritarian-personal control	Mark of sovereignty	Non-colonial
Yemen	4,500,000 est.	Non-colonial	Military oligarchy	Political ruling group	Non-colonial
Syria	4,539,000	1946	Civil-military coalition	Political ruling group	Ex-colonial
Tunisia	3,935,000	1956	Democratic-competitive ‡	Mark of sovereignty	Ex-colonial
Israel	2,061,000	1948	Democratic-competitive	Mark of sovereignty	Ex-colonial
Jordan	1,636,000	1946	Civil-military coalition	Political bloc	Ex-colonial
Lebanon	1,550,000	1941	Democratic-competitive	Political bloc	Ex-colonial

SUB-SAHARA AFRICA

Country	Population	Year	Regime	Sovereignty	Status
Nigeria	35,400,000	1960	Democratic-competitive	Mark of sovereignty	Post-liberation
Ethiopia	21,000,000	Non-colonial	Authoritarian-personal control	Mark of sovereignty	Non-colonial
Congo (Leopoldville)	13,652,000	1960	Civil-military coalition	Political bloc	Post-liberation
Sudan	10,262,000	1956	Military oligarchy	Political ruling group	Ex-colonial
Tanganyika	9,238,000	1962	Democratic-competitive ‡	Mark of sovereignty	Post-liberation
Ghana	6,690,000	1957	Authoritarian-mass party	Mark of sovereignty	Ex-colonial
Madagascar	5,239,000	1960	Not classified	Mark of sovereignty	Post-liberation
Mali	4,300,000	1960	Authoritarian-mass party #	Mark of sovereignty	Post-liberation
Upper Volta	3,537,000	1960	#	Mark of sovereignty	Post-liberation
Cameroun	3,225,000	1960	#	Mark of sovereignty	Post-liberation
Ivory Coast	3,103,000	1960	#	Mark of sovereignty	Post-liberation
Guinea	2,727,000	1958	Authoritarian-mass party	Mark of sovereignty	Post-liberation
Chad	2,730,000	1960	#	Mark of sovereignty	Post-liberation
Ruanda	2,634,000	1962	Not classified	Mark of sovereignty	Post-liberation
Niger	2,550,000	1960	#	Mark of sovereignty	Post-liberation
Senegal	2,550,000	1960	#	Mark of sovereignty	Post-liberation
Sierra Leone	2,400,000	1941	Democratic-competitive ‡	Mark of sovereignty	Ex-colonial
Burundi	2,213,000	1962	Not classified	Mark of sovereignty	Post-liberation
Dahomey	2,000,000	1960	#	Mark of sovereignty	Post-liberation
Somali	1,990,000	1960	Authoritarian-personal control	Mark of sovereignty	Post-liberation
Togo	1,642,000	1960	**	Mark of sovereignty **	Post-liberation
Cameroons	1,621,000	1960	Not classified	Mark of sovereignty	Post-liberation
Liberia	1,500,000	Non-colonial	Authoritarian-personal control	Mark of sovereignty	Non-colonial
Central African Republic	1,185,000	1960	#	Mark of sovereignty	Post-liberation
Libya	1,172,000	1951	Authoritarian-personal control	Mark of sovereignty	Post-liberation

* A significant ex-colonial element from the Japanese army is included.
† Ex-colonial cadres from the French period were joined with post-liberation forces.
‡ Civil control is based on semicompetitive political institutions.
§ An important national liberation component, which served as a guerrilla force, is included.
# Not classified as a civil-military model, since the armed forces are not integral groups because of defense treaty with France.
** Military revolt in 1963 resulted in the army assuming the role of political bloc.
Not classified cases imply either absence of data or indeterminacy of situation because of recent independence.

The military accumulate a considerable amount of material and technological resources. For example, the military serve as a training ground for technical and administrative skills; in a number of countries they maintain economic enterprises, from manufacturing plants to department stores. In Burma the Defense Service Institute, which was mainly concerned with supplies to the military establishment, was expanded in 1961 to include the Burma Economic Development Corporation. Now the army controls commercial concerns involved in steel production, pharmaceuticals, cement, and shipping. The military contribute to the development of public works, roads, and engineering projects. Such projects can be found throughout most new nations, but, with some notable exceptions, their importance is more symbolic than economic.

While there has been a trend toward "civilianizing" the military profession, the difference between military management and the skills of political leadership is still marked. Political leaders are men who specialize in verbal skills and in mass appeals. Military officers have limited contact with the outside public, and it is difficult to transfer military skills to a civilian political career. The argument is that specific military characteristics give the military establishment potential to assume political power but limit its ability to exercise such power effectively.

Common Ideologies

While it is impossible to identify one military ideology in all the new nations, there are common ideological themes which help to explain the professional officer's political behavior.

First, there is a strong sense of nationalism with overtones of xenophobia. Military profession and career seem to produce few experiences which work to counter this xenophobia. As the military become more representative of the social structure, the code of professional ethics operates to repress tribal and separatist ties.

A second element is strong puritanism and an emphasis on anticorruption and antidecadence. The military view of morality prescribes modesty and self-restraint in private life. When the military junta in South Korea took action in July 1962 against inefficient, insubordinate government officials, among charges they levied were not only those of black-marketeering activities, but also of "keeping concubines." This asceticism creates tension with other elites, especially with new political elites, who use conspicuous consumption as one way to justify their authority and position.

A third element is the acceptance of collective public enterprise as the way to achieve social, political, and economic change. A scattering of officers in the Middle East have become outright Communists (Communist penetration in Iraq was probably the most extensive). The Indonesian air force, young and technologically oriented, is strongly leftist. The same appears to be the case in Egypt. More typically, however, the desire for governmental intervention is moderate. In the Middle East this leads to acceptance of socialist goals. After the military coup in Syria in 1962, the officer group in control (hardly radicals) announced their adherence to a "constructive and just socialism." In Southeast Asia, where the military confront leftist political parties, they do not use socialist symbols, although their specific objectives involve extensive governmental control of the economy. In Sub-Sahara Africa political trends within the military are only unfolding, but the inclinations for governmental intervention are apparent.

Fourth, and perhaps the most important theme, is the attitude of "antipolitics." As a result of social background, education, and career experiences, the military of the new nations become interested in politics, but they continue to distrust organized politics and civilian political leaders. Among officers there is no respect or understanding for the creative role of the politician and the political process. This is an expression of the military's resentment of older elites who accumulated profits and privileges in what they believe to have been a weak and ineffective society.

Political Takeover

As agents of political change, the military cannot avoid the popular goal of increased economic activity and a higher standard of living. In fact, modernization is a more overriding political objective than establishing a claim to legitimate authority. But to modernize the economy of a new nation, it is necessary to develop mass participation in new forms of social organization, ranging from village cooperatives to professional associations. If a prime political objective is persuasion rather than coercion, it becomes necessary to judge the effectiveness of a military oligarchy in domestic politics in terms of the military's ability to develop or permit the development of a mass political base.

The ability of the military to act as a political coalition partner often depends upon the extent of their own economic base. The more economic resources they have at their command, the greater is their scope for domestic politics. In turn, the scope of their economic enterprises seems to expand with the broadening of their political involvement. But the economic functions of the military change when the military assume direct political power.

The fundamental issue is the strategic contribution of the military to management of economic development, either in specific sectors in which they concentrate their efforts or in the overall rate of economic growth. While the results on either score are mixed, the outcome indicates basic limitations of the military in supplying economic leadership.

What factors assist or retard the military in developing an apparatus of mass political support? Social origins, education, and military skills help to explain the military's commitment to economic and social change. But the same factors inhibit political change, since they highlight the separateness, if not the exclusiveness, of military leaders from other elite groups, especially from political elites. Likewise, the format of military organization and the absence of appropriate political skills stand in the way of developing new political devices. However, the type of takeover which transforms the army into a military oligarchy becomes as crucial as its social heritage and professional tradition.

There are two types of takeover. The first is designed militarism, which is the premeditated search for political power, and the second is reactive militarism, which is the expansion of military power that results from the weakness of civilian institutions and the pressures of civilians to expand the military role. Reactive rather than designed militarism is the usual case in the new nations—although Egypt has supplied one of the few examples of designed militarism. By contrast, Pakistan is a clear-cut case of the more typical reactive militarism.

International Arena

The mechanics of political intervention of the military in the new nations, as in the old nations, involve both domestic and foreign policy. Clearly, domestic issues and domestic political objectives are overriding, but new nations continue to prepare for military intervention in support of foreign policy objectives. If the task of creating a domestic political apparatus to assist economic modernization seems to present a formidable objective to military oligarchies, and is yet to be solved adequately, the task of supporting a positive foreign policy can only complicate the tasks of political change.

The new nations are hardly underdeveloped in their concern with foreign affairs. One striking characteristic of the nationalism that emerges in new nations is that it immediately involves them in the world-wide arena of international politics. The existence of the United Nations, with its membership principle of one nation–one vote, and the realities of regional politics require each nation, no matter how small, to embark upon foreign policy.

The link between foreign and domestic politics in a new nation is obviously broader than the sources of military assistance and officer training. In fact, foreign military assistance is often only partially related to American or Soviet dependency and more related to national expansionist objectives. Few new nations are immune from some immediate security problem, either real or imagined.

The mercenary military are certainly at variance with the political morality of modern nationalism. Yet too often, political neutrality in the military is disguised opposition to democratic principles. Instead, in terms of democratic theory, the military need to be committed to the basic format of a democratic political system, even though they must remain nonpartisan in domestic politics. They must have a political orientation and, in fact, a political education similar to that of the citizen—one that enables them to act within the broad consensus of the policy. In this sense, then, the democratic model of civil-military relations has application to the political goals of a new nation. Therefore, the basis on which the military broaden their political involvement becomes a central issue. Are the military's political activities an expression of their fundamental commitment to the emerging values of the society? Any useful answer to this question would include the capacity of the political system to generate social and economic change, but would have as its basic dimension the minimization of coercion.

The Example of Ataturk

In summary, the military of the new nations are more politicized than their Western counterparts, and they may even produce a cadre of political activists. The process of education, recruitment, and the attendant emergence of professional cohesion all work to support this politicization of the military. Life career and indoctrination lead military personnel to a broad identification with national interest, but the military do not have appropriate political ideologies. While they are strongly nationalistic and oriented to collective and governmental enterprise, military officers are skeptical and even hostile to organized politics. They must learn the meaning of politics by actual experience. What is lacking in new nations is a basis of mutual trust between politicians and the military profession.

Yet, pressure toward political involvement does not necessarily imply the development of appropriate skills for the broader roles that the military accumulates. In fact, it is most difficult, if not impossible, for the military to manage the politics of a nation in the process of rapid economic development. At best, whether the military operate as a political bloc or as the ruling group, the greater their internal cohesion the greater the likelihood that they can prevent the fragmentation of their political power by means of countercoups.

But the military must be able to do more than merely

conserve their power. In the recent past, Turkey, under Ataturk, represented the one case in which a military oligarchy under an enlightened leader made fundamental contributions to social and economic modernization.

The process of modernization in Turkey was gradual and built on evolving institutions. From the beginning of his national leadership, Ataturk had a sharp sense of the limits of the military in politics. Perhaps his most decisive step was to insist that army officers who wanted to become directly involved in partisan politics had to leave the armed forces.

As the military leaders of the new nations approach the problems of political development, they have the model of Ataturk. Their timetable may be more pressing, but they have the advantage of his historical experiment. And there can be no doubt that the history of Ataturk is not lost on military leaders as they struggle for new political forms which might permit the military to operate as a political umpire rather than as a ruling oligarchy. If political change must wait for the breakdown of a military oligarchy, its outcome will not be conducive to an orderly and humane process of modernization.

Civilian Loyalties
and Guerrilla Conflict

CHALMERS A. JOHNSON

It is not surprising that Western statesmen and students of politics everywhere have recently begun to give major attention to what are variously termed guerrilla warfare, irregular warfare, paramilitary operations, *la guerre révolutionnaire,* insurrectional warfare, resistance movements, and other, allegedly military, doctrines. Of course, irregular armed struggles are not a unique feature of mid-twentieth-century politics; however, they have occurred with great frequency in our time and, more important, they have resulted in baffling victories over vastly better armed, better trained, and more numerous forces. President Kennedy, in response to the apparent superiority in military doctrine possessed by Communist forces in Asia, . . . ordered the rapid expansion of United States "guerrilla and counter-guerrilla forces."[1] On a more prosaic level, the publication in a national Sunday-morning newspaper of excerpts from a celebrated pamphlet on guerrilla warfare by Mao Tse-tung suggests that "guerrilla warfare," along with "massive retaliation," has entered the popular Cold War vocabulary.[2] Before a great deal of money is spent training anti-guerrilla troops, however, American leaders would

[1] Neal Stanford, "U.S. Prepares for Guerrilla Wars," *Foreign Policy Bulletin,* XL (June 1, 1961) , p. 139.
[2] "Mao's Primer on Guerrilla War," *New York Times Magazine,* June 4, 1961.

Reprinted by permission from World Politics, 14, *No. 4 (July 1962),* 646–661.

be wise to find out what is actually meant by "guerrilla warfare," and to determine whether military counter-measures—regardless of the type of training program pursued—are necessarily the appropriate response to it.

To approach the subject of guerrilla warfare as a purely military doctrine is to court disaster. The area of counter-guerrilla policy in which military considerations become relevant is extremely restricted and, even then, the most sophisticated military activities against guerrillas may prove to be fruitless if not pursued in conjunction with political measures. It might be recalled that T. E. Lawrence saw the problem of his war in terms of three categories of related variables: "the algebraical element of things, a biological element of lives, and the psychological element of ideas." [3] His breakdown is not necessarily accurate, only suggestive. What is significant is that he thought of only a third of war as a military, or technical, problem. Because the political two-thirds of guerrilla warfare has been ignored or misinterpreted by many recent commentators, a major confusion has entered into much thinking about guerrilla struggles. Some writers have suggested that armies of the Western Alliance have lost to Communist guerrillas because the former were over-equipped with inappropriate weapons (e.g., the Kuomintang, 1947–1949; or the French Expeditionary Forces in Indochina); other writers contend that "privileged" or "active sanctuaries" adjacent to the scene of guerrilla activity, and from which the guerrillas draw sustenance, are the key to the problem; still others pale at the effectiveness of Communist troops in China and Vietnam and gratuitously elevate Mao's strategic insights into a kind of secret weapon. However, all such criteria are open to exception. There are, indeed, certain general features—such as mobility and surprise—that constitute basic doctrine for the military one-third of guerrilla operations but, as we shall see, the ability of guerrillas to achieve surprise and to maneuver with great freedom depends upon the existence of other conditions that constitute the essence of a guerrilla situation.

Many writers feel that one military feature characteristic of

[3] David Garnett, ed., *The Essential T. E. Lawrence*, London, Jonathan Cape, 1951, p. 99.

all guerrilla warfare is the lack of established fronts. According to these writers, the freedom of guerrilla bands from fixed lines of supply and communications gives them the *sine qua non* of guerrilla victory: an ability to fight only at times and places of their own choosing. Lawrence has given poetical expression to this military "doctrine" in a famous and often repeated metaphor: "Translated into Arabic, the algebraic factor would first take practical account of the area we wished to deliver, and I began idly to calculate how many square miles: sixty: eighty: one-hundred: perhaps one hundred and forty thousand square miles. And how would the Turks defend all that? No doubt by a trench line across the bottom, if we came like an army with banners; but suppose we were (as we might be) an influence, an idea, a thing intangible, invulnerable, without front or back, drifting like a gas? Armies were like plants, immobile, firm-rooted, nourished through long stems to the head. We might be a vapour, blowing where we listed. Our kingdoms lay in each man's mind; and as we wanted nothing material to live on, so we might offer nothing material to the killing." [4] Actually, this was not the whole of Lawrence's doctrine, and certainly not the bedrock upon which it rested, but some writers have supposed that it was and criticized it.

W. E. D. Allen, for example, in a highly praised little book concerned with Wingate's Gideon Force (which invaded Abyssinia from Khartoum in the spring of 1941 and defeated the Italians), takes up Lawrence's tactical doctrine and finds it dated. Allen feels that favorable terrain—i.e., geography which interferes with the movement of heavy weapons and tanks and which affords cover and ambush sites to the guerrillas—is the chief prerequisite for guerrilla operations.[5] In his opinion, Lawrence's terrain was particularly unsuited to guerrilla warfare; and the development of aircraft has reduced the likelihood that Lawrence's operations could ever be repeated. Thus Allen regards Lawrence's doctrine of "war without fronts" as essentially

[4] *Ibid.*
[5] W. E. D. Allen, *Guerrilla War in Abyssinia*, London, Penguin Books, 1943, p. 19.

irrelevant unless geography is in the guerrillas' favor or control of the air is achieved.

Allen's opinion concerning the influence of aircraft on guerrilla tactics was, of course, not shared by Lawrence himself and has been refuted by recent events. Lawrence commented on this subject: "I fancy that air-power may be effective against elaborate armies: but against irregulars it has no more than moral value. . . . Guerrilla tactics are a complete muffing of air-force." [6] And, in a more recent context, Bernard Fall notes that "In view of the French mastery of the air, the Viet-Minh troops had made a veritable fetish out of camouflage." [7] Our interest in raising these points is not to defend one view against the other; it is, rather, to illustrate that if we seek to identify the common denominator of guerrilla wars in terms of military tactics alone, only confusion results. Allen's own contention that guerrilla conflicts are determined by geography is strikingly refuted by an observation of Vladimir Dedijer (official historian of the Yugoslav Partisan movement and one-time editor of the Party journal *Borba*). In his diary entry for July 2, 1943, Dedijer wrote: "Men from Srem [the region between the Danube and the Sava in Serbia] are visiting Tito. . . . I have discussed the development of the rising in Srem with him. The geographical conditions are exceptionally unfavourable for partisan fighting. The area is level as the palm of your hand, bordered by two great rivers, divided by two trunk railways, and with little forest. Tito points out what a first class example it is of the relative *unimportance* of the geographical factor in the development of a rising. The basic factor is studious political work, the attitude of the mass of the people, and the fighting leadership—if these are right, the population will fight to the last man." [8] If Dedijer and Tito are correct, as I believe they are, then the mounting of a guerrilla movement as well as

---

[6] Letter to Col. A. P. Wavell (later Field Marshal Lord Wavell), May 21, 1923, in Garnett, ed., *op. cit.*, p. 260.

[7] Bernard B. Fall, *Street Without Joy: Indochina at War, 1946–54*, Harrisburg, Pa., 1961, p. 60.

[8] Vladimir Dedijer, *With Tito Through the War: Partisan Diary, 1941–1944*, London, Hamilton, 1951, pp. 341–42.

the possibility of guerrilla victory depends upon the loyalties of civilians in the area of operations.

Writers on guerrilla warfare, such as Allen, have failed to distinguish between what is universal in all guerrilla struggles and what are individual military aspects of particular guerrilla contests. As we shall analyze in greater detail below, the irreducible characteristic of successful guerrilla warfare is the close cooperation between full-time guerrillas and a population almost wholly in sympathy with the guerrillas' goals. Both Lawrence and Allen, the former explicitly and the latter implicitly, support this conclusion. The foundation of Lawrence's strategy against the Turks was to mobilize ". . . the ill wills of all the Arab peoples, combined with the active hostility of a few zealots." [9] Similarly, in Wingate's campaigns against the Italians in Abyssinia, the mass of irregulars, led by English soldiers, were Abyssinians who had engaged in guerrilla harassment of the Italians since the collapse of the main Abyssinian forces in May 1936. Italian reprisals, insults, and dislocations of the traditional Abyssinian way of life gave rise to a mass mobilization that Allen himself describes as the "patriot movement." [10] Wingate was fully aware that the element upon which the success of his endeavor rested was the loyalty of the Ethiopians. In his report on Gideon Force, he wrote: *"Given a population favourable to penetration, a thousand resolute and well-armed men can paralyze, for an indefinite period, the operation of a hundred thousand."* [11] Lest it be thought that the foreign origin of Wingate's own force negates this proposition, it should be recalled that the English cadres were accredited to the Abyssinians and legitimatized by the presence in the field with them of Emperor Haile Selassie.

The idea that guerrilla warfare depends upon and is a function of mass civilian mobilization is, of course, not new to writers on guerrilla warfare. The doctrine of *la guerre révolutionnaire* evolved in recent years by French Army officers explicitly recognizes the guerrilla-civilian nexus and bases its

[9] Garnett, ed., *op. cit.,* p. 100.
[10] Allen, *op. cit.,* p. 33.
[11] In Christopher Sykes, *Orde Wingate,* Cleveland and New York, 1959, p. 324; italics added.

counter-guerrilla strategy upon this principle. Peter Paret has summarized French thinking on guerrilla warfare as follows: "Generally in modern war the civilian population does not constitute the main, and certainly not the first, object of attention. It is usually thought necessary to deal with the enemy's armed forces and his war-making potential before the population as such can be subjected to direct pressure. In revolutionary war this order is reversed. Revolutionary or insurrectional war has for its aim the take-over of power in the state—that is, internal conquest—made possible through the active help of a population that the insurgents have 'physically and morally conquered.' Military power plays a secondary role in such a contest; the decisive factor is the population, which is both the strongest force in the struggle as well as its primary object." [12]

Despite this clear perception of the underlying reality of a guerrilla situation, the French writers dissipate their insight as they develop their analysis. In focusing upon the link between active zealots and the population at large, they conclude that guerrilla-civilian cooperation is inevitably compelled by foreign agents and does not in any way manifest the wishes of the population. According to *la guerre révolutionnaire* theorists, the principal tactic employed by the agents of foreign powers in "conquering" the population is *terrorism*.[13] Some passing attention is given to the possible need for political and economic reforms but, generally speaking, contemporary French Army studies have failed to inquire objectively into the bases of mass social mobilization.

An emphasis upon guerrilla terrorization of an allegedly passive population leads directly to policy failures. It is supposed that successful counter-guerrilla operations involve the use of specially trained commandos who are, in effect, authorized to

[12] "The French Army and La Guerre Révolutionnaire," *Journal of the Royal United Service Institution*, CIV (February 1959), p. 59. For a thorough presentation of all aspects of the doctrine, see Michel Déon, *L'Armée d'Algérie et la Pacification*, Paris, Libraire Plon, 1959. One important French military source on this subject is Ximenès (pseud.), "La guerre révolutionnaire et ses données fondamentales," *Revue Militaire d'Information*, No. 281 (February-March 1957), pp. 7–20.

[13] Déon, *op. cit.*, p. 18.

counter-terrorize the same population. Virgil Ney, writing in a similar vein to that of the French Army school, propounds this policy as follows: "In the twentieth century, terrorism has become an orthodox part of guerrilla strategy. . . . Terrorism is . . . the most powerful weapon at the disposal of the guerrilla leader. . . . The enemy [anti-guerrilla forces], in order to forestall casualties and prevent the demoralization of his forces, must be prepared to meet terror with terror. And yet such draconian measures are alien to a civilized power." [14] Unfortunately, neither Mr. Ney nor French Army writers can point to a single case in which the principle of counter-terrorization has been effective in ending a guerrilla war.

In fact, such counter-measures can easily be shown to have quite the opposite result. German experience in Russia during the Second World War is only one case in point; [15] the American war against Aguinaldo in the pacification of the Philippines, 1899–1902, is another. A comment by General Arthur MacArthur during the latter conflict reveals what the Americans were up against: "When I first started against these rebels, I believed that Aguinaldo's troops represented only a faction. I did not believe that the whole population of Luzon was opposed to us; but I have been reluctantly compelled to believe that the Filipinos are loyal to Aguinaldo and the government which he represents." [16] The measures employed by United States forces included village-burning, blockade, reconcentration of civilians, and depopulation of various areas by military means. Yet the war continued even after the capture of Aguinaldo, and sporadic fighting occurred in many areas years after the official end of the war on July 4, 1902.

Japanese operations against Communist guerrillas in China during World War II offer a particularly valuable case study of the effect of terrorism against guerrillas. The Japanese command

---

[14] "Guerrilla War and Modern Strategy," *Orbis*, II (Spring 1958), pp. 75–76.

[15] See Edgar M. Howell, *The Soviet Partisan Movement, 1941–1944*, Washington, D.C., 1956.

[16] Quoted in Leon Wolff, *Little Brown Brother: How the United States Purchased and Pacified the Philippine Islands at the Century's Turn*, New York, 1961, p. 311.

in China was never wholly unified; the North China Area Army in Peking administered a separate area and pursued different policies from the China Expeditionary Army headquartered in Nanking. In both areas the Japanese suffered from guerrilla attacks and from their own inability to distinguish a guerrilla from a villager. However, in north China a policy known as *sankō-seisaku*—the physical destruction of all life and property in an area where guerrillas were thought to exist—was implemented, whereas in central China a policy of establishing so-called Model Peace Zones was pursued. The policy of Model Peace Zones consisted of expelling the Communists from certain very rich agricultural areas and then, following this military phase, of integrating the cleared area into the Japanese satellite economy. Government was placed in Chinese—albeit puppet— hands and the population was led to believe that cooperation with the Japanese was a viable alternative. Over the course of the war, the policy in central China achieved a much greater measure of success. Japanese *sōtō* (guerrilla mopping-up campaigns) were still under way in north China on virtually the day the war ended, and north China became the Communist stronghold in the succeeding civil war.[17]

While one can conclude from these and other case studies that anti-guerrilla terrorism will more than likely *spread* the mass mobilization upon which guerrilla movements thrive, it is true that guerrillas themselves have, in certain cases, resorted to terrorism against the civilian population. When this occurs, however, it is important to determine whether it is selective terrorism against alleged traitors to the movement, particular classes, or economic groups; or whether it is terrorism designed to compel support of an otherwise unpopular movement. There are, to my knowledge, no cases in which guerrilla operations have been successfully based solely on intimidation of the population.[18]

[17] For a full discussion of this history, see my *Peasant Nationalism and Communist Power: The Emergence of Revolutionary China, 1937–1945*, Stanford, Calif., 1962. . . .

[18] Russell W. Volckmann implies the possibility of forced loyalty from the population when he writes: "No resistance movement can flourish for long without mass civilian support. This support may be voluntary, induced, or imposed, but it is absolutely essential to the maintenance of large guerrilla

When guerrillas resort to indiscriminate terrorism, this indicates that they do not have broad mass support, without which their movement flounders. Only a losing or degenerate guerrilla force will risk the loss of all mass support by forcing civilian cooperation at gunpoint.

It is equally clear that those writers who stress "active sanctuary" as the basis of guerrilla success are also generalizing from an erroneous conception. When Bernard Fall writes, "In brutal fact, the success or failure of *all* rebellions since World War II depended entirely on whether the active sanctuary was willing and able to perform its expected role," [19] he is simply ignoring other equally brutal but nonetheless existent facts. The guerrilla victories in China, Cuba, and Yugoslavia did not depend upon the partisans' having unassailable sources of support or refuges within which they were secure. Moreover, in Indochina, the case with which Fall is concerned, he himself observes, ". . . the French were definitely the 'aliens' and the Communist-led Viet-Minh forces could count on the instinctive support of the native population." [20] Active sanctuaries, as well as the existence of guerrilla bases are, of course, not figments of the imagination and may well have an important effect upon a particular conflict; but civilian loyalties within the guerrilla area still determine the effectiveness of such sanctuaries. The postwar guerrilla struggles in Burma and, to a lesser extent, in Greece illustrate conflicts in which active sanctuaries proved to be of limited value because, among other reasons, the population was itself resistant to the trans-border insurgents. [21] Again, with regard to Algeria, where the Morice Line (an electrified barrier) interdicts the Tunisian

---

forces for a prolonged period of time in a country overrun by the enemy." (*We Remained: Three Years Behind the Enemy Lines in the Philippines,* New York, 1954, p. 125.) Colonel Volckmann commanded the United States Armed Forces in the Philippines, North Luzon—a guerrilla corps operating during the period of the Japanese occupation. His own experience indicates that broad-based civilian support was voluntary; only Filipino agents for the Japanese and collaborators were objects of guerrilla attack.

[19] Fall, *op. cit.,* p. 294.

[20] *Ibid.,* p. 15.

[21] See *Is It a People's Liberation? A Short Survey of Communist Insurrection in Burma* (Rangoon, Ministry of Information, Government of the Union of Burma, 1952) , which shows how the rebels alienated themselves from the

frontier, Fall concludes, "The war in Algeria, though far from being militarily as hopeless for the French as Indochina, nevertheless again shows the following equation: on the one hand 35,000 guerrillas with at best heavy infantry weapons; on the other hand 500,000 troops, including crack airborne divisions, 'heliborne' *SkyCav* outfits the Indochina fighters only dreamed about—in short, a luxury of matériel and manpower unequalled in French history for a force that size—yet a solution of the conflict by a decisive French military victory is not readily in sight." [22] Thus, it would appear that in preventing the spread of guerrilla war the Morice Line was of only secondary relevance to the Algerian struggle, as was the de Lattre Line around the Red River delta and the armored Ping-Han railroad of the Japanese in north China.

However, to say that sanctuaries or other military advantages possessed by the guerrillas are of secondary importance is not to say that they are of no importance at all. In our attempt to give definition to the phenomenon of guerrilla warfare, we have stressed the *primacy* of civilian loyalties; but this is not the whole of the definition. All guerrilla struggles are mass movements, but not all mass movements are guerrilla struggles. [23] Therefore, while it is crucial that the military one-third of guerrilla war (using

---

population (pp. 22–23); and Svetozar Vukmanović ("Tempo"), *How and Why the People's Liberation Struggle of Greece Met with Defeat* (London, Yugoslav Information Service, 1950), which criticizes the Greek guerrillas on the same score but from the opposite political point of view. For an objective study of the Greek war and a discussion of the question of privileged sanctuary, see Geoffrey Chandler, *The Divided Land: An Anglo-Greek Tragedy*, London, Macmillan, 1959, pp. 180–81 and *passim*.

[22] Fall, *op. cit.*, p. 297. The Morice Line was, of course, penetrated on occasion. See photographs of FLN operations against the Line in *New Statesman*, June 6, 1959, pp. 782–83. Nevertheless, the most effective French maneuver was "to cut off the nationalist fighters from their roots by preventing them from getting food and shelter from the peasant population" (*New York Times*, December 13, 1959, p. 2).

[23] There are obviously types of mass risings against governments other than guerrilla movements. Gwynn distinguishes at least three main classes of "disorders" in the experiences of British colonial troops: "1. Revolutionary movements organized and designed to upset established government. 2. Rioting or other forms of lawlessness arising from local or widespread grievances. 3. Communal disturbances of a racial, religious or political character not directed against Government, but which Government must suppress." It is

Lawrence's division figuratively) be understood as contingent
upon the question of popular attitudes, this military segment can
by no means be ignored. In fact, it can be much better understood as springing from guerrilla-civilian cooperation. The union
of active zealots and mobilized population gives rise to those very
features of guerrilla warfare—such as near-perfect intelligence,
extreme mobility, freedom from logistic anchors, and surprise—
that the true guerrilla force enjoys.

This becomes clear when one looks at the writings of individuals such as Lawrence, Mao, and Guevara. All of them stress
the need for close ties between guerrillas and civilians because of
the great military control this gives the guerrilla leader over the
course of hostilities, regardless of the enemy's potential.[24] Nowhere is this more evident than in the realm of intelligence, an
element stressed by Lawrence both as a military necessity and as a
major prop for morale.[25] Knowledge of what the enemy is doing
or staging at all times enables guerrillas to fight only at moments
of their own choosing, to guarantee superiority at the moment of
attack, and to escape anti-guerrilla mop-ups. The obtaining of
such intelligence depends upon intimate guerrilla contact with
the population, usually to the extent of creating a rebel "infra-
structure." The military implications of guerrilla intelligence are
obvious. Fall states: "It must be understood that practically all
French troop movements in Indochina took place in a 'fish bowl.'
Since practically no troop movements could take place at night

---

only the first that may imply "guerrilla warfare, carried on by armed bands
acting possibly under the instructions of a centralised organisation, but with
little cohesion." (Maj. Gen. Sir Charles W. Gwynn, *Imperial Policing*, London, Macmillan, 1934, pp. 10–11.) The Boxer Rebellion in China and the
Mau Mau rebellion in Kenya, for example, should be considered as "communal disturbances" and not as guerrilla movements.

[24] It is common in large-scale guerrilla movements to distinguish mobile
forces, full-time partisans restricted to a given area, and militia (organized
civilians who leave their regular occupations for military activity only in
emergencies). Chinese Communist usage designates these forces as *cheng-shih-
tui* (regulars), *yu-chi-tui* (guerrillas), and *min-ping* (militia). Wingate's
doctrine does not envisage armed forces other than regulars, but still stresses
the need to have the loyalty of the population on the side of the raiders. See
Sykes, *op. cit.*, pp. 324 ff.

[25] Garnett, ed., *op. cit.*, p. 101.

for fear of costly ambushes, even the smallest movement of troops, tanks or aircraft was immediately noticed by the population and brought to the attention of Viet-Minh agents." [26] Similarly, the providing of food, shelter, communications, stretcher bearers, labor for mine-laying, and the like by the civilian population all go to make up that ubiquitous word of guerrilla catechisms: mobility. On this point, Allen concludes: "The advantage which a guerrilla leader must retain and exploit over regular forces is *mobility*. Mobility favours surprise, and surprise is the basis of irregular tactics." [27]

These and other principles of guerrilla fighting have in recent times been most fully explored in the works of Mao Tse-tung. His famous lectures delivered in the early years of the Sino-Japanese War to students of the Anti-Japanese Military-Political University (*k'ang-jih chün-cheng ta-hsüeh*), located near the Communist base of Yenan, and other pamphlets prepared earlier during the period of the Kiangsi Soviet, constitute the largest body of doctrine on guerrilla warfare in existence. The most important of Mao's studies on guerrilla warfare are *Strategic Problems of China's Revolutionary War*,[28] *Strategic Problems in the Anti-Japanese Guerrilla War*,[29] *On the Protracted War*,[30] and *Problems of War and Strategy*.[31] His analyses fully bear out the understanding of guerrilla fundamentals established here. Mao continually stresses the need for close cooperation between guerrillas and the population at large: "Because guerrilla warfare basically derives from the masses and is supported by them, it can neither exist nor flourish if it separates itself from their sympathies and cooperation." [32] Similarly, one of the outstanding characteristics of his doctrine is the demand for rigid discipline and

[26] Fall, *op. cit.*, p. 73 n.
[27] Allen, *op. cit.*, p. 24.
[28] December 1936. See Mao Tse-tung, *Selected Works*, New York, 1954, I, pp. 175–253. For a competent military history covering the same period as this work, see Gen. Lionel Max Chassin, *L'Ascension de Mao Tse-tung*, Paris, Payot, 1953.
[29] May 1938. Mao Tse-tung, *op. cit.*, II, pp. 119–56.
[30] May-June 1938. *Ibid.*, II, pp. 157–243.
[31] November 1938. *Ibid.*, II, pp. 267–81.
[32] "Mao's Primer on Guerrilla War," *loc. cit.*, p. 13.

scrupulously correct behavior by fully mobile guerrilla troops in order to prevent their alienating the rural population through excesses.

The sensitivity of the Chinese to civilian loyalties is further revealed in their use of political commissars. Differing from the early Russian commissars, whose function it was to supervise ex-Tsarist officers in the Red Army, the Chinese *chengchih weiyüan* (political officer) had an educative function. His primary task was to heighten political awareness of the objectives of the war and of the means of achieving those objectives, both among the troops and among the civilians who backed up the troops. A Communist spokesman told the Yenan press party of July 1944: "No guerrilla army can fight successfully, or even last long, without the support of the people of the areas in which they campaign. Eighteenth Group Army [the Chungking designation for the Communist army] indoctrination is primarily aimed at training the troops to act in such a manner that they will gain this total support." [33] An indication of the literalness of Mao's aphorism that the relation between the guerrillas and the people is like that of fish to the sea is seen in the fact that the Japanese called certain of their north China operations "draining the water."

Despite the great richness of Mao's works on guerrilla warfare, the meaning of these works continues to be misunderstood in many quarters. Interpreters of Chinese guerrilla warfare commonly fail to consider the question of mass attitudes and, as a result, they tend to overestimate Mao's own role in producing a Chinese Communist victory. For example, one writer has said: "Mao Tse-tung has done for war what Lenin did for imperialism and Marx for capitalism: he has given war 'scientific schemata.' . . . [Mao] is the man who has written it down for others; the man who has presented the Communist revolutionary with the workable blueprint." [34] And, with even less caution, another writer asserts: "This 'scholar-soldier,' this man of intelligence,

[33] "The 18th Group Army: Training, Medical Care and Supply," U.S. Office of War Information, General Intelligence Division, *OPINTEL Report No. 324* (December 15, 1944) , p. 1.

[34] Edward L. Katzenbach, Jr., and Gene Z. Hanrahan, "The Revolutionary Strategy of Mao Tse-tung," *Political Science Quarterly,* LXX (September 1955) , pp. 322, 324.

patience, strength, and faith in himself put his end-justifies-the means philosophy to work without scruples, morals, or ethics and strove steadily for power. Without Mao Tse-tung there would have been no Communist conquest of China." [35] However, as Mao's own long experience shows, no matter how well a leader perceives the nature of guerrilla tactics, his movement will flounder until he has a mass following. Mao Tse-tung was writing on guerrilla warfare as early as 1927, and the Red Armies in the Kiangsi Soviet were noted for their exemplary employment of his guerrilla methods; yet the Kiangsi Soviet was crushed in 1934. It was not until after 1937 that Mao's movement was able to capitalize upon his insights into guerrilla tactics; and then it was based on widespread Communist-peasant collaboration against the Japanese, which was ultimately strong enough to overwhelm the Nationalist government in 1949. Mao's "scientific schemata" for war span these two periods; the crucial development was the achievement of a mass basis during World War II.[36]

This brings us to the primary consideration in an evaluation of any guerrilla conflict: the potentiality of the population for supporting the guerrillas or the formal government, or for remaining passive. In determining this potentiality, one must bear

[35] Francis F. Fuller, "Mao Tse-tung: Military Thinker," *Military Affairs,* xxii (Fall 1958) , p. 139.

[36] The maximum population of the various districts under the direct control of the Soviet central government in 1934 was estimated by Mao Tse-tung for Edgar Snow in 1936 as follows:

Kiangsi Soviet	3,000,000
Hupeh-Anhui-Honan	2,000,000
Hunan-Kiangsi-Hupeh	1,000,000
Kiangsi-Hunan	1,000,000
Chekiang-Fukien	1,000,000
Hunan-Hupeh	1,000,000
Total	9,000,000

Snow recalled that "Mao laughed when I quoted him the figure of '80,000,000' people living under the Chinese Soviets, and said that when they had that big an area the revolution would be practically won." (*Red Star over China,* Modern Library edn., 1938, p. 73.) By April 24, 1945, at the Seventh Chinese Communist Party Congress, Mao Tse-tung could announce that "China's liberated areas under the leadership of the Chinese Communist Party have now a population of 95,500,000." ("On Coalition Government," *Selected Works of Mao Tse-tung,* London, Lawrence and Wishart, 1956, iv, p. 259.)

in mind the particular configuration of guerrilla warfare—
namely, armed operations by a relatively small number of full-
time combatants against an objectively more powerful force.
Guerrilla warfare is not synonymous with generalized insurrection, civil war (of the American or the Spanish variety), or
general strike, in which all individuals of the war area may be
regarded as overt participants. The condition upon which guerrilla warfare is predicated is that the civilian population is regarded by the defending force as neutral but is, in fact, hostile to
the defending force. (Even if the population is known to be
hostile, so long as the defending force grants it non-belligerent
status the conditions for guerrilla warfare are established.) It is
this presence of an overtly neutral but covertly engaged population that provides the "ocean" in which the "fish" maneuver and
hide, thereby crippling the stronger force and depriving it of the
advantages of occupation. The conversion of the "ocean" into a
"desert" is, as we shall see, the primary consideration in anti-
guerrilla operations.

The willingness of the population to support the guerrillas
depends upon the intensity of its hostility to the guerrillas'
enemies; it is not necessarily related to the ultimate goals of the
guerrilla leadership—e.g., to the establishment of a Communist
or other nation-state, or to the carrying out of a broad-based
social revolution. The population will support the guerrillas if it
is convinced that the guerrillas are operating effectively against
the enemies of the people: e.g., agents of a tyrannous or economically unjust government, foreign invaders, or colonial troops.
The actual mobilizing influence is the hated condition—the presence of foreign troops, economic exploitation, and so forth—that
alienates the population from the formal authorities. The guerrilla leadership, however, may well entertain objectives beyond
the immediate removal of the people's burden. It may, moreover,
transmit these objectives to the population by propaganda; and
it may have its objectives made legitimate by successfully overcoming the enemies of the population in battle. But it must not
be thought that long-range political objectives of revolutionary
elites are the usual *reason* why a population initially gives aid to
the guerrillas. As has been frequently observed, communism is
more often the result, or beneficiary, of revolution than its

cause.[37] Successful counter-guerrilla operations may well include the advancement and support of political objectives similar to, but distinct from, those of the guerrilla leadership (such as the creation, by a colonial power, of a popular national government that is willing to cooperate with the former colonial authority). But counter-guerrilla military activities divorced from a policy designed to remove, or mitigate, the basic causes of mobilization will surely fail.

In view of these facts, the nature of mass grievances must be considered in the development of any counter-guerrilla strategy, and the alleviation of such grievances has gone hand in hand with most successful anti-guerrilla campaigns. The suppression of the Communist-led Huks in the postwar Philippines is a well-known case in point. The economic and political reforms associated with the name of Ramon Magsaysay improved the life of the Filipino peasant and secured his integration into the political life of the nation—thereby cutting off the Huk zealots from their basis of support and driving them to employ terrorism against the population. The policies of resettlement and re-education of surrendered insurgents further added to the solution of what had seemed an almost endemic problem. These measures were, of course, accompanied by military operations against the Huks; but military suppression was not effective until used in conjunction with political and economic reforms. Probably the single most important factor in the Philippine government's favor was that it, itself, was not incapable of winning popular support. Thus, by incorporating the aspirations of the Filipinos into its own program, the government effectively emasculated the proposed policies of the Communists.[38]

A less clear-cut but nonetheless instructive case is that of operations during the "Emergency" in Malaya. Guerrilla units in Malaya were formed (as in the Philippines) in response to the Japanese invasion. Japanese persecution of the Chinese, together with a conscious policy of pitting the Malay population against

[37] See, e.g., Harry J. Benda, "Revolution and Nationalism in the Non-Western World," in Warren S. Hunsberger, ed., *New Era in the Non-Western World,* Ithaca, N.Y., 1957, p. 20.

[38] See Alvin H. Scaff, *The Philippine Answer to Communism,* Stanford, Calif., 1955; and Frances L. Starner, *Magsaysay and the Philippine Peasantry,* Berkeley, Calif., 1961.

the Chinese, gave rise to a wholly Chinese guerrilla resistance movement.[39] The guerrillas did not succeed in gaining support across the ethnic division; nevertheless, as a result of the size of the Chinese community in Malaya (almost 50 per cent, exclusive of Singapore, where Chinese predominate), they still had widespread civilian backing. In 1948 this trained nucleus of guerrilla fighters was reactivated by its Communist leadership in order to wage war against the British colonial authorities. The Chinese villages on the edge of the jungle again supported the guerrillas, this time in the belief that they were defending Chinese rights against British pro-Malay policies. In broad outline, British strategy against this movement took three forms: in addition to strictly military operations against the guerrillas, (a) some half-million Chinese were resettled onto good land, which was isolated from and defended against active insurgents; (b) non-revolutionary Chinese leaders were urged to participate in the constituted government, thereby preventing a Communist monopoly on Chinese loyalties; and (c) plans were laid for the eventual independence of Malaya, thereby removing the colonial complication from a pluralistic community in which the groups were, and are, basically more complementary than antagonistic. These policies were not pursued as part of a coherent plan, and British reprisals certainly lengthened the war at one time. But the overall result of British-civilian cooperation was the isolation of the guerrillas, thus eliminating the possibility of a guerrilla victory.

A third example of a type of "successful" anti-guerrilla operation is the suppression of Antonio Conselheiro's rebellion in northeastern Brazil (1896–1897), described in Euclides da Cunha's classic history of guerrilla war, *Rebellion in the Backlands*.[40] The significance of this example lies not in its symboliz-

[39] Willard H. Elsbree, *Japan's Role in Southeast Asian Nationalist Movements,* Cambridge, Mass., 1953, p. 148.

[40] To call *Os Sertões* (translated as *Rebellion in the Backlands* by Samuel Putnam) a classic history of guerrilla warfare slights the moral, humanitarian, and scientific significance of this work, considered to be Brazil's greatest literary classic. It is at the same time, however, a major study of military history and of guerrilla conflict. See Euclides da Cunha, *Rebellion in the Backlands,* University of Chicago, Phoenix edn., 1944 and 1957.

ing one kind of viable policy alternative; rather, it shows that the logical outcome of anti-guerrilla military operations divorced from any political measures whatsoever is the total destruction of both the active fighters and their sustaining population. And, as da Cunha has shown, this is not an easy thing to do. Antonio the Counselor was a religious fanatic who led the backwoodsmen of the São Francisco region in open rebellion against the Brazilian government at the end of the nineteenth century. The economic, geographical, racial, and religious bases of the *sertanejos'* (natives of the backlands) and *jagunços'* (the "actives" among the *sertanejos*) mobilization against the government are analytically distinct from the nationalist and Communist revolutions considered earlier.[41] Nevertheless, the conditions that developed around Canudos—Antonio's capital—were identical to those met with in more recent guerrilla conflicts: total hostility of the people to the anti-guerrilla forces; guerrilla knowledge of the difficult terrain, which was exploited with devastating effectiveness by them against the troops; ignorance of the basis of guerrilla warfare by the attacking forces; perfect intelligence on the side of the guerrillas, surprise and ambush; and the consequent demoralization of the anti-guerrilla army. Since the counter-guerrilla forces had no understanding of their adversary and had no intention of attempting to remove the causes of mass mobilization, the war assumed a scale of savagery and destruction entirely out of proportion to the numbers of guerrillas involved. Four expeditions were launched against the area held by Antonio and, as da Cunha laconically observes, Canudos never surrendered—the guerrillas were simply exterminated with great loss of life to both sides. Such a Pyrrhic solution must be understood as implicit in anti-guerrilla operations where complete identity between rebels and civilians is achieved and where solely military counter-measures are pursued.

Although it is easy to demand that counter-guerrilla policy incorporate political measures which will isolate the guerrillas and restore strategic initiative to the defenders, it is less easy to put such measures into practice. General political and economic

[41] Antonio Conselheiro's rebellion bears a striking similarity, on a lesser scale, to the Taiping Rebellion of mid-nineteenth-century China.

considerations must be taken into account, such as the abilities of local elites, the nature of a country's economy, its class structure, and a host of other variables that can only be altered by long-term reforms. By the time guerrilla warfare has actually broken out, the conflict may already be lost to the defenders and require a negotiated or stalemate solution. Thus it would seem that prevention is the better part of cure. The recognition of this fact provides one further support for those foreign policy measures undertaken by Western governments that seek long-range solutions to endemic problems via controlled social change. Moreover, an understanding of the political basis of guerrilla warfare should dictate against Western governments' further militarizing certain conflicts by granting unrestricted arms support for already discredited regimes. However, in cases where guerrilla conflict is unavoidable, a sensitivity to civilian loyalties in guerrilla warfare should facilitate the effective employment of troops, thereby minimizing the tendency this all too commonly has to drive the guerrillas and civilians closer together.

Part III

The Military and Politics:

Specific Nations

The Conflict between Old and New
in the Chinese Army

ELLIS JOFFE

Ap / Jun 1964

One of the most pressing needs of the Chinese Communists
when they established their régime, was to convert the sprawling
semi-guerrilla force which had brought them to power into a
modern army capable of maintaining that power. China's leaders
were acutely aware of this need and they lost little time in
launching the armed forces on the long march to modernisation.
No modernisation, however, could have succeeded without large
numbers of officers skilled in running a complex military establishment. The Red Army commanders, though resourceful and
battle-tested, were by and large not equipped for this task. It was
necessary, therefore, to develop a professional officer corps.

The leadership made a conscious and concerted effort to
meet this need, and this effort has been reinforced by the very
process of military modernisation which has been conducive to
the growth of professionalism. But if this solved one problem, it
created another. The professional officers [1] developed views and
values which have brought the army into conflict with the Party

[1] For reasons of style, the phrases "the professional officers" and "some
professional officers" are used interchangeably throughout the article. This,
however, does not imply that I am referring to the entire professional officer
corps. Although it is impossible to determine what percentage of the officers
may be termed "professionals," it is clear that only a part of the officer corps
has been involved in this conflict.

Reprinted by permission from The China Quarterly, *No. 18 (April–June
1964), pp. 118–140. The article is based on a study which is being prepared
for the East Asian Research Center, Harvard University.*

on a number of issues. Essentially this is a conflict between generations differing in experience, outlook and responsibilities. The protagonists are the veteran leaders of the "guerrilla generation" on the one hand, and the younger officers of an increasingly "professional generation" on the other. Although both generations are Party members,[2] and although both desire a modern army, they tend to see things in a different light; the viewpoint of the officers is more "expert," that of the Party leadership more "red."

What were the circumstances which produced the "professional generation"? What are their views and how do they differ from those of their superiors? How has the leadership met the challenge to its beliefs? This article is a preliminary attempt to shed some light on these questions.

Modernisation and Professionalism

The growth of a professional officer corps, and its consequent conflict of views with the Party, is inextricably connected with the modernisation of the armed forces. For it was this transformation that has nourished professionalism. Before this the revolutionary nature of the army militated against the development of professionalism.[3] The army's primitive equipment and rudimentary staff system obviated the need for, and indeed precluded, specialisation. Its irregular, and "democratic" character, and its intimate relationship with the population blurred the distinctions between ranks, and between soldiers and civilians. The close merging of political and military doctrine and tasks led to the fusing of political and military leadership.

It has sometimes been asserted that China's leaders, irrevocably committed to a "guerrilla mentality," have underestimated the importance of modernising the army. This is an oversim-

---

[2] No figures are available on how many officers are Party members, but it may be safely assumed that all the high-ranking officers and the overwhelming majority of the junior officers belong to the Party.

[3] There is no space to sketch the salient features of the Chinese Red Army before 1949. Its "non-professional" nature in terms of weapons, training, organisation and political work is examined in some detail in Ellis Joffe's "The Chinese Red Army 1927–1949 and the 'Man-Over-Weapons' Doctrine," unpublished paper, Harvard University, January 1964.

plification. Although the revolutionary concepts of the veteran leaders have been decisive in their conflict with the officers, there is no evidence that they denied the need for transforming the army into a modern force. On the contrary, there is ample evidence to show that they were fully aware of the need to usher the army into the modern era [4]; realised that professional officers were required to do the ushering [5]; and initiated measures to meet these needs. What were these measures and what impact did they have upon the growth of professionalism? This question must be approached on several levels.

Technological Modernisation

First of all weapons had to be modernised and standardised. In 1949, however, the Chinese Communists were in no position to carry out a swift and sweeping transformation of their weapons and probably they turned immediately to the Soviet Union for help. There are indications that the Sino-Soviet Treaty of 1950 contained secret provisions for military assistance,[6] but it is unlikely that the suspicious Stalin was in a hurry to give weapons to the Chinese. There is no doubt, however, that the intervention of the Chinese in the Korean War to wage a costly fight not of their own making forced the Russians to come to their aid with large quantities of military hardware.[7] This aid served as a springboard for the Chinese Army's leap into the era of modern conventional warfare.

It is more difficult to evaluate the less tangible aspects of the Korean War's impact on the Chinese military leaders, but there

---

[4] See, for example, New China News Agency (NCNA), July 31, 1951, in *Current Background* (CB) (Hong Kong: U.S. Consulate-General), No. 208; NCNA, July 31, 1952, *ibid.; Jen-min Jih-pao* (*People's Daily*) editorial, NCNA, July 24, 1954, *Survey of the China Mainland Press* (SCMP) (Hong Kong: U.S. Consulate-General), No. 856, pp. 54–55.

[5] See, for example, *People's Daily* editorial, NCNA, February 15, 1955, CB, No. 314, p. 18; *Eighth National Congress of the Communist Party of China* (Peking: 1956), II, Speeches, pp. 29–30.

[6] See, for example, *Kung-jen Jih-pao* (*Daily Worker*), July 31, 1955, SCMP, No. 1163, p. 261.

[7] *Cf.* Raymond L. Garthoff, "Sino-Soviet Military Relations," *The Annals* (of the American Academy of Political and Social Science), September 1963, pp. 84–85.

can be little doubt that it was a traumatic experience for them. It hammered home the fact that their army had to undergo a thorough transformation before it could lock horns with a modern military force. It exposed them to the manifold problems of modern warfare for which their vast storehouse of experience provided no solutions. And it dramatically demonstrated the limitations of their hitherto successful strategy and tactics.

From the Korean War to 1960 the modernisation of the Chinese army proceeded at a steady pace. With the aid of advisers and modern, although not the latest, Soviet equipment, the Chinese transformed their infantry force into a complex, well balanced, conventional army with numerous specialised arms and support and service units, backed by a network of military industries.[8]

Training Professional Officers

To run this huge and increasingly complex military machine required vast numbers of officers with special skills. To meet this need the Communists set up military academies in the early months of their rule.[9] The graduates of these academies formed the backbone of the new officer corps. With the growing complexity and diversity of the armed forces the original handful of schools have mushroomed into a network of at least 67 military academies, covering a wide variety of specialised subjects.[10] The main training ground of the professional officer is, of course, the military academy, but special efforts are also made to promote research in military science and to disseminate information

[8] For an estimate of China's armed forces, see *The Communist Bloc and the Western Alliances: The Military Balance 1962–1963* (London: The Institute for Strategic Studies, 1964), p. 8; *The Christian Science Monitor,* February 21, 1964.

[9] Derk Bodde, *Peking Diary: A Year of Revolution* (New York: 1950), pp. 117–118; NCNA, December 1, 1950, SCMP, No. 21, pp. 13–14; *People's Daily* editorial, NCNA, December 1, 1950, *ibid.* pp. 15–16; NCNA, December 9, 1950, SCMP, No. 27, pp. 17–18; NCNA, December 25, 1950, SCMP, No. 37, pp. 20–22.

[10] *Communist China: Ruthless Enemy or Paper Tiger?* (Department of the Army, Pam 20–61: 1962), Appendix G (Chinese Communist Military Organisation).

to keep the officers in the units abreast of the latest developments.[11]

Formation of a Professional Officer Corps

No single event probably contributed more to the growth of professionalism than the adoption of the "Regulations on the Service of Officers" in February 1955.[12] The introduction of these regulations fundamentally altered the informal, egalitarian, "democratic" and non-professional nature of the Chinese Communist officer corps as it had been moulded during more than two decades of revolutionary warfare.[13]

For the first time officers in the Chinese Red Army were classified according to their fields of specialisation, and ranks were established.[14] Regular channels were set up for entry into the officer corps and for advancement on the basis of professional competence.[15] The regulations also required the officers to wear shoulder-boards and insignia in accordance with their rank.[16] Shortly after the regulations were adopted, the old system of providing both officers and men with food and a small allowance in lieu of salaries was replaced by cash payments. The present scale of pay—which ranges from U.S. $2.50 per month for a private to $192–236 for a full general [17]—is indicative of the new differentiations. With the conferment of military titles and honours on the army leaders in September 1955,[18] the Chinese officer corps acquired all the trappings typical of a regular army.

The introduction of conscription in July 1955 capped the process of putting the army on a regular footing. Until then, the Communists had relied on "volunteers." Under the Conscription

[11] *Chung-kuo Ch'ing-nien Pao* (*The Chinese Youth Newspaper*), November 3, 1956, SCMP, No. 1416, pp. 7–8; NCNA, March 16, 1958, SCMP, No. 1736, p. 2.
[12] NCNA, February 9, 1955, CB, No. 312.
[13] See Joffe, pp. 35–39.
[14] Regulations, Articles 4, 7, 8.
[15] Articles 11, 15, 17.
[16] Article 24.
[17] Edgar Snow, *The Other Side of the River: Red China Today* (New York: Random House, 1962), p. 289.
[18] CB, No. 368, pp. 1–2.

Law,[19] all male citizens have the duty to serve in the armed forces upon reaching the age of eighteen, and it is estimated that some 700,000 are called up for military service each year.[20] Conscription has thus brought into sharp focus the distinction between the amateur citizen-soldier and the professional officer.

Cumulatively, these developments spelled the end of the irregular, egalitarian and informal guerrilla officer, and cleared the ground for the emergence of a status-conscious, professional officer corps.

Soviet Aid and Advice

Despite the immense importance of the Soviet Union's role in creating a modern and professional Chinese army, it is difficult to detail, much less document, Soviet military aid and advice because this aspect of Sino-Soviet relations has been shrouded in a veil of official secrecy.

There is little doubt that most of the new Chinese military establishment has been built with Soviet equipment. To be sure, this was no handout; Peking paid for what it got, and these payments were financed by loans from the Soviet Union, which by mid-1957 reportedly amounted to about U.S. $2 billion.[21] Nevertheless, Soviet aid did lay the foundation and provide the vital push for the modernisation of China's armed forces.

With aid, came advice. Until the late fifties, Chinese leaders went all out to heap praise on the Soviet army and to underline the need for studying its "advanced experience." Concretely this meant that Soviet personnel played an important part in modernising the Chinese armed forces. Soviet advisers arrived in China in late 1950 and remained, probably in declining numbers, until 1960.[22] Many Chinese officers are believed to have been sent to

---

[19] CB, No. 344.

[20] *The Communist Bloc and the Western Alliances*, p. 8.

[21] Allen S. Whiting, *Contradictions in the Moscow-Peking Axis* (Santa Monica: The RAND Corporation, RM-1992, September 24, 1957), pp. 5–6.

[22] No details are available, but the establishment of a Russian language school among the first Chinese military academies was probably in response to the pressing need for interpreters and for Russian-speaking Chinese officers in anticipation of their dispatch to the Soviet Union.

study in the Soviet Union.[23] The importance of the Russian influence is reflected in the reorganisation of the Chinese military establishment along essentially Soviet lines.

No less important has been the impact of Soviet counsel and guidance on the Chinese officers, although of course this cannot be evaluated in tangible terms. Through their Soviet advisers and through Soviet military writings, the Chinese officers inevitably became acquainted with and assimilated doctrines and practices which in some basic respects differ markedly from those considered sacrosanct by their own leaders. This has led them to question the wisdom of their leaders on fundamental issues of military organisation and strategy. The Soviet organisation is more hierarchic and bureaucratic than the Chinese—particularly in its emphasis on unity of command compared with the Chinese stress on collective leadership—and, therefore, more acceptable to a professionally-oriented Chinese officer.[24] Soviet strategic influence assumed far-reaching implications in the mid-fifties, when it began to acknowledge that in a nuclear war military factors, rather than political ones, are decisive. Some Chinese officers apparently accepted this revision, which was tantamount to rejecting the revered military thought of Mao Tse-tung.[25] In sum, the precise nature of Soviet influence on the Chinese officers is a subject for speculation, but there is little doubt that it had an important impact on the growth of professionalism in the Chinese army.

A New Division of Labour

Of no less importance than the specific steps taken to build up a professional officer corps have been the changes stemming

[23] Here too no details are available, but in 1954, for example, it was reported in Hong Kong that twenty regimental staff officers had been sent to the Kiev staff school. S. M. Chiu, "The Chinese Communist Army in Transition," *Far Eastern Survey*, Vol. XXVII, November 1958, p. 171.

[24] See, for example, *Chieh-fang Chün Pao (Liberation Army News)*, June 16, 1959, *Joint Publications Research Service* (JPRS), No. 10343/59, p. 4; *Liberation Army News* editorial, August 18, 1958, JPRS 10240/59, p. 40; *Liberation Army News*, August 29, 1958, JPRS 10239/59, pp. 31–33.

[25] Alice Langley Hsieh, *Communist China's Strategy in the Nuclear Era* (Englewood, New Jersey: Prentice-Hall, 1962), Chap. 2.

from the nature of the post-revolutionary environment. Throughout the revolutionary period and for several years after 1949 there was little to distinguish the political from the military leaders. The military and political élites were inextricably intertwined, and their tasks and experience were identical to a great extent. There was little ground, therefore, for the emergence of basic conflicts of views between the political and military leaders.

As the Party gradually came to grips with the manifold problems of state administration, tasks and responsibilities became increasingly specialised. Whereas in the insurrectionary milieu the same leader could be—and usually was—simultaneously qualified to handle several key jobs in different fields, today this is no longer possible. The efficient management of state affairs has necessitated a clear division of labour between the managers.

The new division of labour is illustrated in the shifts which have taken place in the functions of the élite since 1949.[26] Many top level leaders have drifted away from the daily direction of military affairs. On the other hand, those leaders who are concerned with the armed forces have become specialists. In other words, overall military policy at the highest levels is determined largely by men whose intimate relationship with military affairs has been limited in the main to the days of revolutionary warfare. While they are undoubtedly aware of the need for a modern military machine, they have only limited first-hand knowledge of modern warfare and the day-to-day problems of a complex army. In contrast to this, several of the important second-level leaders have, for a number of years, tackled these matters from day to day, and it is reasonable to assume that, their "guerrilla" background notwithstanding, some of them have become fully aware of the problems of modern warfare and have adopted a "professional" viewpoint.

In sum, the professional officers may be grouped in two broad categories. First, young men who joined the army, or became officers, after 1949 and who were trained and became

---

[26] Donald W. Klein, "The 'Next Generation' of Chinese Communist Leaders," *The China Quarterly*, No. 12, October–December 1962, pp. 65–66.

professionals as the army was being modernised; these officers presumably occupy the lower levels of the command structure. Secondly, veteran guerrilla officers who were assigned to specialised military duties in the early fifties and who have since been intimately involved in the complex problems of the modernised army; these officers hold positions on the General Staff and occupy important command posts.

The Elements of Conflict

It is difficult to pinpoint when tensions first appeared between the Party and the professional officers or to gauge their intensity at a particular time. The best barometer of these tensions is the Party's various campaigns to curb professionalism in the army. In broad outline, these campaigns appear to tie in with developments in the country at large, and especially with the rectification campaigns and the drives against intellectuals. In the army they seem to have started in 1956, gathered momentum in 1957, reached a climax in 1958 and continued through 1959. There is little doubt that friction between the Party and the officers over issues which we shall examine below was responsible for the dismissal of Marshal P'eng Teh-huai as Minister of Defence and General Huang K'o-ch'eng as Chief of the General Staff.[27] Under P'eng's successor, Marshal Lin Piao, a new attempt has been made to strengthen Party control over the armed forces. Lin's leadership, together with the scrapping of the great leap forward, the waning of the anti-professional euphoria which had accompanied it, and, perhaps, the drastic deterioration of Sino-Soviet relations, probably account for the muting of tension. There is no sign, however, that many of the sources of tension have been removed.

Before analysing these sources of tension, several caveats are in order. First, it cannot be overemphasised that this "conflict" over professionalism exists within a broader context of unity and harmony which is indeed striking. Secondly, it must be stressed again that the overwhelming majority of the officers are Party members, so that whatever conflict exists, it is strictly an intra-

[27] See below.

Party affair. Thirdly, we have chosen to deal with issues without associating them with personalities, primarily because given the fragmentary evidence, such an attempt must be relegated in large part to the realm of speculation and inference.[28]

Man or Weapons?

Underlying all the points of conflict between the Party and the officers are two fundamentally different points of view on the relationship between man and weapons and, consequently, on the nature of the modernised army. The officers argue that in modern warfare material and technological factors are more important that the human element. They assert that, in contrast to the guerrilla period when primary reliance had to be placed on the human element, the outcome of a modern war depends primarily on the material resources of an army and the way in which they are used. For this reason, the development of weapons and their efficient operation should take priority over political considerations. In short, professionalism must take precedence over politics.[29]

Not so, insist the Party leaders. They do not deny the importance of weapons, but they believe in the inherent superiority of man over machines. To translate this superiority into reality, man has to be properly mobilised, indoctrinated and used—and only the Party is competent to do this. Hence politics must be placed above professionalism.[30]

It may be argued that this doctrine is merely the Party leaders' rationalisation for China's lack of atomic weapons, a smokescreen for the painful reality of military and technological inferiority. This is undoubtedly true. There is overwhelming evidence that China's leaders are acutely aware of the importance of nuclear weapons, that they are deeply distressed by the fact that China has none, that, whatever their bellicose statements, they have a healthy respect for an adversary who does, and that

---

[28] For an attempt to identify issues with personalities see Hsieh, *passim.*

[29] See, for example, *People's Daily,* July 28, 1961, SCMP, No. 2556, p. 2.

[30] See, for example, Lin Piao, *March Ahead Under the Red Flag of the Party's General Line and Mao Tse-tung's Military Thinking* (Peking, 1959), p. 17.

they are making every effort to join the nuclear club.* But that is only one side of the coin. To stop short at this explanation and to consider this question solely in terms of the leadership's current needs is to disregard their whole historical experience, and there is every indication that this experience has left an indelible imprint on their thinking.[31]

What is that experience? Put simply, it is not the gun, but the man behind the gun that is decisive in determining the outcome of war, and the conditioning of man depends on political factors. The validity of this experience, assert the leaders, is not altered by the passage of time and the advance of technology. Although this view has been expressed in numerous statements, it can be argued that the leaders really do not believe what they say publicly, and such pronouncements are intended only for the population at large and for external consumption. Such an argument, however, is on shaky ground. The available issues of the army's secret *Kung-tso T'ung-hsun* (*Bulletin of Activities*) clearly show that there is a remarkable identity between published views and those voiced in inner Party circles.[32]

It is important to keep in mind that these differences between the leaders and the officers are basically a matter of degree. Both the officers and the leaders concede the necessity of being both "red" and "expert"; the gulf between them lies essentially in the emphasis which they place on the "red" and the "expert." These divergent approaches underlie their conflicting viewpoints on the nature of the modernised army. The Party leaders agree, of course, that the army must be modernised, but they

* Written before the Chinese nuclear tests in 1964.—W. C. McW.

[31] Joffe, *passim*.

[32] See, for example, a document prepared by the Academy of Military Sciences, *Kung-tso T'ung-hsun* (*Bulletin of Activities*) , No. 29, August 1, 1961. In an excellent analysis of these documents Professor Ralph L. Powell points out that "they provide convincing evidence that previously published statements of doctrine have generally represented official policy, even when they have been considered to be unrealistic in the atomic age. . . . The doctrine still claims that the two basic and unchanging factors in war are the dominance of men and of politics. . . ." Ralph L. Powell, *Politico-Military Relationships in Communist China* (Policy Research Study, External Research Staff, Bureau of Intelligence and Research, United States Department of State, October 1963) , p. 19.

assert that modernisation must not basically alter its traditional doctrine, characteristics and practices. The "revolutionary" essence of the army must not change in the midst of change.[33]

The army must change with the changing times—this is the basic contention of the professional officers. In their view, modernisation is not something that can simply be tacked onto the "guerrilla" army; the substance of that army must change too.[34] In the following sections we shall see how these opposing viewpoints apply to concrete issues.

Relations between Officers and Men

The far-reaching changes which have taken place in the army since 1949 have brought about an estrangement between some officers and the rank and file. The main reason for this is that officers believe that the efficient operation of a modern, technically complex army requires discipline and "centralism," rather than "democracy" and individual initiative.[35] Other, less tangible, factors also undoubtedly contributed to the worsening of relations. The introduction of conscription and, consequently, the frequent rotation of enlisted men, has precluded the formation of ties which formerly grew out of long and intimate association. The whole range of measures adopted to make the officers professionals has tended to make them status-conscious and remote from the men. Finally, relations moulded during a revolutionary era of idealistic fervour and constant danger are bound to be very different from those formed in a period dominated by the dreary duties of a peacetime army.

These factors have combined to produce a situation which has caused grave concern to the Party leaders. They have blasted the officers for flagrantly flouting the cherished traditions of the revolutionary army. Some officers, it was said, looked upon discipline and "democracy" as diametrically opposed things, and stressed the former to the exclusion of the latter. They regarded

[33] *Liberation Army News* editorial, August 17, 1958, JPRS, No. 6471/59, p. 1.
[34] *Liberation Army News*, August 29, 1958, JPRS, No. 10239/59, p. 31.
[35] See, for example, *Eighth National Congress of the Communist Party of China*, p. 264.

the new status accorded them as a sign that the egalitarian
traditions of the army had been abandoned, and felt free to lord
it over the men. They set themselves on a pedestal, failed to mix
with the men, showed no concern for their welfare, and abused
their authority. They became armchair bureaucrats, neglected
the "mass-line," and retaliated against critics. They exaggerated
the importance of their professional training and hierarchical
status, and scoffed at the practice of soliciting the opinions of the
rank and file.[36]

Relations between Officers and Civilians

The estrangement between the ranks has been paralleled by
a loosening of the close ties which had traditionally existed
between the Chinese Communist forces and the peasant masses.
Over-conscious of their new status and no longer dependent on
the support of the population, some officers began to treat civilians in a high-handed and haughty manner. Such behaviour has
drawn strong fire from the Party leaders. Some officers, it was
said, blatantly disregarded the needs, well-being and feelings of
the population. They requisitioned property from the peasants
and destroyed crops during manoeuvres. They callously ignored
safety rules on the road. They dabbled in black market operations. They and their dependants lived a life of luxury which
alienated the masses. They used their position to pursue their
romantic ambitions with village girls, even married ones. And
they and their families showed contempt for physical labour.[37]

Political Controls in the Army

Nowhere has the clash between politics and professionalism
been more apparent and acute than in the friction generated by
Party control in the army. This control is exercised through a
hierarchy of Party committees, political commissars, political
departments and Party members, a hierarchy which parallels the

[36] See, for example, *People's Daily*, August 1, 1955, SCMP, No. 1106, pp.
4–9; *Liberation Army News* editorial, August 18, 1958, JPRS, No. 10240/59,
p. 42; *Liberation Army News*, August 29, 1958, JPRS, 10239/59, p. 32.
[37] See, for example, *People's Daily*, August 1, 1955, SCMP, No. 1106, p. 7;
NCNA, May 12, 1957, SCMP, No. 1547, p. 27; *Liberation Army News*, March
30, 1958, JPRS, No. 10239/59, p. 14.

military chain of command from the highest to the lowest level. The Party committees are granted wide powers to formulate measures relating to the implementation of directives received from above and to supervise their enforcement. The decisions of the Party committee are handed over to the military commander and the political commissar for execution. Between these two there ostensibly exists a division of work to the effect that one is responsible for everything concerning military matters, the other for political affairs.[38]

Theory is one thing, practice another. Problems are bound to arise in the functional relationship between the military and political leaders, whatever the theoretical division of labour between them. These may stem from matters which are not clearly under the jurisdiction of either, or they may pertain to areas where the decision of one will affect the sphere of responsibility of the other. More important, when "politics take command," all other considerations are subordinate; this implies that the political functionary is entitled to meddle in everything that goes on within the unit.

In the event of a dispute between the officer and the commissar, the matter is presumably referred to the Party committee for resolution. It is extremely doubtful, however, whether the committee will judge a case on its merits. First, it must be remembered that the commissar is also the secretary of the committee,[39] i.e., the top Party man on the spot, and from this position of power he wields great authority over the Party members. Second, it may be safely assumed that the committee is composed of the more "activist" elements among the Party members, and they can be expected to view everything through politically tinted lenses and to be receptive to the commissar's, rather than to the officer's opinions. In view of this, it is safe to say that in practice it is the commissar who manipulates the actions of the committee rather than the reverse. As a result, the officer may find himself in the frustrating position of being in effect subordinate to the man with whom nominally he shares command. If he and the commissar see eye to eye, things will work smoothly; however, in cases

---

[38] See, for example, *Eighth National Congress of the Communist Party of China*, pp. 32–33; *Bulletin*, No. 3, January 7, 1961.

[39] *Liberation Army News* editorial, May 8, 1963, SCMP, No. 2984, p. 4.

where they are at loggerheads, the existence of political controls may well hamper the ability of the military commander to exercise effective leadership and will generate friction.

Despite the potential incompatibility of political controls with professional leadership, there is little doubt that the system functioned well during the period of guerrilla warfare and in the early years of the Communist régime. Three reasons seem to account for this harmony. First, both the commanders and the commissars were veteran Party members with much the same experience and background in both political and military work. Second, the close interrelation of political and military tasks in the milieu of insurrection gave little basis for conflict. Third, in many cases the commander and the commissar were one and the same person.

With the modernisation of the army and the growth of professionalism, the latent elements of conflict have come to the surface. Some officers have assailed the system of political controls on the grounds that it is incompatible with a command structure that will function swiftly and smoothly, a requirement they deem vital in modern warfare.[40] Not only do they consider the Party committees and the commissars an obstacle to organisational efficiency, but they consider them incompetent to handle military affairs. In their view, it is the professional military men and not political functionaries who are best equipped to render judgment on military matters.[41] These officers did not stop short at criticising the political control system, but in some cases at least took direct action. Although only fragmentary evidence is available, it is clear that in certain instances the commanders pushed the commissars into the background or simply abolished this institution.[42] Perhaps more serious, from the Party's viewpoint, than the

[40] See, for example, *Liberation Army News* editorial, July 1, 1958, SCMP, No. 1881, p. 4; *Liberation Army News* editorial, August 1, 1958, SCMP, No. 1881, p. 2; NCNA-English, Peking, July 31, 1958, CB, No. 514, pp. 1–2; *Hsin Hunan Pao (New Human Daily)*, November 22, 1959, SCMP, No. 2155, p. 11.

[41] See, for example, *Liberation Army News* editorial, August 18, 1958, JPRS, 10240/59, p. 40.

[42] *Liberation Army News* editorial, July 1, 1958, SCMP, No. 1881, p. 4; *Liberation Army News*, May 23, 1958, SCMP, No. 1900, p. 9; *Liberation Army News*, June 16, 1958, JPRS, No. 10343/59, pp. 4–6; *Liberation Army News*, September 4, 1958, JPRS, No. 10240/59, pp. 18–19.

friction generated by the operations of the political control system was the startling fact, revealed in the *Bulletin of Activities*, that as late as 1960 many of the lower-level units simply had no such system.[43]

Such views and actions have been vehemently denounced by the Party leaders. They are deeply committed to the predominance of political considerations over all others, and assert that politics should always "take command." [44] They interpret the officers' contention that collective leadership is unsuitable for modern warfare as a camouflage for the officers' desire to loosen the Party's hold over the army, and they reject the argument that collective leadership is incompatible with efficiency on the grounds that even in a modern army collective decision-making by non-specialists is superior to individual decision-making by a specialist.[45]

Employment of the Army for Non-military Purposes

The increasing tendency of the professional officers to view things through "expert" rather than "red" lenses has led them to assail another cherished policy of the Party leadership: the use of the army in the execution of economic and socio-political tasks.[46] Their objections to this policy were voiced on the grounds that the diversion of troops to non-military activities dissipates their energies and interferes with training. In a modern army, they maintain, training is a full-time job and the soldiers should devote all their time to this task, leaving the execution of non-military projects to civilians.[47]

Quite the contrary, assert the Party leaders. The employ-

[43] *Bulletin*, No. 23, June 13, 1961, cited in Powell, p. 8; *Bulletin*, No. 3, January 7, 1961.

[44] See, for example, *Liberation Army News* editorial, July 1, 1958, SCMP, No. 1881, p. 4.

[45] See, for example, *Liberation Army News*, August 29, 1958, JPRS, 10239/59, pp. 31–32.

[46] For a brief discussion of the army's non-military activities see Ellis Joffe, "The Communist Party and the Army," *Contemporary China*, IV, 1961, pp. 55–59.

[47] See, for example, *Hung Ch'i* (*Red Flag*), No. 15, August 1, 1959, *Extracts from China Mainland Magazines* (ECMM) (Hong Kong: U.S. Consulate-General), No. 182, p. 7.

ment of the army in construction, they maintain, has two important advantages: first, the socialist construction of the state will benefit from the use of troops on economic projects; second, participation in non-military activities is essential to the political and ideological conditioning of the troops, for it will heighten their appreciation of labour and will raise their Communist consciousness.[48]

The Militia

The disfavour with which the officers have looked upon the turning of soldiers into peasant masses has been paralleled by their distaste for turning the peasants into soldiers through the militia. In the autumn of 1958, it will be recalled, the militia movement was revived with intense vigour and a frenetic campaign for a nation-at-arms swept the country.[49]

This campaign was anathema to the professional officers. In an era when combat is waged with complex and refined instruments of destruction manned by highly trained personnel, the spectre of hordes of peasants lugging rifles into battle can give little comfort to a professional officer. But the task of training the militia fell upon the army, and this involved diverting men and precious equipment to the militiamen.[50] To the officers this meant disrupting the regular programmes of the army and allocating sparse resources to what many evidently considered a worthless cause. They left no doubt that in their view the complex business of war should be left to the troops trained for this task and not to incompetent civilians.[51]

Nothing could be farther from the convictions of the Party leaders. Their deeply rooted, almost mystical, belief in the power and potentiality of mobilised masses was clearly brought out in their explanations of the militia programme. Fighting between armies, they contend, is only one form of warfare. In the war against Japan and the Nationalists it was mobile and guerrilla

[48] See, for example, NCNA, Peking, April 25, 1959, CB, No. 579, p. 2.
[49] Cf. Ralph L. Powell, "Everyone a Soldier—The Communist Chinese Militia," *Foreign Affairs*, XXXIX, October 1960, pp. 101–111.
[50] NCNA, December 31, 1958, SCMP, No. 1934, p. 10.
[51] See, for example, *Che-hsueh Yen-chiu*, No. 1, January 10, 1959, ECMM, No. 159, p. 29.

but cf. McW that training (boot camp) is a mere matter of weeks.

warfare, based on the mobilisation of the masses, that emerged victorious. The conclusion is clear to the Party leaders: a "people's war" can defeat any enemy, whatever his weapons.[52]

Nuclear Strategy and Sino-Soviet Relations

A key element of disagreement involving the highest echelons of the Party and the army has been the question of nuclear strategy. This debate has been closely intertwined with the issue of economic versus defence priorities and the nature of Sino-Soviet strategic relations.

It appears that, as we have already observed, by 1954–55 some ranking Chinese officers had become fully aware of the implications of nuclear weapons for modern warfare, partly as a result of the revision in Soviet military thinking which was taking place at the time. They stressed the threat of a surprise attack and the decisiveness of the first blow in a nuclear conflict and, by implication, denied the feasibility of Mao's doctrine of protracted war. They called for a rapid improvement in China's defences and the maintenance of a large standing army. The adoption of these proposals would have required the diversion of resources from economic development—and it was primarily on this score that their proposals were rejected by the leaders. They asserted that economic construction must take precedence because a sound industrial base is a prerequisite for strong defence. Like the officers, they recognised that until China had a nuclear capability of her own, she would be decisively dependent on the Soviet Union.

Recognition of this dependence coupled with an awareness of the West's military superiority may account in part for the cautious course which China pursued in foreign affairs after 1954.[53] But this shift was short-lived. The successful testing of an ICBM and the orbiting of an earth satellite by the Russians in the autumn of 1957 had a profound effect on the Chinese. They now believed that the balance of power had shifted decisively in favour of the Communist bloc and thought that this superiority

[52] See, for example, *Kiangsu Ch'ün-chung* (*Kiangsu Masses*), No. 5, October 1, 1958, ECMM, No. 150, p. 6.
[53] The preceding section is drawn from Hsieh, Chap. 2.

should be exploited through a more aggressive policy in support of "national liberation" wars. The Russians, however, thought otherwise. They did not share Peking's optimistic evaluation of the strategic balance, and were reluctant to foment local wars for fear of "escalation." [54] The cracks which had appeared in the alliance after Khrushchev's denunciation of Stalin in 1956 were growing wider.

Khrushchev was apparently unwilling to go too far in alienating the Chinese, at least at this time. The Soviet camp was still shaken by the dramatic developments of 1956—the Polish October and the Hungarian Uprising—and the Soviet leader had just emerged from a power struggle at home. He may have decided that at this juncture it was necessary to placate Peking. Perhaps for this reason Moscow made a momentous move: on October 15, 1957, the Chinese subsequently revealed, the two countries signed an agreement on "new technology and national defence," according to which the Soviet Union would give China a sample of an atomic bomb and technical data for its manufacture.[55] But far from placating Peking, the aftermath of this agreement was to have exactly the opposite effect.

Why this came about can only be speculated upon. It is conceivable that the Russians were far from eager to see Peking join the nuclear club and the pace of their assistance only frustrated the Chinese. Some time in 1958, perhaps on the eve of the Formosa Straits crisis, the Chinese may have outrightly asked the Russians for nuclear warheads; the Russians, it appears from later Chinese charges, refused—unless they maintained control over the weapons.[56] By this time the Chinese probably realised that they would have to go it alone. Perhaps partly due to this, their economic programme based on self-reliance, which was already under way, was pushed to the extreme, culminating in the "great leap forward" and the communes. Aggravated by the paucity of Moscow's aid and angered by Khrushchev's move toward a détente with the West, the Chinese began to challenge the Soviet leader's ideological primacy in the Communist move-

[54] Hsieh, pp. 76–96.
[55] *Peking Review*, No. 33, August 16, 1963, p. 14.
[56] Quoted in *The New York Times*, September 14, 1963.

ment and, possibly, to undermine his leadership by drumming up support against him in the bloc. By mid-1959 the Russians apparently had had enough; on June 20, the Chinese later claimed, they "unilaterally tore up" the agreement.[57] The conflict was moving inexorably towards a climax.

It is possible that some Chinese military leaders had grave misgivings over a policy which led to rapidly mounting tension between Peking and Moscow. Moscow was not exactly generous with her nuclear arsenal to be sure, but she was obviously prepared to give something, and to military men, keenly aware of the importance of nuclear weapons and deeply apprehensive over China's vulnerability, that was better than nothing. For better or for worse, Russia was China's sole supplier of nuclear data and materials, and cutting off that source would retard China's chance of acquiring her own capability. No less important, the Russians still provided China with vital conventional equipment and supplies, and the officers may have feared that Moscow would be antagonised to the point of stopping this flow.

From their viewpoint, it may have seemed preferable to make political concessions to gain immediate military benefits, small as these might be, and they may have argued that efforts should be made to retain, and perhaps increase, Soviet assistance —at a price. That such a controversy was going on was indicated by the intensity of the campaign against the officers in mid-1958, a major theme of which was the need for self-reliance and opposition to dependence on the Soviet Union.[58] It is possible that Marshal P'eng Teh-huai, the then Minister of Defence, communicated his dissatisfaction to Khrushchev, perhaps in an attempt to head off the abrogation of the agreement; then, supported by some officers and other leading personalities, he blasted the leadership at the Lushan plenum of the Central Committee in August 1959.[59]

In September 1959 Marshal P'eng and the PLA's Chief of Staff, General Huang K'o-ch'eng, were removed from their posts.

[57] *Peking Review*, No. 33, August 16, 1963, p. 14.

[58] See, for example, *Liberation Army News* editorial, August 1, 1958, SCMP, No. 1881, p. 2; *Liberation Army News* editorial, September 20, 1958, JPRS, No. 6471/59, pp. 21–24.

[59] David A. Charles, "The Dismissal of Marshal P'eng Teh-huai," *The China Quarterly*, No. 8, October–December 1961, pp. 63–76.

The circumstances surrounding this shake-up are veiled by official secrecy. In the *Bulletin of Activities,* P'eng and Huang are accused of many misdeeds relating to issues with which we have dealt in the previous pages.[60] They are not directly charged with colluding with the Soviet Union, though the documents speak of the need for eradicating their "erroneous line" and "modern revisionism" in one breath.[61] However, official Chinese charges in 1963 and 1964 that Khrushchev supported anti-Party elements in the CCP and praised them for opposing the Party's economic policy [62] lend credence to the speculation that P'eng and Khrushchev may have been up to something. It was this economic policy and its doctrinal implications that aroused Khrushchev's wrath, and it was perhaps for this reason that, it is believed, P'eng attacked the leadership on economic rather than military grounds. The full story of this episode, however, has yet to be told.

The Party Strikes Back

The reaction of the Party leaders to the challenge posed by the professional officers, needless to say, has not been limited to criticism and verbal rebuttals. As the officers began to fire broadsides at Party leadership and doctrine, the Party high command moved quickly to clamp down on them.

Tightening of Political Controls

First and foremost, the Party tightened its grip over the armed forces. Essentially this has been done along two lines: the

---

[60] In the *Bulletin of Activities,* P'eng and Huang were charged with representing the "military line of the propertied class," supporting an "erroneous or false line" not in accordance with Mao's ideology (*Bulletin,* No. 3, January 7, 1961; No. 1, January 1, 1961, cited in Powell, p. 2), promoting "dogmatism," "warlordism," "feudalism" and a "simple military point of view." They were blamed for disobeying the ideology and military thought of Mao while believing in and imitating foreign countries (*Bulletin,* No. 24, June 18, 1961; No. 29, August 1, 1961, cited in Powell, *ibid.*). Criticisms which probably include P'eng and Huang attacked "unreasonable military systems and formalities" (*Bulletin,* No. 11, March 2, 1961, cited in Powell, *ibid.*). In essence, as Powell observes, P'eng and Huang were accused of military professionalism (*ibid.* p. 3).

[61] *Bulletin,* No. 1, January 1, 1961; No. 7, February 1, 1961.

[62] Quoted in *The New York Times,* September 14, 1963, and February 7, 1964.

intensification of indoctrination in the officer corps, and the consolidation of Party organisations in the military establishment, especially at the lower levels. This, of course, has always been the Party's preoccupation, but with the growth of professionalism its efforts have been stepped up.

By 1956 a full-scale campaign to indoctrinate the officers was under way.[63] Simultaneously, Party organisations in the armed forces, and especially the Party branches, were enlarged and overhauled in order to augment their position of leadership vis-à-vis the officers.[64] In the first half of 1957, the tone for the rectification campaign in the army, as elsewhere, was set by Mao's speech on contradictions.[65] There is no evidence that the torrent of devastating criticism which poured forth from intellectual circles during the short-lived "hundred flowers" period extended in any considerable degree to the army.[66] Nevertheless, it appears that during the subsequent anti-rightist campaign the Party took the opportunity to strike out at the officers, branding them "right-wingers" and ominously linking their views with the ultimate crime of opposition to Communism in general.[67]

In 1958, and especially in the latter half of the year, the movement against professionalism soared to new heights of vehemence. The inculcation of Mao's military writings was pushed with unprecedented vigour [68] and special stress was put on the leadership role of the Party committees.[69] The military academies, where professional attitudes were most likely to originate and be nurtured, were a prime target of the drive. It is also likely

[63] NCNA, February 21, 1956, SCMP, No. 1241, p. 5; NCNA, December 22, 1956, SCMP, No. 1455, p. 7.

[64] Liberation Army News, January 12, 1957, SCMP, No. 1616, pp. 14–15.

[65] NCNA, May 12, 1957, SCMP, No. 1547, p. 27; NCNA, April 20, 1957, SCMP, No. 1524, p. 7.

[66] This is also suggested by the fact that, as far as it is known, the anti-rightist campaign did not claim any important victims in the army—with one notable exception, Ch'en I, Director of the Cultural Department of the General Political Department, who was purged. See People's Daily, March 1, 1958.

[67] Liberation Army News editorial, NCNA, July 30, 1957, SCMP, No. 1588, p. 9.

[68] Liberation Army News, January 16, 1958, SCMP, No. 1786, pp. 6–7; NCNA-English, July 31, 1958.

[69] Liberation Army News, January 16, 1958, SCMP, No. 1786, p. 7.

that the influence of Soviet advisers was strongest in these schools, and perhaps this is one of the reasons why they bore the brunt of the campaign to instil Mao's teachings and to eradicate "dogmatism." The reports on what had to be eradicated in some of these academies indicate to what extent professionalism had taken root.[70]

After Lin Piao took over as Minister of Defence a new and extensive effort was made to reorganise and revitalise the political control system; this provides another indication that the system had deteriorated to a considerable degree. From July 1960 to February 1961 inspections, investigations and a purge were carried out in the army. Then the Party launched a campaign to recruit new members and to establish branch committees and Party groups in companies and platoons which had previously lacked Party organisations.[71]

Measures to Improve Relations with Civilians

Hand in hand with the house-cleaning in the army, the Party moved to forestall what it considered a dangerous drift of the officers from the population at large. Here perhaps the most prickly problem was the glaring gap which had developed between the living standard of the officers and their dependants on the one hand and the populace on the other hand.

Since the adoption of the pay system thousands of officers' dependants had left their rural homes to stay at military posts. This, it was said, caused difficulties in providing supplies, services and employment, and adversely affected the work of the officers. More important, perhaps, was the awkward situation created by the fact that at a time when the peasants were under perennial pressure to increase production and cut down on consumption, the dependants were not only sideline spectators of their efforts but also led a much better life. Such a situation, it was said, dampened the enthusiasm of the peasants for work and alienated

[70] NCNA, June 19, 1958, SCMP, No. 1802, p. 12; *Liberation Army News,* June 24, 1958, SCMP, No. 1817, pp. 16–17; *Liberation Army News,* May 5, 1958, JPRS, No. 10343/59, p. 39; *Liberation Army News,* June 20, 1958, JPRS, No. 10239/59, p. 34; *Liberation Army News,* August 8, 1958, JPRS, No. 10240/59, pp. 4–6.

[71] *Bulletin,* No. 23, June 13, 1961, cited in Powell, p. 8.

them from the armed forces. Taking all this into account, the
Party ordered, in late 1957, that the dependants should go home
and get down to work. Consequently, a mass migration of officers'
families back to their villages was set in motion.[72]

Other measures aimed at levelling the living standards included a reduction in the quantity of provisions supplied to the
armed forces and a lowering of the dependants' rations to the
level for the population as a whole,[73] a reduction in the salaries
of officers of divisional level and above,[74] and exhortations to the
officers to be thrifty and to refrain from buying up commodities
which were in short supply.[75] At the same time, steps were taken
to put an end to the callous treatment of civilians by the military.[76]

"Officers to the Ranks"

The whole campaign against professionalism was epitomised
in the "officers to the ranks" movement, laid down by a General
Political Department directive of September 20, 1958, which
required every officer to spend a month as an ordinary soldier.[77]
By February 1959 over 150,000 officers, including more than 160
generals, were reported to be cheerfully doing their stint as
privates.[78] It was said that battle-hardened veterans of three
decades of soldiering shed their gold-braided uniforms, donned a
private's kit, and took orders from greenhorn corporals[79]; heads
of logistics departments served as cooks[80]; divisional political
commissars stood sentry duty[81]; colonels swept barrack floors and
cleaned spittoons[82]; a major-general sang songs to entertain the

[72] NCNA, November 27, 1957, SCMP, No. 1668, pp. 18–19; also pp. 17,
19.

[73] Lanchow, *Kansu Jih-pao (Kansu Daily)*, September 18, 1957, SCMP,
No. 1626, pp. 24–25.

[74] *Liberation Army News*, February 26, 1957, SCMP, No. 1625, p. 27.

[75] NCNA, January 12, 1957, SCMP, No. 1460, pp. 9–10.

[76] NCNA, June 14, 1957, SCMP, No. 1557, p. 6.

[77] NCNA-English, September 21, 1958.

[78] *People's Daily*, April 27, 1959, CB, No. 579, p. 5.

[79] *People's Daily*, June 24, 1958, SCMP, No. 1812, p. 1.

[80] *Ibid.*

[81] *Ibid.*

[82] See note 78, p. 6.

troops accompanied by another general on the fiddle [83]; and so on. Few will argue that this phenomenon is probably unique in the annals of modern armies.

Essentially this movement was intended as a panacea for the problems arising from the growing caste-consciousness of the officers. The Party sought to recreate the revolutionary climate of the past and to demonstrate forcefully to both officers and men that regardless of how the army has changed, its time-honoured traditions have not.[84] Assessing the programme, the Chinese have noted, to no great surprise, that it made the troops very happy.[85] The same could hardly be said for the officers. The strange metamorphosis forced upon them not only ran counter to what a professional officer would consider the requirements of status and discipline, but was probably also a source of considerable physical discomfort to them. That the officers were not exactly elated with the movement is evident in the fact that the Party felt compelled to defend it at length.[86] In any case, it appears that since the "great leap forward" was abandoned, this programme has been quietly dumped.

After the "Leap"

In late 1960 the Party leaders scrapped the "great leap forward" and reluctantly returned to more sober and sensible policies. One reason for this has been the realisation that sheer muscle-power cannot perform miracles and that expertise cannot be dispensed with. Consequently, the stock of "experts" in relation to "reds" has risen markedly on the political exchange. There has been a renewed emphasis on expertise, and the scorn heaped on professional men in past years has given way to an admitted appreciation of the need for their talents.

This shift in attitude toward specialists has been reflected in the army. The deluge of denunciations which had descended on professional officers in previous years, especially in 1958, has

---

83 NCNA, October 19, 1958, SCMP, No. 1891, p. 3.
84 See, for example, note 78, pp. 6–8.
85 *Ibid.*, pp. 7–8.
86 *Hung Ch'i* (*Red Flag*) , No. 4, February 16, 1959, JPRS, No. 9176/59.

almost stopped. In fact, since 1960 there does not appear to have been a campaign aimed specifically at the officers, though indoctrination drives intended for the army as a whole have, if anything, been stepped up.[87]

There are no indications, however, that the Party leaders have made any key concessions to the viewpoint of the professional officers. To be sure, it appears that in two important areas of disagreement the Party has modified its policy. First, the employment of troops in economic construction has been drastically curtailed. Whereas in 1958 the army devoted some 60 million work days to industrial and agricultural work,[88] in 1961 the number fell to 22 million.[89] But this may have been due as much to the Party's reluctance to use troops in the countryside at a time of severe food shortages, and to the abandonment of many projects initiated during the "leap," as in deference to the officers' demands. Second, the militia movement appears to be on the wane, but this also is probably due to the abandonment of the "leap" and to the monumental mess into which the militia had deteriorated [90] rather than to the objections of the officers. In short, while these may seem to be concessions, there is no evidence that they are the direct result of pressure by the officers, and there is no hint that any of the officers' arguments have been accepted.

Quite the contrary is true. The Party has reaffirmed its basic views regarding the army and has taken steps to ensure their implementation. The "Regulations for PLA Management and Education on the Company Level" [91] and the "Four Sets of Regulations on Political Work in Company-Level Units of the PLA" [92] promulgated in 1961 were designed to strengthen the

[87] S. M. Chiu, "The PLA and the Party: Recent Developments," *Military Review*, XLIII, June 1963, pp. 58–66; *Bulletin*, No. 3, January 7, 1961.

[88] *Shih-shih Shou-ts'e (Current Handbook)*, No. 3, February 6, 1959, ECMM, No. 167, p. 15.

[89] NCNA-English, February 4, 1962.

[90] For an illuminating report on the sorry state of the militia in Honan, see *Bulletin*, No. 4, January 11, 1961.

[91] NCNA, July 5, 1961, SCMP, No. 2540, pp. 1–3.

[92] NCNA, November 21, 1961, SCMP, No. 2630, pp. 1–3.

Party's political and organisational hold over the basic-level units of the armed forces. But the most forceful and far-reaching reassertion of Party principles and practice was the publication in March 1963 of the "Regulations Governing PLA Political Work." [93]

The importance of these Regulations—the first such Regulations to be issued apart from a 1954 draft [94]—can hardly be exaggerated. But their most striking feature is that they contain nothing new. They bring together and formalise things which had been said many times before, but in no way do they diverge from previous patterns. That it was necessary to do this is, as has been observed, a clear indication that much of what was supposed to be operational was in fact not so. But at the same time the Party has left no doubt that it will bend every effort to remedy the defects and that it has no intention of modifying its stand, whatever the views of the professional officers. Commenting on the Regulations, the army newspaper went through the whole gamut of issues which have been in dispute and restated emphatically and unequivocally that the Maoist doctrine remains the guiding light for all of them. [95] The Party, in short, has conceded nothing in principle, but it is apparent that it has a long way to go before all its principles become practice.

How the drastic deterioration of Sino-Soviet relations has affected Party relations is an open question. It is likely that the removal of Marshal P'eng and his supporters has not removed the apprehension of some officers over the consequences of the rift. For one thing, the defensive value of the Soviet nuclear shield for China can now only be very limited. More important, outside aid, especially aircraft parts and aviation and vehicle fuel, is still indispensable for keeping China's military machine at maximum efficiency, to say nothing of modernising it. Such

[93] The text of these Regulations has apparently not been made public. For a detailed description of their content, see *Liberation Army News* editorial, May 8, 1963 (reprinted in the *People's Daily*), SCMP, No. 2984, pp. 1–8.

[94] The 1954 draft has been referred to several times, but apparently it has not been made public.

[95] Note 92, p. 3.

aid, however, has not been forthcoming. It is known that in mid-1960 the Soviet Union withdrew its military as well as non-military technicians, and drastically diminished its shipments of military equipment and supplies.[96] This has undoubtedly hit the army hard.[97]

Just how hard is suggested by China's apparent efforts to overcome the difficulties. One sign was the establishment in 1963 of three new Ministries of Machine Building, presumably to take charge of expanded military production. Another was the visit in September 1963 of a Chinese military delegation to Sweden, possibly to shop for supplies. A third is Peking's preoccupation with increasing petroleum production and importing oil.[98] However, in view of the country's sparse resources and economic priorities, it is unlikely that China's military industry can rapidly make up for the hardware which previously came from abroad. The efficiency of the armed forces will probably continue to decline in the near future, and it is possible that some officers are deeply distressed over this state of affairs.

There is no sign, however, of tension between the Party and the military. On the contrary, since 1960 there has been a notable absence of public criticism of the army, and recently the army has come in for unusual praise.[99] Could one reason for this harmony be that Moscow's disregard for Peking's views, especially on the test ban treaty, has convinced the officers that China has only herself to depend upon? If so, then, ironically, the widening of the Sino-Soviet rift, which several years ago tended to drive the military and political leaders apart, has now drawn them closer together.

But if there is no sign of tension, there is also no sign that the sources of potential tension have been eliminated. "Redness" and "expertise" do not, in the final analysis, go together and

[96] United States Department of State press release, August 20, 1963: *The Military Balance 1963–1964* (London: Institute for Strategic Studies, 1963), p. 9.

[97] *The New York Times*, December 4, 1963, and March 1, 1964; *The Christian Science Monitor*, February 21, 1964.

[98] *The Christian Science Monitor*, February 24, 1964; *The New York Times*, December 27, 1963.

[99] See, for example, *Far Eastern Economic Review*, February 13, 1964.

some way out will eventually have to be found, perhaps by a new generation of more technically oriented leaders. However, given the Party's firm control over the army and its constant concern with maintaining that control, there is no reason to expect any major crisis in the relations between the Party and the army in the present circumstances.

Generals and Politicians in India

1964

LLOYD I. RUDOLPH AND SUSANNE HOEBER RUDOLPH

India has been transformed from the leading exponent of peaceful initiatives to a nation vitally concerned with military security.[1] Her military defeat by China has led to large increases in defense spending and substantial projected expansion of the military services. In new states, the modern professionalism of the military with its apparent promise of order and efficiency— and the ineffectiveness of nationalist political classes—has often led to military take-overs. This has not been the case in India, but will it be so in the future?

How is it that the Indian military services have played a limited professional role when in neighboring Pakistan, also part of the old British Raj, the present regime is headed by a military man, General Ayub Khan? Both military and political leaders in India agree that the variable is not the army itself. Senior Indian officers who attended Sandhurst with their Pakistan counterparts remember a shared military past and see little difference between themselves and Pakistani generals. Prime Minister Nehru and Defense Minister Chavan concur. They agree it was not inordinate ambition or a special taste for politics but the failure of the political classes to govern effectively that persuaded the Pakistani army under Ayub Khan to seize power. It took power, Mr. Nehru

[1] This article profited from a series of interviews conducted in India in the spring of 1963. We are grateful to Prime Minister Jawaharlal Nehru, Defense Minister Y. B. Chavan, former Defense Minister V. K. Krishna Menon, civil servants presently or formerly connected with the Defense Ministry, and present and former members of the military establishment for their comments and views.

Reprinted by permission from Pacific Affairs, 37 *(Spring 1964)*, *5–19.*

believes, "naturally," "automatically," when politics failed. It seems reasonable to senior Indian officers that when politicians "play ducks and drakes," as they did in Pakistan, rather than shoulder their responsibilities, the army should step in to "put things right." But in the absence of a serious failure of politics Indian army men will adhere to a standard learned under the British, to "know their place."

So far, Indian politics has by no means failed. Its relative success is the product of long experience with modern political ideas and practice and the integration of these with traditional Indian values. The assimilation of modern political ideas began almost one hundred and thirty years ago with the introduction of "English" education. Indians have been electing legislators for over fifty years. Indian parties formed provincial cabinets, responsible to elected legislatures, twenty-five years ago.

Indian politics has profited from the experience of three nationalist generations: the generation which espoused Gandhi's statement of transformed traditionalism; its predecessors the "moderates," loyalist in their sympathies and committed to such liberal ideas as fundamental rights and parliamentary government; and its successors the socialists, concerned with social and economic justice and planned development. If there was tension and conflict among these nationalist generations, there was no fundamental break, no alienation of the modern liberals and socialists from Gandhi's more traditional following. The adherence to Gandhi of the Nehrus (Motilal, the liberal-moderate father, and Jawaharlal, the socialist son) illustrates Gandhi's ability to keep these generations in harness with him, even if he did not convince them of the ultimate truth of his ideas. They followed him without fully believing, partly because of his extraordinary human and moral qualities, partly because of his concern and ability to be heard by traditional India, the India of villages, castes and regional languages.

Nehru too unites the three nationalist generations, but not in the same way as Gandhi. He has governed in the spirit of the grandfathers and the sons, of the liberals and the socialists, yet he retains much of Gandhi's traditional support and authority as the Mahatma's political heir, if not his moral disciple. The gap between tradition and modernity, between village and city, oral and written communication, *dhoti* and trouser, so often found in other new states, has been closed not only by the amalgamation of traditional and modern ideas and generations, but also by the pervasiveness and depth of party and associational life. The dominant Congress Party, heir to the nationalist movement and independence, has won large legislative majorities at the center and governed in most states, yet has polled less than half of the popular vote in India's three general elections. The four major opposition parties, along with an active and independent press, provide the lively and telling public dialogue which makes democracy meaningful. At the mass level, it is the caste associations and linguistic states which provide channels of communication and bases for leadership and representation, that have made political participation understandable and effective.

Political democracy in India has steadily enlarged the chances of its continued existence by educating India's huge electorate in the skills and values of self-government, yet its fate is by no means secure. Of the many difficulties that persist, the propensity to popular authoritarian rule is most likely to play into the hands of military leadership. The authoritarian character created by the traditional family, the attraction of cultural fundamentalism to the urbanized lower middle classes, and the appeal of order, discipline and efficiency to the professional classes, now marginal features of Indian political life, are susceptible of mobilization by military leadership under the right circumstances. But the expressions of authoritarianism (the memory of Subhas Chandra Bose's effort to identify Indian nationalism with fascism during World War II; the R.S.S., a uniformed cultural cadre behind the right radical Jan Sangh party; the DMK, the Tamilian fundamentalist and secessionist opposition in Madras State; and unreconciled elements of the old feudal order) show neither signs of common purpose nor military leadership. The efforts of General Cariappa, the first Indian to hold the office of Commander-in-Chief, to lead the forces of order and cultural fundamentalism have made little impression nationally or regionally.

The Viceroy and Parliament, one autocratic, the other democratic, represent the two great traditions of modern politics which the subcontinent experienced under British rule. The differences between the role of the military in India and Pakistan are related to the fact that after independence Pakistan under Jinnah identified with the Viceregal tradition while India under Nehru embraced parliamentarism. The English Viceroy and Governor-General headed an administrative state which, at its best, approximated the ideal of platonic guardians, paternal, benign, and efficient. The Commander-in-Chief stood second to the Viceroy under the British Raj, powerful yet subordinate to the Crown's civilian representative in India. Representative democracy developed side by side with the Viceregal tradition. In Pakistan a kind of Viceregal government by civil servants in the guise of politicians was toppled by a general who has tried to rid the state of parties, politics, and politicians. In India, parliamentary nationalists might have yielded to the opposite temptation, ousting the remnants of the Viceregal tradition, the military officers who had fought for England and the civil servants who had jailed the nationalists. Had they done so, they would have seriously jeopardized governmental effectiveness and created a potentially subversive political class. But the Congress leaders recognized the value of these professional services to the new state. There was some readjustment of their status in state and society, but no purges.

At independence, India's new rulers were under some pressure to replace the "military mercenaries" who served the British Raj with a political and nationalist army. Of the 60,000 Indian troops captured by the Japanese in Malaya, 25,000 went over to the Indian National Army, a force built by the Japanese to aid its South Asia offensive, and described to Indian soldiers as a nationalist liberation force for India.[2] The army was eventually led by Subhas Chandra Bose, a prominent nationalist from Bengal who had been President of the Indian National Congress and who thought well of Hitler Germany. Bose was killed in a 1945 plane crash, but in the nationalist upsurge at independence, the

---

[2] Hugh Toye, *The Springing Tiger: Subhas Chandra Bose;* and Stephen B. Cohen, "Subhas Chandra Bose and the Indian National Army," *Pacific Affairs,* Winter 1963–64.

INA and its leaders were given great prominence and glory. Their reputations were enhanced when the British tried to convict them in widely reported public trials of desertion, mutiny and other serious crimes.[2a] Bose had promised them that "out of your ranks will be born the future General Staff of the Army of Free India." [3] A less prudent leadership might have been pressed in the excitement of freedom to replace "mercenaries" with "dedicated fighters for freedom." But this was not done. None of the INA's "heroes" were retained as officers, a decision which not only cemented the loyalties of the old officers to the new regime but also strengthened the idea that professional competence, not political initiatives, was the first requirement of the Indian Army.[3a] The INA was not dishonoured: for example, Shah Nawaz Khan, one of its leaders, is today Deputy Minister of Railways; the late J. K. Bhonsle, another, headed the National Discipline Scheme. But unlike Indonesia and Burma, India did not start its independent life with a political army that claimed a share in the nationalist movement and the winning of independence.

Because India's political classes were able to master the civil and military services of the Viceregal tradition and because they had the wisdom to conciliate them, they have benefited by certain of their "English" prejudices. The senior civil servants and military officers were highly anglicized, the military perhaps even more than the civilians.[3b] A Sandhurst man accounted for the

[2a] For examples of the sentiments the INA leaders evoked, see Jag Parvesh Chander, *Meet the Heroes,* Lahore (n.d. 1946?) .

[3] *Selected Speeches of Subhas Chandra Bose.* Government of India, 1962, p. 183.

[3a] As a member of the Interim Government, Nehru ably gave a difficult speech supporting the Commander-in-Chief, Auchinleck, in resisting demands in the Legislative Assembly for immediate release of former INA men still in prison. See John Connell, *Auchinleck: a Biography of Field-Marshal Sir Claude Auchinleck,* London, 1959, pp. 869, 871; and Alan Campbell-Johnson, *Mission with Mountbatten,* New York, 1953, p. 53. For an officer's view, see Sir Francis Tuker, *While Memory Serves,* London, 1950.

[3b] The problems and consequences of assimilation are suggested in Humphrey Evans, *Thimayya of India: A Soldier's Life,* New York, 1960. Some of the concern with whether the proper patterns are still being observed in the post-independence period emerges from Lord Birdwood, *India and Pakistan: A Continent Decides,* New York, 1954, Chapter V.

high number of drop-outs in his generation of officers by describing the severe demands for English cultural assimilation, in large things as well as small. "The Civil Servants could at least go home at five o'clock to their wives and children. But we went 'home' to our messes. We ate, drank and lived with the British. We had more chances to make bloopers."

Among Indian officers, the assimilation displays itself today not merely in the exquisitely tailored lounge suits of officers in mufti, in a penchant for understatement, for beautiful silver, and for cavalry moustaches, but also in a belief that really civilized politics, like that of the Small Island, requires civilian control and parliamentary processes. Furthermore, under the Raj, Indian officers learned the prudence of having no political views. Older officers recall complicated cat and mouse conversations with British superiors in which they averred they had no opinions about the Congress. That doesn't mean that a recessive belief that "all politicians are scallywags" would not assert itself were the scallywag qualities of political leaders to become too apparent. British mess talk in the thirties did not neglect to point out frequently that the leaders of Indian nationalism were no-account men. Retired General Cariappa has taken the view, it was alleged in parliament,[4] that India could stand two years of President's rule with army support, the civil administration being made subordinate to the army. "Look at Pakistan," he is said to have told a public meeting, "people there are happy, and everything is clean." But most Indian officers prefer to serve under a civilian government, providing that it is sufficiently competent and effective that one can do so honorably.

The army's position has been down-graded both administratively and socially. In British days, the Commander-in-Chief of the Indian Defense Forces, a high-ranking military officer, sat as a member of the Viceroy's executive council, the administrative state's equivalent of a cabinet. His position as number two man in the executive suggested that the circumstances of empire required a much more prominent position for the army in India than at home in Britain. The pre-independence army

---

[4] *Lok Sabha Debates, 1961.* Second series, LIV, 41, p. 10589.

felt itself a very important part of the governing class. Immediately after the war, the process of down-grading began. The Commander-in-Chief was replaced in the Cabinet by a civilian Defense Minister responsible to an elected legislature.[4a] This, the Constituent Assembly believed, was no more than a logical consequence of responsible government. Thereafter the Defense Ministry, at least until Krishna Menon took over, did not count, as it generally does in the West, as one of the two or three key portfolios. The President of India became the Supreme Commander of the armed forces, a ceremonial supersession which symbolized civilian control. In 1955 the military office of Commander-in-Chief was abolished altogether, and now there are only three Chiefs of Staff, one each for the Army, Navy and Air Force. The move reflected some nervousness concerning the military's potential role and a consequent desire "to trim their tails." Ceremonial rankings reflect these changes. Lieutenant-Generals who were entitled to gun salutes are no longer. Only some Lieutenant-Generals are entitled to travel in saloon cars, and the democratic state encourages them not to. The Warrant of Precedence places the Army Chief of Staff, the senior military officer in India, in twenty-fifth place, behind such offices as the Comptroller and Auditor General, Chief Justices of State Courts, members of the Planning Commission and State Cabinet Ministers.[5] Officers are moving away from the idea of a mess, from dressing for dinner and wine and fine silver, to the idea of Officers' Clubs, where wives can be brought of an evening to save cooking dinner.

The relatively modest standing of the military is a logical consequence of non-alignment. Some of India's most distinguished officers made their reputations under U.N. rather than Indian commands. Best known is former Chief of Staff Thimayya, who was in charge of the POW Repatriation in Korea. Others have served in Gaza, the Congo, and Cyprus. The present Chief of Staff, General Chaudhuri, made his reputation in limited engagements at home: the "integration" of Hyderabad just after independence and the more recent Goa take-over. In India

---

[4a] When the Interim Government took office in 1946, Sardar Baldev Singh replaced Field Marshal Sir Claude Auchinleck, who had been War Member.

[5] Warrant of Precedence. in *India, 1962*. Government of India, 1962.

one of the leading justifications of non-alignment has been that it permits India to devote her efforts and resources primarily to economic justice and growth rather than military weapons and personnel. Both Nehru and Menon see the failure of politics in Pakistan as in part a result of the opposite emphasis. Far more resources, prestige and national effort have gone into planned development than the military establishment; both before and after the Chinese invasion, military security has been seen as a function of rapid and effective development. After reviewing the Third Plan in the light of the emergency, the Prime Minister declared that it was 85 per cent defense-oriented while the National Development Council stated that "the country's Plans of development [are] an integral part of national defence." [6]

The reorientation of Indian foreign policy in light of the Chinese threat is apt to bring with it some changes in the political role of the army. Increased resources are likely to have similar effects on the standing of the Indian armed forces as did large-scale U.S. aid under CENTO and SEATO on Pakistan's, raising their prestige and power *vis-à-vis* other social forces in the state. The fact that Defense has become a desirable and eagerly sought-after portfolio already suggests a shift. So far the emergency has, however, produced no men on horseback. Those who rode to the frontier returned as something less than heroes. Short of large-scale and protracted fighting, which at the moment seems unlikely, the scope for men on white horses is limited. There was some indignation among retired senior officers at the extent of the debacle. For a while it looked as if they might give some direction to public indignation in a way that could affect the civil-military balance by demanding a public inquiry. But then two former Chiefs of Staff and another retired officer, the late Rajendrasingji, Thimayya and Thorat, were absorbed in the National Defense Council, set up to advise the government in the emergency. The Council's Military Affairs Committee has not been very effective or active, but it has satisfied the generals and the public that available military talent is being consulted. Most of the retired officers expressed themselves content with a confi-

[6] *Asian Recorder*, 1962, p. 4911.

dential internal inquiry into the military reverses on the north-east frontier.

The public position of an army is not only affected by the strength of politics and the quality of foreign policy, but also by its relative status in society. If armies in the West still profit by historical traces of feudal honor and social standing, this is hardly true of the Indian Army. The historical eclipse of the *kshatriya*—the ancient warrior-ruler caste—has dimmed the traditional glamour associated with the fighting man, while his standing as a modern professional is still somewhat tainted by his association with British power and culture. Among India's three great caste cultures, *kshatriya* (warrior-ruler), *brahman* (priest, teacher), and *vaishya* (merchant), *kshatriyas* have lost the most in the transition to independence and modern times. They declined because they failed in their ancient duty: for centuries they could not prevent large sections of Hindu India from falling under alien rule. *Brahmans,* who had served the *kshatriyas* as priests and administrators, survived foreign rule better: some took to the new learning, whether Persian under the Moghuls or English under the British. While *brahmans* adapted to modern culture and learned to turn liberal and nationalist ideas to Indian account, *kshatriyas* survived as rulers of princely states, frequently indifferent to the changes in society and political ideas occurring in British India. Having stood aloof from nationalism, *kshatriyas* at independence were identified with monarchy and feudalism rather than nationalism and its major components, democracy, parliamentary government, social justice and planned development.

The *kshatriya* ideal also survived among the "martial races," —though not all "martial races" are *kshatriyas*—those communities considered fit by the British Raj to fight for the empire abroad and, if necessary, at home. Not only did the "martial races" serve the cause of British imperialism, but they were least involved with and frequently opposed to the cause of nationalism and independence. The British recruited officers initially only from "loyal classes," from families known to support the Raj. Often these officers shared British disapprobation for bookish, pen-pushing *vaishyas* and *brahmans* like Gandhi and

Nehru, who formed the backbone of the modern middle classes which dominated Indian nationalism. By taste and culture they found themselves outsiders as Gandhi transformed traditional *vaishya* and *brahmanical* non-violence for use in contemporary political settings. Nationalists considered the army an instrument of British imperialism, cultural as well as political. After independence, Nehru's peace policy for quite different reasons continued to emphasize non-violence.

In those new states where ambitious young men are blocked from politics, business and the professions because they are the closed preserves of entrenched elites, the army has become a significant outlet for talent and a revolutionary force. In India, alternative careers open to merit compete strongly with the army. Politics in India's fifteen states has become a vehicle for ambitious men, offering them the opportunities American urban and state politics did to emerging ethnic groups at the turn of the century. The professions beckon talent: the senior civil service (IAS) attracts able youths from all backgrounds. There is an increase in bright but unpolished IAS probationers (9 per cent over the past twelve years have come from families who earn less than $60 per month) [7] who learn upper middle class social graces from the sophisticated wives their prestige can command on the marriage market. Other central and provincial services also recruit by merit. The modern professions, particularly engineering and, to a lesser degree, medicine, are also getting a very substantial portion of the talented youth. Business, too, is offering increasing scope for ambitious young men. While traditional family firms still favor family and caste, modern firms, many of them the outriders of British and American companies—Lever, Burma-Shell, Esso, Imperial Tobacco—recruit more by merit and to some extent by class style. In this career competition, the army runs a weak third, if its position is that high. This is a considerable contrast to its pre-independence status, and is partly due to the fact that pay and perquisites are below those of the civilian all-India services. The marriage "market," a reasonably faithful

[7] D. N. Rao, "Disparities of Representation Among the Direct Recruits to I.A.S." *Indian Journal of Public Administration*. Vol. IX, No. 1, January-March 1963, p. 91.

barometer of career status in a society where marriages are still arranged, rates young men in the "foreign firms" highest, in the Indian foreign and administrative services next, and then perhaps those in the defense forces. (The army's position in the marriage market registered a disastrous decline with the Chinese invasion; mothers prefer to see their daughters married to safe professions.)

The army has complained of difficulties in officer recruitment for some years. There is little by way of service traditions in officer families, although there is a strong tradition of this kind among enlisted men. Senior officers are as apt to send their sons to foreign firms or modern professions or coffee plantations as to the military services. To be sure, the position is improving since the Defense Ministry initiated, in Krishna Menon's time, so-called Sainik Schools which offer the equivalent of an English Public School education for boys wishing to enter the National Defense Academy at Khadakvasla. These schools should increase the supply of good material to the officer corps. But so far, the Indian military services, unlike those in many other underdeveloped countries, are by no means the most obvious path for the ambitious and talented in search of honor and power. Nor are officers socially isolated. Sons of business and professional men choose the military as a career, and military, professional and business families inter-marry. The army is merely one honored occupation among many.

But suppose that the military's built-in feelings of restraint should weaken, that it should receive more resources—as it will —and that the political policies and leadership should cease to command respect. Suppose some leaders in the army wanted to seize power. One consideration that would restrain them is Indian federalism, a federalism which expresses the country's size, diversity and diffusion of power. The fifteen states, eleven with larger populations than California and one with a population larger than any European country save Russia, are more powerful *vis-à-vis* the center—not perhaps on paper, but politically— than any American state, and as such constitute obstacles to military rule. Defense Minister Chavan, who knows the meaning of state power from his years as Chief Minister of Maharashtra, points out that while control of Karachi could mean control of Pakistan—and even there there are problems—Delhi could not easily control unwilling states. Most of the state Chief Ministers are sufficiently self-confident politicians and administrators to take a dim view of military claims that officers govern better.

Army organization itself militates against the possibility of a coup. The subcontinent is divided into four Commands (Southern, Western, Central and Eastern) each reasonably self-sufficient and each under a General Officer Commander-in-Chief. An effective coup would have to bring in all the commanders, a formidable concert which seems implausible even under most difficult circumstances. The temptations of easy access to power do not presently exist in India.

On October 26, 1962, President Radhakrishnan, for the first time since independence, declared a State of Emergency under Article 352 of the Constitution.[7a] He did so of course on the advice of the government, as constitutional convention requires, and so far the government has used few of its extensive powers. But it is not impossible to imagine an Indian president, confronted by a weak, divided and ineffective government and a serious crisis, stretching or ignoring the convention to act on government advice, declaring a State of Emergency and calling upon the military services as well as the civilian administration to support him as Supreme Commander and Head of State. If military or quasi-military rule is to come to India, it is much more likely to do so under the cover of legality than through a *coup d'état*. But even with the possibility of legal justification, the same factors which inhibit a coup will also profoundly inhibit such a presidential-military venture. While it should not be ruled out as a future possibility, it yet remains quite unlikely.

In post-independence India few people worried about the army as a political force. The military services and their budget remained small and the Defense Minister a relatively unimportant member of the cabinet. It was only after Krishna Menon took over as Defense Minister in 1957 that the press, parliament and public began to take political notice of the military establish-

[7a] See Benjamin Schoenfeld, "Emergency Rule in India," *Pacific Affairs*, Fall 1963, for the powers which may be exercised.

ment. Even though the new minister's responsibilities at the United Nations and at the Planning Commission (as Member for International Trade and Development) prevented him from concentrating all his time and energy on defense matters, he early on began to draw public attention to himself and the services by hustling about the country inspecting installations to the accompaniment of considerable photographic and written press coverage. His policies towards defense production and research and development drew praise and criticism as the ordnance factories turned their unutilized capacity to the manufacture of items for civilian consumption, as the supply of trucks from the private sector was supplemented by a defense sector venture in that field and as defense research efforts were considerably expanded. Critics charged that a defense sector was being added to the public and private sectors of the country's economy, while friends argued that the defense establishment was for the first time receiving the imaginative and effective leadership it required. The critics were concerned that Menon was adding a new dimension to the power factors in Indian politics by identifying himself with the generals and building up the defense establishment. While it is difficult to assess the validity of these concerns, a combination of the Menon left, with its sources of strength both in and out of the Congress, and the military establishment was seen by some as a potential source of danger, particularly in the context of settling the succession issue.

Mr. Menon's strategic doctrines concerning Pakistan and China and the relationship of those doctrines to professional standards in the services represent another large area of political controversy. In briefest form, the Defense Minister's speech and action reflected the view that Pakistan was the real and most likely enemy while China was a friend who shared similar domestic and international concerns. Ideology and strategy combined to shape Menon's perceptions and attitudes toward Pakistan's military pact allies on the one hand and China's great ally Russia on the other; on such key issues as non-alignment and Kashmir the East seemed to be more favorably disposed to India than the West. That these strategic views were not universally shared in the defense establishment seems certain. It is less clear to what extent senior officers believed that their professional future depended on overt or passive adherence to these views. Under such circumstances it becomes particularly difficult to judge Mr. Menon's handling of promotion policy. Did he promote men congenial to his strategic and political views, disrupting the professional spirit of the army in the process, or did he recognize and encourage imagination and talent, refusing to adhere rigidly to the blind dictates of seniority?

The capacity to know and even anticipate his political chief's mind while maintaining an independent capacity to give professional advice is one of the tests of a good civilian or military officer. But this delicate relationship requires sensitivity and appreciation of responsibilities on both sides, from the chief as well as the subordinate. There is evidence to suggest that under Mr. Menon at the Defense Ministry this relationship broke down under the pressure of Menon's known and strongly held political opinions and personal evaluations. The fact that a number of senior officers now holding positions of highest responsibility were placed on the retirement list and remain in service today only because of Mr. Menon's abrupt departure supports this view. So too does the degree to which seniority was ignored in promotions. In Parliament, Mr. Nehru argued that it was proper that top posts be filled by the political executive "ignoring seniority—not ignoring it, but certainly not attaching too much importance to it" [8] while Mr. Menon observed that officers like General Thimayya, the then Chief of the Army Staff, had superseded several senior officers without difficulties being raised. The opposition held that retirement and promotion policy were being used in a way that went beyond a legitimate concern to recognize professional talent. In particular, opposition members charged that retirement and promotion policy were being used to clear the way for General B. M. Kaul, a man highly valued by both Nehru and Menon.

Like the Prime Minister, General B. M. Kaul is a Kashmiri *brahman* and endowed with a good many of the intellectual qualities which such a background often produces. Even some

---

[8] *Lok Sabha Debates,* 1961. Second series, LIV, 42, p. 10827.

conservative officers who resented his rapid advance respect him. It seems plausible that it is these qualities plus strategic and political views which paralleled his political chiefs' that account for the preference which they showed him over his bluff, straight-forward and less brilliant colleagues. It is generally believed that his rapid promotion was designed to place him in a position to succeed General Thapar in the top post of Chief of the Army Staff and that, but for the events following upon the Chinese invasion, he would have done so.

In 1959, under rather dramatic circumstances, the then Chief of the Army Staff, General Thimayya, offered his resignation on the issue of General Kaul's promotion to Lieutenant-General.[9] The President of Pakistan was about to pay a flying visit to India and, as it turned out, the Prime Minister had to deal with the resignation of his senior military officer on the very day on which he was greeting General Ayub. It was rumored that the Air and Naval Chiefs were on the verge of following suit. The parliamentary opposition charged that Kaul's promotion over the heads of more senior officers was more a matter of personal and political preferences than it was of professional merit.[10] According to the usual practice, the Chief of the Army Staff, after consultation with the area commanders, had offered the names of three officers, Generals P. S. Gyani, P. P. Kumara-mangalam, and B. M. Kaul, as fit for promotion to Lieutenant-General. Of these, Kaul was the most junior. The Chief of the Army Staff had placed Gyani first on the list but Defense Minis-ter Menon and his cabinet colleagues chose Kumaramangalam and Kaul only.

The decision on its face was a legitimate exercise of civilian authority but General Thimayya interpreted the action differ-ently by submitting his resignation to the Prime Minister. Mr. Nehru quickly persuaded him that his action on behalf of the career service was ill-advised and the General withdrew his resig-nation even before the news reached the public and parliament. In parliament, the Prime Minister justified Gyani's exclusion on

[9] *Statesman*. New Delhi, September 1 and 2, 1959.
[10] See *Lok Sabha Debates*. Second series. Remarks ranging from August 31 to September 12 in Volume XXXIV. See especially page 5588.

the ground that he had not yet commanded an infantry division, a normal requirement for promotion to Lieutenant-General. But Gyani was an artillery officer with extensive experience and senior commands in that branch; his professional colleagues apparently did not regard his not having held command of an infantry division as a bar to promotion nor, eventually, did his civilian superiors. He was made a Lieutenant-General a few months after the public outcry over General Kaul's promotion.[11]

While promotions were the immediate occasion of Thimayya's resignation, strategy was also at issue. *Link,* a popular weekly friendly to Krishna Menon, wrote of whispers about the inadequacy of defenses in NEFA, whispers quieted, it said, by the Prime Minister's remarks in the debate which followed the Chief of Staff's resignation. "The North East Frontier," said *Link* in memorable prose, "was safe as houses." Finally, the events of 1959 raised questions concerning lines of communication and responsibility in the defense establishment. General Thimayya was in the habit of seeing the Prime Minister directly from time to time and some say that at one time at least he had had a special relationship with Mr. Nehru. The Kaul promotion seems to have been the occasion for Thimayya to find out whether he or the Defense Minister, from whom he had become progressively estranged, commanded the greater confidence of the Prime Minister. At stake was an issue of some enduring importance for civil-military relationships in India: whether, as in Britain, Chiefs of Staff were to have direct access to the Prime Minister when they disagreed with their political superiors.

In 1961, when General Kaul was appointed Chief of the General Staff, the top staff appointment in the Army, he again became an issue before parliament.[12] Promotions, it was said, were "according to the whims and fancies of the Defense Minister or what will suit his political or ideological purposes." [13] But the opposition acquitted itself badly. Senior spokesmen in their

[11] *Asian Recorder,* 1959, p. 2944.
[12] *Statesman.* New Delhi, February 20 and 28, 1961.
[13] Mr. Kripalani in *Lok Sabha Debates—1961.* Second series, LIV, No. 41, p. 10059.

eagerness to beat Mr. Menon with any stick that came to hand had not taken the elementary precaution of reading General Kaul's biography in the standard references and were duly caught short when they accused him of not having combat arms experience.[14] The debate became a test of parliamentary review of appointments as the opposition fought for the right to canvass promotions case by case, naming names.[15] But the Speaker forbade the naming of military officers: "If I allow this," he said, "there will be eternal lobbying. Member after member of the Armed Forces will come and catch hold of all the 500 odd members here. . . ."[16]

In 1962, the Kaul affair came to an abrupt and tragic close. On October 5, some weeks after the Chinese had intensified their military activity on the northern frontier but before they launched their main offensive on October 20, General Kaul was appointed commander of a newly formed corps with responsibility for the Northeast Frontier area. The appointment confirms that Nehru and Menon had high confidence in his abilities since the government, at the end of September, had decided to oust the Chinese from what it believed was Indian territory. When Mr. Nehru left for Ceylon in the second week of October, he announced: "Our instructions are to free our territory. I cannot fix a date. That is entirely for the army." [17] The government seemed convinced that a determined but limited effort would deter the Chinese: General Kaul is credited with being an exponent of this forward policy believing, unlike some of his military colleagues, that army preparedness was commensurate with the risk.[18] In the event, the worst happened; instead of driving the Chinese back and deterring them from further advances, the Indian advance probably precipitated China's well-planned attack, an attack that quickly over-ran India's surprised, poorly led, and ill-prepared forces. The Delhi casualties of the Chinese offensive included Defense Minister Krishna Menon, Chief of the Army Staff Tha-

[14] *Debates.* LIV, No. 42, p. 10829.
[15] *Debates.* LIV, No. 41, p. 10551.
[16] *Debates.* LIV, No. 42, p. 10812.
[17] *Statesman.* New Delhi, April 12, 1963, and *Indian Affairs Record,* October 1962, p. 261.
[18] Romesh Thapar in *Economic Weekly,* February 1963.

par and Corps Commander Kaul.[19] On April 1, 1963, Defense Minister Chavan disclosed to parliament the terms of reference for the investigation of the debacle to be conducted by senior army officers, terms that included "the capacity of the commanders at all levels to influence the men under them." [20] The inquiry eventually concluded that, while commanders up to the brigade level exercised command adequately, "at higher levels . . . shortcomings became more apparent." Defense Minister Chavan stated "that some of the higher Commanders did not depend enough on the initiative of the lower Commanders, who alone could have the requisite knowledge of the terrain and local conditions of troops under them." The judgment suggests, in its own officially circuitous way, that the highest command, presumably including General Kaul, may have been more in touch with its political chiefs than with the lower commands, and ignored professional advice which might have warned that troops and equipment were inadequate to the expulsion policy. Another finding of the inquiry strengthens the impression that professional criteria were inadequately consulted, so that troops were committed to an enterprise which they could not successfully complete. "Even the largest and the best equipped of armies need to be given proper policy guidance and major directives by the government . . . these must bear a reasonable relation to the size of the army and state of its equipment from time to time." [21] Among the lessons taught by the Chinese invasions seems to be the importance of respecting the professional integrity and independence of the military service.

Finally, Mr. Menon's role as Defense Minister must be viewed in the context of the succession issue. In the spring of 1962, it was very much on the public mind because of Mr. Nehru's illness. Any prominent and ambitious member of the cabinet is interested either in himself succeeding or insuring that the man who does is not unsympathetic to his views. Krishna Menon is not immune from such sentiments. When G. B. Pant, the Deputy Leader of the Congress Parliamentary Party, died

[19] *Times of India.* New Delhi, December 1, 1962.
[20] *Statesman.* New Delhi, April 2, 1963.
[21] Text of speech in *Hindustan Times,* September 3, 1963.

over two years ago, those with ambitions and hopes for the first place, Finance Minister Morarji Desai and Transport and Communications Minister Jagjivan Ram, maneuvered to fill his party post while Home Minister Lal Bahadur Shastri stood ready in case of a stand-off. After several postponements, the Prime Minister decided to sweep the problem under the rug by abolishing Pant's old post. At the time of Mr. Nehru's illness in the spring of 1962, then, there were at least three known aspirants for the succession as well as a less visible consortium of well-established state Chief Ministers who were contemplating joining the central cabinet en bloc and establishing their collective leadership at the center.

Krishna Menon, who has never been strong with the professionals of the Congress Party, was not even prospectively in the running. Nor were any of the possible aspirants particularly friendly to Menon personally or politically. Menon's best hope for remaining an influential man after the Prime Minister leaves the scene lies in maintaining the Nehru family leadership, that is, the leadership of the Prime Minister's daughter, Indira Gandhi. He is not alone in this. The amorphous but visible Congress left made up of ideologically self-conscious socialists, younger intellectuals with leftist leanings and disdain for what they regard as the parochial and philistine professional politicians, and some top men in the central party organization who see Indira Gandhi as the only person in the country possessing the popularity to keep powerful state Chief Ministers in line, believe that the Prime Minister's daughter is their best hope. A part of this unassembled jig-saw puzzle could have been Krishna Menon, heading a powerful defense establishment with a sympathetic professional like General Kaul at its head. No one believes that Kaul would have helped or supported Menon in furthering personal political ambitions. But it is not out of the question that he would have been sympathetic to any Menon efforts aimed at blocking some current contenders for the succession and, as one close to the Nehru family, would have looked favorably upon those who might support Indira Gandhi for Prime Minister. But the Chinese invasion changed the political climate and destroyed the particular constellation of power on which these speculations were based.

Military rule is more the result of civilian political failure than of the political ambition of military men. The Indian Army's traditions, unlike those of armies in some other Asian countries, are professional rather than political. Government in India has been sufficiently effective that the military have had little cause to question their place in the state. The future of the military will depend in part on the continued success of political leadership. It will also depend upon the conduct of political leaders toward the military. If politicians, instead of exercising self-restraint, yield to the temptation to strengthen themselves by developing friends or allies among military men they will inevitably draw the military into politics. The future course of Indo-Chinese relations will also have a bearing on the future standing of the military in Indian public life. Persistent tension will sustain large defense budgets and give added prominence to military opinion and leadership. And large-scale, sustained fighting will not only accentuate these trends but also open the way for a re-orientation of Indian politics. Violence and chauvinism could strengthen existing authoritarian tendencies and create opportunities for military heroes.

The Political Role
of the Army in Indonesia

1963

DANIEL S. LEV

The major problem which Indonesia's military leadership
has had to face during the past decade has been to develop a role
for the army in the national political structure that would satisfy
its political, economic and social aspirations. It was never a
passive professional army and its revolutionary origins and continual operations since 1948 against domestic political rebellions [1] have made its officer corps fully aware of national politics.
Moreover, as a non-traditional institution [2] the army has provided an alternative ladder to success—until 1957–1958 a short
one—for men whose origins did not give them a place among the
new republic's political-social élite. From 1957 on the opportunity existed for these officers to become openly involved in politics. For a variety of reasons, some of which will be discussed
here, they avoided seizing power and were forced instead to
compete for it. Indeed, only gradually did an awareness that they

[1] The Communist rebellion at Madiun in 1948; the fanatical Darul Islam
insurrection, beginning in West Java in 1948, later in South Sulawesi Atjeh,
until 1962; the Republic of the South Moluccas after the transfer of sovereignty
in 1950; the Sumatra-Sulawesi PRRI rebellion, 1958–1961. On domestic violence
and the political role of armies, see S. Andrzejewski, *Military Organization and
Society*, London, 1954, pp. 125–126; also S. Huntington, *Changing Patterns of
Military Politics*, Glencoe, 1962, p. 22.

[2] Cf. E. Shils' comments on non-traditional armies in J. J. Johnson (ed.),
The Role of the Military in Underdeveloped Countries, Princeton, 1962, pp.
31, 54.

Reprinted by permission from Pacific Affairs, 36 (*Winter 1963–1964*),
349–364.

were competing for power dawn upon most politically inclined officers. So far the result has been an evolution of the army's political role that is unlike that in any other country of Southeast Asia, an evolution in which the intelligent guidance of General Nasution (Chief-of-Staff of the Army from 1955 to 1962) has played an important part. This article examines a few aspects of that evolution and attempts to interpret some of the problems which it has produced.

Until 1956 the army was on the political defensive.[3] It did retaliate against parliamentary interference, as in October 1952 when Nasution and several officers tried to force President Soekarno to assume strong presidential powers to the detriment of Parliament.[4] But even this defensive act indicated that the officer corps was seriously divided, a weakness which caused the failure of the attempt and cost Nasution his position for three years. On the whole, with the exception of a few officers like Nasution, Simatupang, and Zulkifli Lubis,[5] the army possessed no ideology, program, or defined political goals.[6] It was constituted as a military not a political organization.

Nevertheless its officers were politically dissatisfied. In 1955–1956 there was general discontent throughout the country, resulting partly from the failure of the national elections of 1955 to clear up the political situation, reduce the multiplicity of political parties, end political and ideological strife, eliminate corruption, and put a brake on high-living politicians. Soekarno expressed this discontent late in 1956 when he called for the

[3] For a fuller discussion of the army's early development and its relations with the government, see G. Pauker, "The Role of the Military in Indonesia," in Johnson, *op. cit.* Also G. McT. Kahin, *Nationalism and Revolution in Indonesia*, Ithaca, 1952, and *Major Governments of Asia* (2nd. ed.), Ithaca, 1963; H. Feith, *The Decline of Constitutional Democracy in Indonesia*, Ithaca, 1962.

[4] The October 17 affair was far more complicated but this was an element in it. See Feith, *The Wilopo Cabinet*, Ithaca, 1958; and Pauker, *op. cit.*

[5] Colonel (later Maj. Gen.) T. B. Simatupang was Chief-of-Staff of the Armed Forces until late 1953, when his position was abolished. It was revived in 1962 and given to Lt. Gen. Nasution, who was replaced as Army Chief-of-Staff by Maj. Gen. Jani. Zulkifli Lubis was a dynamic young colonel who later joined the Sumatran PRRI rebellion in 1958, after a period of considerable intrigue including at least one attempted coup.

[6] Cf. Shils, *op. cit.*, p. 58.

abolition of political parties and proposed a new "Guided Democracy" to replace divisive and dilatory "liberal democracy."
Army officers, many of whom had been angered by political
interference, inadequate supplies, and bad material conditions
within the army, shared also in this national discontent. Some
officers felt that they themselves must assume the responsibility
for saving the nation, as they had done in the revolution against
Dutch colonialism (1945–1950). At the head of the nation's best
developed and most powerful organization, they sought to bring
the army's presumed dedication, honesty, and skills to bear where
civilians had failed utterly.

This powerful feeling was reinforced by the army's own deep
involvement in the national crisis of 1956–1957. Commanders of
military districts in Sumatra and Sulawesi were at the head of
regional protest movements against the central government's economic policies and what they labelled Javanese domination of
the archipelago. Huntington's comment that a military involved
in politics reflects political divisions seems very relevant here,[7] all
the more so because the Indonesian army's territorial organization, consisting of largely autonomous divisions most of whose
troops came from the areas in which they served, encouraged a
political identification under stress between soldiers and civilians
of the same ethnic groups. Central control over regional units
had never been complete, in part because the various divisions of
the army had developed differently in the several islands during
the Japanese occupation and the revolution.[8] Territorial structure reflected and reinforced the regional differences. Civil discontent in the regions thus easily spread to local army personnel,
and then, as the most likely men for the job, regional officers took
over its leadership. The central army command in Djakarta and
most of the officer corps believed that only the army could handle
the problems posed by these outer island commanders. Ultimately the problems could not be handled by anyone, and rebellion broke out in February 1958.

[7] Huntington, op. cit., p. 36. In another sense the army was also influenced at various levels by political parties, but—though this has been argued
—this did not go deeply or extensively. The air force was also politically
affected, the navy much less so. Neither is discussed here, for their importance
has been far less than the army's.
[8] Pauker, op. cit., pp. 196–197.

In March 1957 Prime Minister Ali Sastroamidjojo resigned after he and Soekarno had agreed to a proclamation of nation-wide martial law (state of siege). Nasution had pressed for this after Colonels Simbolon (in North Sumatra) and Sumual (in Sulawesi) on their own initiative had declared martial law in their regions. The state of siege gave the army commanders of every district immense authority, subordinating civilian administration to military orders and making it possible everywhere except in Djakarta for officers to exercise paramount influence in government. In Djakarta too the army was all-important but here Nasution and his staff (and the city command) were officially subordinate and politically respectful to Soekarno, the Supreme Commander of the Armed Forces. It is not clear how most army commanders in non-dissident areas regarded their new powers initially. During the first several months they applied themselves to such efforts as starting development projects, trying to make civilian administration more efficient, outlawing gambling, and arresting scores of corrupt civilians.

But martial law was to become the army's political charter, forming the basis for its full participation in the political life of Indonesia—as the political parties were to realize before long. By the end of 1957 martial law also turned out to be the army's economic charter. In December 1957 Dutch business firms in Djakarta and other major cities were taken over by their employees in connection with Indonesia's campaign to force the Dutch from West Irian. A few days after the action began, the army stepped in to prevent the situation from getting out of hand and assumed control of all the firms with the approval of Prime Minister Djuanda. Army officers were soon appointed to sit alongside the civilian managers of these companies, which the general staff regarded as a legitimate place for surplus officers. From then on, as one Indonesian writer on the "new [army] elite" has put it, "This group of officers who entered the economy became a new social group with a special place in Indonesia's economic life." [9] It was not long before these officers, and many

---

[9] See E. Utrecht, *Pengantar dalam Hukum Indonesia* (Introduction to Indonesian Law), 5th ed., Djakarta, 1959, pp. 450 ff., for a discussion of the army's role in the economy after 1957 and its connection with Guided Democracy and Guided Economy, Soekarno's alternatives to "liberal de-

others who exercised administrative power, became as intoxi-
cated with the social and (often illegal) economic perquisites of
their new positions as their civilian predecessors had been.

Army officers brought to politics a political outlook shaped
by their army experience. It was by no means a well formulated
outlook, nor did all officers think carefully about it. But such as
it was, it put great emphasis on national consensus, unity, obedience, and discipline. These predilections were very much in
tune with Soekarno's presentation of Guided Democracy, to
which many officers gave their full support—short of accepting
Soekarno's demand for a cabinet which would include the Communist Party (PKI). Nasution and the general staff were aware
of the possibilities which existed under martial law for putting
their political ideas into practice. The first major indication of
this, beginning in June 1957, was their attempt to introduce
army influence into specialized organizations affiliated with political parties. National military-civilian "cooperation bodies"
(Badan Kerdja-Sama, BKS) were organized by the army among
youth groups attached to the several parties, and eventually
among peasant and labor organizations, religious leaders, and
women's groups. In part this was an attempt to open up communications between the army and significant civilian organizations.
It also represented the beginning of an army drive to weaken
political parties, unify major interest groups, and put a stop to
the proliferation of political organizations. Because of their special relationship with the army, veterans were the one group with
which the general staff felt free to deal firmly. In 1958 all veterans organizations save one, most of them tacitly affiliated with
political parties, were abolished and reorganized into a single
national body controlled by the army.

Neither the cooperation bodies (BKS) nor the National
Front for the Liberation of West Irian (FNPIB)—into which
the BKS were later organized—were successful, partly because
some officers connected with them were corrupt and inept and
partly because Soekarno and the political parties opposed them.

---

mocracy" and "liberal economy." The Dutch firms were nationalized in 1958
and later became state enterprises. Criticism of the malfeasance of some
officers eventually forced Nasution to deactivate the new class of officers,
making them liable under civil law for their actions in the firms.

In 1960 the FNPIB gave way to a new National Front, which might have been intended as the basis for a future single state party, but which until very recently was stalemated by competition for its control between Soekarno and army leaders.

The political parties were justifiably horrified as the army's new role took shape in 1957 and 1958. Military restrictions on party activities and the daily press, not to mention arrests for corruption, made the army threat perfectly clear. The martial law statute became a subject of intense interest.[10] Late in 1957, after two weeks of hard debate, Parliament created a new statute, somewhat different from the old colonial law on the state of war and siege, but this still left the army in control for another year. In December 1958 martial law was renewed for six months; at the end of that time another law was passed but martial law remained, and it was extended several times more. The army held tenaciously to martial law, explicitly threatening a coup late in 1958 if it were not extended. Understandably the parties wanted it lifted and the army withdrawn from political and economic affairs. Only a very few young leaders understood the inevitability of a politically involved army.[11]

President Soekarno's discomfort with the army was only slightly less than that of the parties. His special relationship with the army requires some explanation. As several writers have pointed out, the dominant political configuration since 1957 has been tri-partite, with Soekarno deftly balancing the army against the PKI. Two alliances have been in operation. The first, that between Soekarno and the army, has been the more important. Directed against political parties ("liberal democracy"), it accomplished a major reform of the political system, replacing the parliamentary government in operation from 1950–1957 by the

---

[10] For military leaders as well as civilians. Since 1957 a small flood of books and pamphlets on martial law has appeared. See, for example, Koesnodiprodjo, *SOB* (State of War and Siege), 2 vols. and supplement, Djakarta, 1957.

[11] Imron Rosjadi, a young MP from the Islamic party, Nahdatul Ulama, said in Parliament in 1957 that "There is sufficient evidence that to leave [the army] outside the fence of government is not possible. To separate them from politicians is a holy dream which may be realized by the next generation, who have not participated in the revolution to free Indonesia from Dutch colonialism." *Ichtisar Parlemen* (Parliamentary Debate Summaries), 1957, no. 31, p. 293, session of May 22, 1957.

far more authoritarian presidential system of Guided Democracy.[12] To this alliance the army brought physical power, whereas Soekarno brought legitimacy and an ability to articulate ideas and mobilize popular support. Neither Soekarno nor the army has completely dominated this alliance; the rule has been negotiation. It was to avoid being engulfed by the army's power that Soekarno developed the second alliance with the PKI, the best organized and strongest of the political parties. The PKI was and remains the natural enemy of the army, not only because officers regard it as being internationalist, atheist, and under foreign control, but also because the PKI—as a well disciplined organization with deep roots in Indonesian labor and peasantry, and dedicated to radical change—poses a threat to all the political, social, and economic interests of the army élite.[13] In exchange for Soekarno's protection against the army, the PKI has supported his policies both at home and abroad, including a few which were too radical for the taste of some army officers. Moreover, the well-known honesty of PKI leaders has made their occasional finger-pointing at the army a useful, though limited, means of control. Also, by threatening to insist on a larger PKI role in the government, Soekarno has been able to add to his bargaining power with the army. The Soekarno-PKI alliance has not been an equal one, the PKI having got itself caught in a debilitating web which permits it only to go along almost completely with Soekarno and be drained gradually of its power, or to rebel and be pounced on by a well trained and equipped army.[14]

[12] On the development of Guided Democracy, see the chapter by Feith in R. McVey (ed.), *Indonesia,* New Haven, 1963.

[13] Failure to recognize this implicit antagonism of interests led Dr. Pauker to the analysis that after becoming accustomed to Communists in government, army officers might begin to feel that only the Communists could "give the country strong and powerful government and obtain from outside the kind and amount of aid" Indonesia needed; see Pauker, "Current Communist Tactics in Indonesia," *Asian Survey,* No. 3, 1961, pp. 33–34. Long before army officers conclude that the PKI alone can lead the country, they will conclude, as some already have, that only the army can do so. The considerable Soviet military and economic aid since 1959 has made no difference to their judgment.

[14] For a discussion of the PKI's plight under Guided Democracy, see D. Hindley, "President Soekarno and the Communists: The Politics of Domestication," *American Political Science Review,* December 1962.

The Sumatra-Sulawesi regional rebellion, which began in February 1958 and lasted three years,[15] had at least two major consequences for the army. The first was that it eliminated the most radical of the army's officers, among them Cols. Lubis, Simbolon, Husein, and Sumual. Gen. Jani, at present army Chief-of-Staff, once described the pre-rebellion division within the officer corps in radical-moderate terms on the following issues: [16] (1) radicals had no compunctions about a coup whereas moderates believed a coup would start a tradition of coups that could not be repressed; (2) a variation of (1), moderates believed that army unity was essential to national political stability, and that a coup would destroy army unity by setting off a fierce struggle for power within the officer corps; (3) radicals felt that if Soekarno stood in the way of their demands, he should be removed, while moderates believed that under no circumstances should Soekarno, Indonesia's foremost leader and symbol of unity, be removed from office or power. If we accept this analysis, it is clear that after the 1958 rebellion moderates were in undisputed control of the army and committed to a Soekarno government. The position of General Nasution in particular was greatly strengthened by the rebellion, several of whose leaders had also favored replacing him with another Chief-of-Staff.

A second major consequence of the rebellion (and its fairly rapid reduction to guerrilla proportions) was that it emphasized the importance of the army and gave it a stronger position in the national government, in addition to justifying the continuation of martial law. Led by a more secure and confident Nasution, politically conscious officers were more than ever determined to alter the structure of the government which they claimed had divided the country and led it downhill for a decade. Especially were they resolved to destroy or weaken permanently the political parties, which they felt to be the chief source of domestic conflict and national frailty. The political and administrative

[15] Although it lasted that long, it was as guerrilla action after the first six months. The royal army was able to drive the PRRI (Revolutionary Government of the Republic of Indonesia) rebels from major cities of Central Sumatra and North Sulawesi by June 1958. See H. Feith and D. S. Lev, "The End of the Indonesian Rebellion," *Pacific Affairs,* Spring, 1963.

[16] Interview of October 18, 1961.

integrity of the country would have to be restored, the central
government strengthened, party influence weeded out at all levels, and discipline and unity inculcated throughout. These goals
the army leaders intended to accomplish under Guided Democracy. Soekarno agreed with this program but there was a great
though muted difference between him and the army leaders on
the question of how large a political role the army should ultimately be allowed to play.

General Nasution was the driving force behind the events
which culminated in the restoration in July 1959 of the presidential constitution of 1945. He had always favored this constitution,
which actually was in effect for only a few months in 1945 before
it gave way to a parliamentary cabinet form of government.
Nasution thought that it had been a mistake to remove Soekarno's constitutional powers, for it divided the leadership of the
revolution. Soekarno, as the revolutionary leader of greatest personal authority and popular appeal, should also exercise the
greatest constitutional authority. The parliamentary cabinet
(which was retained in the 1950 Constitution) made Soekarno a
symbol, but the 1945 Constitution had made him the center of the
government, promising strong and unified leadership.[17] In mid-
1958 the National Council, a body appointed by Soekarno in 1957
to advise him and the Cabinet, began to discuss the implementation of Guided Democracy. Nasution, a member of the Council,
proposed restoration of the 1945 Constitution. It is interesting to
note that at that time Soekarno was reluctant to go along with this
proposal—much as he had been in October 1952—preferring instead to press for reform of the government, simplification (nu-
merically and ideologically) of the party system, and a re-structur-
ing of Parliament to make it more amenable to Cabinet leadership. It may have been that Soekarno did not feel capable of
shouldering the full burden of the presidency under the 1945

[17] Nasution's views on the 1945 Constitution and national leadership are
in his book, *Tjatatan2 sekitar Politik Militer Indonesia* (Notes on Indonesian Military Policy), Djakarta, 1955, especially pp. 20, 99, 104. This very
important book is filled with Nasution's frank and perceptive analyses of the
army's development, its relations with the government, army politics, and
Indonesia's problems since the revolution. It is an excellent introduction to
post-1945 Indonesian history and to Nasution.

Constitution but it is also likely that he was worried about his ability to control the army if the political parties were precipitately weakened. The National Council was compelled to take up Nasution's proposal when the political parties proved recalcitrant about accepting drastic parliamentary reform. Soekarno then sped to the vanguard of the movement to return to the 1945 Constitution, using the initiative to strengthen his position vis-à-vis the army. In July 1959, after the Constituent Assembly had refused to approve the 1945 Constitution and Nasution had temporarily banned all political activities, Soekarno returned from abroad and decreed the Constitution into effect.

Thereafter much of Nasution's program was fulfilled. In the new Cabinet (with Djuanda as First Minister), which Soekarno appointed in July 1959, there were twelve officers of the armed forces (including police), eight of them from the army.[18] The political party system was overhauled later, all but ten parties being abolished and the rest partly indebted to Soekarno for their continued existence. Central authority over regional government was reasserted.[19] Army efforts to consolidate labor organizations were not successful but Nasution's general policy of unifying organizations representing similar interests took hold. One of the first groups to be consolidated was the Boy Scout movement, which before had been divided among several parties.

Finally, an intense ideological program was begun in 1959–1960. Soekarno's Independence Day speech of August 1959 was elaborated by the National Council as his Political Manifesto (*Manipol*), and this, along with the Pantjasila and USDEK,[20]

[18] The state police force is recognized as part of the national armed forces. In this cabinet the chief of the state police became minister of police. The army, navy, and airforce chiefs-of-staff were appointed to the cabinet ex-officio. Nasution was also appointed Minister of Security and Defense.

[19] However, at the same time the powerful position of regional military commanders pushed in the opposite direction, giving the regions more independence than they had enjoyed before martial law.

[20] The Pantjasila is Soekarno's five-point state philosophy: Belief in God; Nationalism; Humanitarianism; People's Sovereignty; Social Justice. USDEK represents (1) the 1945 Constitution, (2) Indonesian Socialism, (3) Guided Democracy, (4) Guided Economy, (5) National Identity. Nasution has always been impressed by the need for a powerful ideology to which the entire nation would be devoted. See his *Perang Gerilja* (Guerrilla Warfare), 2nd ed., Djakarta, 1954, p. 22, and *Tjatatan2, op. cit. passim*.

became the basis for an intensive ideological indoctrination effort throughout the nation. This has been nothing less than an attempt to force the consensus which both Soekarno and Nasution see as Indonesia's greatest need. The army has been the chief impetus behind the ideological campaign, taking an implacable stand on Pantjasila-Manipol-USDEK as an ideology for itself—something which the army had lacked in the past. The attempt to force an ideological consensus has also served as a weapon against the parties, compelling them to conform publicly to official doctrine and making it somewhat more difficult (though not insuperably so) to justify their multiple existence.

Since 1959 the dominating theme of political conflict in Indonesia has been that of the army and the PKI. For vehement anti-Communist parties and groups (including the United States Government) the army became the center of attention. Among these parties were the modernist Islamic party (Masjumi), the small intellectual-led Socialist Party (PSI), the Catholic and Protestant parties, and the League of Upholders of Indonesian Independence (IPKI).[21] These parties, while themselves apprehensive about the army's anti-party commitment, turned to it to achieve their old aim of crushing the PKI. The Nationalist Party (PNI) and the conservative Islamic Nahdatul Ulama (NU) were also anti-PKI, but the closer attachment of their older generation leaders to Soekarno, in addition to their continued participation in the government, distinguished them clearly from the first group of parties. For the hostility of the Masjumi and others in this first group was directed not only against the PKI, but also against Soekarno, whose protection of the PKI and whose radical nationalism were equally unacceptable to leaders of these parties. In time, they hoped, a democratic government would be restored, after martial law was lifted, with the PKI threat gone and Soekarno weakened (or perhaps also gone).

---

[21] IPKI, an army-based group, was founded by Nasution in 1954 after he was relieved of his post following the October 17 affair. After his reappointment in 1955 he gradually pulled away from IPKI, maintaining some influence over it but not being influenced very much by it. Masjumi and the PSI were abolished by Soekarno in August 1960 on the ground that members of the two parties had supported the PRRI rebellion.

Army leaders looked at the PKI from a different perspective: (1) as the one remaining powerful political party, whose threat to Indonesia's future was made more serious by its foreign ties; and (2) as a threat to the army's own position. Soekarno's protection of the PKI was resolute, for he saw its destruction as a dangerous threat to national unity and to his own independence.

A second radical-moderate split developed in the army over the PKI issue. The radical position was represented primarily by regional commanders in Java and the outer islands who wanted either outright abolition of the PKI or the imposition of extreme restrictions on it. A few officers on the general staff, including the head of Army Intelligence, also took this position. They were actively supported by the Masjumi, PSI, and other parties, whose leaders were increasingly preoccupied after 1959 with the attempt to exercise influence over officers in Djakarta and the regions.

The year 1960 saw the greatest tension in this conflict. Soon after the suspension of Parliament in March 1960,[22] the Masjumi, PSI, Christian parties, IPKI, and a few members of the NU and other parties formed a Democratic League, with the help and encouragement of Army Intelligence. The League campaigned for restoration of the old Parliament, abolition of the PKI, and, implicitly, for restrictions on Soekarno—an impolitic mixing of goals as it turned out. Nasution permitted the League to exist but kept it at arm's length, perhaps using it as a political threat for a while in his relations with Soekarno. In the middle months of 1960, while Soekarno was away on a world trip, certain members of the League pressed the army assiduously to take over the government, hoping perhaps that there would be a place for League parties in a new government. But there was no coup, for Nasution was unwilling. Soekarno returned from his trip to deal firmly (though cautiously at first) with the League, forcing Nasution to withdraw his support from officers involved in it. Thereafter Soekarno let the League atrophy for a year before abolishing it with ridiculous ease.

[22] It was later replaced by a *Gotong-Rojong* (mutual help) Parliament appointed by Soekarno from political parties (excluding Masjumi, PSI, and unacceptable members of other parties) and functional groups, including the army.

During this period, while the League was doing its utmost to convince the army of the necessity of a coup, officers in the regions were moving steadily against the PKI. The radical-moderate split in the army concerning the PKI came to a head in September 1960. The regional commanders of South Sumatra, South Kalimantan, and South Sulawesi, for whom the absence of tough opposition in their areas made politics seem a rather simple matter, undertook the uncomplicated policy of banning the PKI and its subsidiary organizations in those areas. (The PKI in East Java was also harassed, but its strength in that province made banning it a dangerous policy.) So explosive did the situation become that Soekarno called a national conference of all martial law authorities, including high civilian officials and military commanders, to ease the tensions. Regional commanders had prepared for a showdown with Soekarno on the PKI issue, several of them having met in East Java beforehand to discuss strategy at the conference. They argued during the conference that, while Soekarno might be able to control the foreign-dominated and atheistic PKI during his lifetime, no one could guarantee what would happen after his death. Soekarno replied forcefully that the PKI was a national party, that it accepted the state ideology, and that therefore it should not be abolished. The regional commanders could not cope with Soekarno or his arguments, and they received no help from Nasution, who, caught between the opposing pressures of Soekarno and the regional officers, remained silent. As a compromise, the conference decided to ban temporarily all political activities throughout the nation. Following the conference, at which they had failed to achieve anything permanent, the regional commanders began to withdraw partially from national politics into the local affairs of their regions. The army's national political leadership was thus left to the moderates of the general staff.

During 1959–1960 the army could not abolish the PKI unless it was willing also to consider at least the possibility of a coup against Soekarno.[23] This Nasution and most other officers would

[23] This does not exclude the possibility that the general staff feared that a Communist rebellion would follow upon an attempt to ban the PKI. PKI Chairman Aidit had warned the army of this several times after 1957. Such a

not do. There were several reasons for this, in addition to those apparent in Jani's remarks mentioned above. One was that Soekarno was popular and the army was not. Since 1957, as Nasution was well aware, the army had become increasingly unpopular because of its heavy handedness in dealing with civilians and because of the corruption of some of its officers. Most people wanted the army to withdraw from sight, not to become more involved in the government. Second, Soekarno as paramount leader relieved the general staff of the onerous burden of responsibility which it would have to bear if it tried to run the government alone. It was not only that the army had no program for running the country; also with Soekarno there it was easy to put the responsibility on his shoulders for many trying issues that might cause political disruption within the army. Third, the officer corps was divided in its attitudes towards Soekarno, many Javanese officers in particular being personally quite loyal to him. Fourth, these conditions may have led Nasution himself to fear that he would lose in a struggle with Soekarno, as he had in 1952.

These are obvious reasons, much commented on by others; but there is another that merits great emphasis in a discussion of the army's political evolution. This has to do with the way Nasution himself has tried to formulate the army's role—undoubtedly after taking the above factors into consideration—and how he has attempted to direct its participation in the political process on terms other than a coup.

Nasution clarified his conception of the army's role at the end of 1958, when despite the opposition of the political parties he was urging profound changes in the political system. He perceived two fundamental facts in the army's political existence. One was that a coup would create more problems than it would solve. The second was that army officers would not brook being forced out of the political and social life of Indonesia. They had fought for independence and they wanted some of its fruits. In an anniversary speech at the National Military Academy in

---

rebellion could not hope for success, but on top of the PRRI it might have caused considerable disorder.

Magelang in November 1958, Nasution declared that the Indonesian army would emulate neither the politically active militaries of South America nor the "passive instrument" armies of Western Europe. Between those two poles, it would follow a course which Nasution termed the "army's middle-way." The army as such would not be politically active but its individual members must participate in determining state policy, even at the highest levels. They must be given an opportunity to make use of their skills in the Cabinet, the National Council, the National Planning Board, diplomatic posts, and elsewhere in government. Otherwise, Nasution threatened, the army might react violently to discrimination against its officers.[24]

The difficulty was that martial law was temporary and under attack. To make permanent the army's right to participate in the direction of national affairs, Nasution claimed for it a new and explicitly political status. At the end of 1958 he insisted that whatever the form of government—whether a revised parliamentary system or one based on the 1945 Constitution—the army must have a place in it as a functional group. The functional-group concept originated in 1945, when it was introduced in the Constitution as one category of representation. Soekarno had reintroduced the idea of functional groups in 1957, partly as an alternative source of political support, and had appointed to the National Council representatives of such groups as labor, peasantry, youth, intellectuals, and veterans. Neither in 1945 nor in 1957, however, was the military considered a functional group. It was assumed that the army would have authority only so long as martial law was in force. In 1958 Nasution's demand for functional-group status for the military was conceded in the National Council. Later the National Council tried to persuade the political parties to allocate to functional groups half of Parliament's seats, including 35 seats (out of approximately 260) for the armed forces (army, navy, airforce, police). The subsequent refusal of the parties to grant the functional groups control of more than one-third of Parliament was part of the reason for the National Council's decision to restore the 1945 Constitution.

Since mid-1959, under the resuscitated Constitution of 1945,

[24] Nasution's speech was prominently reported in the daily press; see *Pos Indonesia* (a Djakarta daily) , November 13, 1958.

the military (and especially the army) has taken its place in Parliament, the People's Consultative Assembly, the Supreme Advisory Council (successor to the National Council), and increasingly in regional government, several officers having been appointed governors and second-level district heads. Functional-group status has given the army rudimentary form as a political organization, guaranteeing it a basis for political participation independent of martial law.

In one sense, this was a crucial reason why there was never a coup. The army's élite was integrated into the political structure of the nation and was satisfied. Little was denied it in the way of political power, economic perquisites, and the social prestige which followed upon political and economic influence. Moreover, the exercise of power—especially among officers appointed to national government bodies—has had a moderating influence. Many officers have in effect been absorbed into the national élite, whose attributes, good and bad, they have assumed. This, as well as the restraining influence of Soekarno, has for the time being inclined the army to compete peacefully with its enemies rather than to try violently to obliterate them.

In this competition the army's most important goals have been to consolidate its political position, to keep political parties generally from ever resuming the control of the government they once had, and in particular to weaken and finally destroy the PKI. This latter goal the army leadership undertook to pursue alone after hoping briefly that the PNI and the NU might help. Those two parties, however, appeared to be too weak, disorganized and demoralized, and too eager to get rid of the army incubus to be effective allies. Since 1959 the army has been able to restrict the PKI's activities almost (but not quite) at will, obstructing Communist organizational work, forbidding strikes, controlling the PKI press, and in other ways seriously hampering the party. Furthermore, PKI Chairman Aidit's commitment under Guided Democracy to President Soekarno (who is not equally committed the other way) has made a considerable weakening of the PKI almost inevitable. The pace of its decline has been slower than that of the other parties because of its greater initial strength and integrity.

From the army's point of view, however, the mere fact that

the PKI could be controlled or gradually weakened was not enough to assure its final demise. More important, the army was not assured of an increase in its own political appeal in the cities and villages where the PKI had been strong. And for army officers this is the other crucial side of the question. In addition to defeating the PKI, they must also buttress their legitimate right to take part in the political life of the nation, and for this they require popular support.

Army leadership has approached this twofold problem at two levels of strategy. At a high level of politics, army-sponsored organizations have attempted to compete with the PKI for control of significant groups in the population. The army was at first not conspicuously successful in this effort: it failed to win full control of the National Front, headed by Soekarno, and it also failed to organize the other functional groups under its wing, partly because political parties also maintained an influence in them. Recently, however, a more significant role has emerged for the functional groups, more or less in alliance with the army but subject to Soekarno's influence. Working through the National Front,[25] younger men who see for themselves a better political future attached to a functional group block than to political parties, are becoming active in organizational work. Also, other recent organizational efforts of the army have had more success than in previous years. The SOKSI, an army-encouraged organization of labor and management (both "functional workers") in state enterprises, has been able to attract members away from the Communist labor federation (SOBSI), apparently largely because of its ability to distribute government-subsidized commodities in short supply.[26] There is no guarantee that SOKSI will maintain its growth, particularly if economic conditions improve and it fails to offer its new members other satisfactions, but it is nevertheless more promising than other such efforts have been.

Army leaders, moreover, have played an important role in drafting new legislation for the next national elections, which

[25] The National Front consists of organizations of every sort, including political parties, as its constituent members. The parties, however, have little to gain from its success and have acted independently of it.

[26] On the initial organization of SOKSI and its stated purposes, see *Suluh Indonesia* (a Djakarta daily), December 27, 1962.

may be held any time after 1964. Although not yet approved, and although the elections may be deferred for some time, the new law provides that functional groups and the regions, as well as political parties, will send representatives to national legislative bodies.[27] One can assume that the parties' role will be held to the minimum possible, and that the army will support functional groups in the elections, hoping to maintain its influence among them. The army's own representatives in the government will be appointed by the government, presumably with the advice of the general staff or a special army committee.

The other level of army political strategy results from the view which army officers have of the necessity for establishing contact with that great majority of the Indonesian people who live in villages. Nasution and the general staff have been anxious to compete with the PKI where it is strongest. They feel, as do many officers, that by demonstrating its interest in the people's welfare, by helping villagers to develop their roads, dams, bridges, and agriculture, the army can win the respect and devotion of the people. These officers believe that army units were very well received in occupied rebel territory when they set about lending a hand to the local population. If the army could win the same goodwill everywhere, it could easily undercut the political parties, even the PKI. And, according to this reasoning, there would then be little resistance to the army's continued participation in the government.

The first doctrine to justify a military descent to the villages was territorial warfare (*perang territorial*). As Nasution explained it in 1955, territorial warfare is a defensive strategy in which every area of the country is organized and equipped independently to defend itself against foreign attack with a minimum of central tactical direction and logistical support. It is well planned guerrilla warfare, requiring that the army give the country not only military but also proper political, social, and economic organization.[28] After 1959 the army did in fact begin to concern itself with village affairs in some regions, replacing vil-

---

[27] *Suluh Indonesia*, February 2, 1963. The chairman of the government committee to draft a new election law is Brig. Gen. Wilujo Puspojudo.

[28] On territorial warfare, see Nasution, *Tjatatan2, op. cit.*, pp. 199–200; also articles in a new army journal, *Territorial*, first appearing in June 1961.

lage heads, training administrative officials, and later putting whole village administrations through indoctrination sessions. As a political program, however, territorial warfare never quite became popular, perhaps because its perspectives were limited by military definitions. But it remained important as a doctrine and is the basis for a new approach to the same problem—"civic action"—now much in vogue in some army circles.

Civic action received its first big boost as a result of Indonesia's successful campaign to wrest control of West Irian from the Dutch. As long as the campaign continued there was every reason to have a large military force, and the army undertook a recruitment program that brought its already bloated size up to approximately 350,000, exclusive of thousands of hastily trained volunteers and short-term "draftees." After the Dutch agreed in mid-1962 to leave Irian peacefully, the argument for a large army suddenly evaporated. Army and government leaders decided that demobilization of scores of thousands of soldiers was out of the question. Unemployed and discontented in the bad economic conditions that have beset the country, they would undoubtedly be the source of disorder and unrest.[29] Therefore it was decided that the army's manpower would be put to use in a gigantic civic action program, a policy which Nasution and other officers insisted upon. The army engineer corps, which had already proved its effectiveness in several projects, would undertake to build roads, dams, and bridges around the countryside. Troops would join in and help on simpler projects, wielding hoes and picks instead of guns. The army's civic mission would be dovetailed into national development plans, easing the burden—one might suppose—of the state budget.[30] Civic action pilot projects were

[29] The army has been aware of the danger of unemployment in Indonesia. See Maj. Sajidiman, "Faktor Pengangguran dan Masalah Keamanan" (The Factor of Unemployment and the Security Problem) in *Madjalah Sedjarah Militer Angkatan Darat* (Journal of Army Military History), No. 7, 1960, pp. 18–28.

[30] For a detailed discussion of the civic action program, see Brig. Gen. Sokowati, *TNI dan Civic Mission: Suatu Aspek Pembinaan Wilajah* (The Army and its Civic Mission: An Aspect of Regional Development), Djakarta, Ministry of Information, 1963. Sokowati, also a member of the National Front executive council, has long been a popularizer of the territorial warfare doctrine.

carried out in West Java by Brigadier General Adjie, commander of the regional division, in areas where the recently crushed Darul Islam rebellion had raged.[31]

Civic action may prove useful in economic development but that is not its only purpose. Army leaders themselves believe it has profound political significance. The army, they insist, must be "to the people as fish in water," [32] a quotation from Mao Tse-tung that Nasution has long favored. That the United States Government has decided to assist the army in its civic mission, having already provided numerous military technicians, equipment, and technical training opportunities in America for Indonesian military personnel, also attests to its political significance. In effect, it will be an attempt by the army to compete with the PKI at the grass-roots level.

In May 1963 martial law was finally lifted and it has been announced that the military budget for the coming year will be much lower than it has been since 1959. Though no great changes have occurred yet, there are signs that the political parties are stirring and that army leaders feel somewhat insecure. It is probably going too far to say that the determined effort of General Nasution against Malaysia is motivated by a desire to restore martial law, but there may be a slight element of truth in that contention. Nasution has put increasing emphasis on the army's status as a functional group and on its civic mission, reminding everyone that the disappearance of martial law does not mean that the army will withdraw into the barracks.

The development of the army's present political position has not been without internal dissent and tension. There have always been field officers who believed that the army should not be concerned with politics and who resented other officers with political and economic interests. In the civic action program there is also considerable dissent, in part from officers who do not want to put their troops to work hoeing in the villages and who

---

[31] *Ibid.* Actually Adjie began these projects before the civic action program was conceived. Cf. *Territorial*, pp. 38 ff. See also *The New York Times* report by Seth S. King, August 22, 1963, on civic action in Sumatra and its political significance.

[32] Sokowati, *op. cit.*, p. 52.

feel that their men will resent such unmartial activity. Nasution has called attention bluntly to a division between officers who want a "conventional" army and those, like himself, who want an "unconventional" army, one whose functions are not limited to the military. The Indonesian army, he has said, will not again become a "passive instrument" as it was during the colonial and liberal (pre-1957) periods.[33]

That the army must participate politically is clear; its officers will not relinquish the authority they now exercise. They feel they have as much to contribute as civilian leaders to the nation's development, perhaps more, and ultimately they have the power to maintain an influential position for themselves. But the problem is whether the army can overcome its immersion in the political system to make its role a productive one. No one has yet found a remedy for corruption and high living among the officer corps—natural concomitants of the army's gradual absorption into the political and social structure of Indonesia. Eventually, however, these problems will have to be dealt with if the army is to fulfill the ideal Nasution has set for it. Otherwise it may become a half-army, half-party organization, increasingly divisive and ineffective as both. Many officers are aware of this and they are trying to fashion a place for the army within the broader framework of national political development. How successful they are will depend to a considerable extent on the wisdom (and political caution) civilian politicians display; this is a responsibility that must devolve increasingly to younger leaders as the older ones continue to fall away.

One cannot predict the final outcome of a political experiment—and this one has much stacked against it—but the evolution of the Indonesian army as a political organization has so far been unique. It *may* prove to be an excellent solution to the problems posed by a modern army in a rapidly changing society.

---

[33] Foreword in Sokowati, pp. 9–10.

Burma's Military Government: A Political Analysis

1962

JOHN BADGLEY

The Union of Burma no longer has a parliamentary democracy. All governmental powers were seized by the military when U Nu, his cabinet, party leaders, and the Shan MPs were imprisoned. By special decree, the Constitution was voided, Parliament dissolved, the Supreme Court suspended while new judges were appointed, and the State placed under the rule of an eighteen-member Revolutionary Council.

The coup was greeted with reserved approval by most articulate Burmese. The incoming leaders were well-known and respected for their integrity. The Premier, or Chairman as he chooses to be called, is once again General Ne Win. His Council includes prominent army colonels and the chiefs of the naval and air forces. This government, however, is not a continuation of the military Caretaker regime of 1958–60. The theme of rule has changed from "caretaking" to revolution. In a systematic if not spectacular manner, the Council has launched an administrative and economic revolution. There can be no doubt as to who rules Burma. The military has a firm grip on political power and an unchallengeable status in Burmese society. Its leadership candidly admits that it is serving as guardian of the State.

Reprinted from Asian Survey, 2, No. 6 *(August 1962)*, *24–31, by permission of the Institute for International Studies, University of California.*

171

I

The causes of the military coup in Burma were not superficial, but were intimately related to two problems running far back in Burmese history. Under the monarchy, Burma enjoyed unity among its several racial communities only when the central authority had a powerful military force at its disposal. During the latter years of the Konbaung dynasty in the mid-nineteenth century, steps were taken to modernize Burmese administration radically, and there was hope for much greater social and economic integration. A young and inexperienced king, however, lacked the energy to carry out the necessary reforms. His weakness hastened the collapse of the monarchy and brought the British into central and upper Burma. Fifty years of British rule introduced a unified administration but failed to bring social or political integration. Indeed, in certain respects, British administration was premised upon the continuing separateness of the various tribal and racial components of Burmese society. Nor did the economic developments of this era foster inter-community ties.

The nationalist movement which began to flower after 1920 encouraged the growth of political parties, but even these had little cross-racial membership until the Anti-Fascist People's Freedom League was created in 1944. The League's president, Aung San, personalized the new unity of Burma. He was "the just man," the leader who supposedly placed national interests before the interests of the Burman majority. After Aung San's assassination in 1947, U Nu worked assiduously to inherit the fallen leader's mantle. As long as the AFPFL was a unified party, the forces of centralization were sufficient to counterbalance the pressures of separatist communal groups. But the AFPFL split in 1958 weakened the political force of unity and U Nu's Pyidaungsu Party, formed during the subsequent Caretaker period, was not able to stem the tide of communalism. Karens, Arakanese, and Shans were driving for internal autonomy, the latter with powerful economic resources.

The second major cause for the coup, like the communal issue, runs deeply in Burmese politics: provincial distaste for central authority. This problem was manifested in a strange manner. U Nu had long been troubled by the corruption encouraged by the governmental system of issuing licenses to control imports. Often Burmese who purchased the licenses resold them to more experienced Chinese or Indians who in turn passed on the cost to consumers. Thus the practice also had an inflationary effect. In January the government proposed to eliminate the system. There was a political aspect to this matter, however, for Nu's party had just split into a district, town-based, "uneducated" faction versus a more urban, Rangoon-based, "educated" faction. The nature of the crisis was similar to that of 1958 with second-line politicians struggling for control in their districts. The rural-oriented faction won in party elections and immediately faced the problem of how to finance themselves. Much of the money available for political purposes has come from Rangoon and Mandalay businessmen, and their interests were best represented by the more sophisticated AFPFL and the urban faction of the Pyidaungsu. The new dominant faction, who called themselves Thakins, pushed U Nu to eliminate private importers with the understanding that their men would control the proposed government import companies. A portion of the profits would finance their party.

The Pyidaungsu Thakins had wide support in many Burman districts where local leaders exercised influence through their popularity or power, but the top leadership of this group showed little capacity for national leadership. Although declared socialists, these leaders, like the minority community leaders who pressed for autonomy, represented a rural, conservative viewpoint. And like too many politicians in Burma since independence, the Thakins were prepared not to lead, but only to represent—and often to profit personally from their position as representatives.

II

The military, with the exception of pro-AFPFL colonel clique ousted in 1960, stood aloof as the parties engaged in their pyrrhic battles. It is apparent from their actions since the March 2 coup, that the Revolutionary Council leaders are severely disillusioned not only with the party system but with democracy itself as it has functioned in Burma. What then are their beliefs and political objectives?

The Council subscribes to a domestic policy labelled "The Burmese Way to Socialism." It is too early to determine with any precision the theoretical basis of this "ideology," despite publication of a vaguely-worded pamphlet attempting to set this forth. However, one can turn to the actions of the Council and thereby gain some insight into the direction being taken and the general values being held by the new government.

In domestic affairs, the Council has emphasized the concept of socialism, not some unique "Burmese Way." Yet socialism in practice is following a pragmatic course. Physical security, administrative efficiency, and increased agricultural production are the immediate goals. The Council's style is more that of the austere realism being displayed by the Pakistan and Korean military regimes than that of involved developmental schemes characteristic of earlier Burmese governments. Security councils, which include army, police, and civil representatives, were immediately established at division, district, township, and village tract levels. Their function has been two-fold: to provide greater flexibility in meeting local needs, and to insure that a direct chain-of-command exists to administer priority programs of the central government. To date, these programs include direct dissemination of loans to farmers, improved roads and irrigation facilities, and increased yields through mechanization and distribution of standardized high quality seeds and breeding stock. Two months after the coup, all of these activities were moving at a more rapid tempo.

In commerce and industry, the Burma Economic Development Corporation, with 34 subsidiary firms, has become the major productive organ in the public sector. The BEDC itself only engages in management selection and broad policy decision-making. Its individual concerns retain control over their operations, pricing, and expansion plans. Established in 1953 as a commissary for military personnel, the organization proved more efficient than its counterpart in civil government, the Civil Supplies Corporation, which had much greater scope. With powerful support from the military, the BEDC was allowed to turn its profits into expansion during the Caretaker period and under the last Nu government. By 1961, it had purchased outright control over most foreign-owned businesses and began acquiring management control of other government productive firms.

The most formidable, and profitable, branch of government still remains the State Agriculture Marketing Board. Its agents purchase rice throughout the country at controlled prices, and SAMB then sells this rice abroad as a state monopoly. Despite its importance, SAMB has been markedly inefficient in purchasing, transporting and storing rice. The Council is certain to reorganize or replace the system and has already authorized private millers to compete in the sale of high quality rice. As with the BEDC, military officers have taken over key management positions in SAMB.

Joint ventures with private foreign firms in oil, mining, and the State Timber Board form the other major government enterprises. They have been relatively successful enterprises and continue to operate without military interference. The Council has, however, taken over all public transport. The Inland Water Transport had been particularly skillful in evading safety regulations and had several disasters. The new Marine Department director cancelled the operating permits of a majority of both public and private launches on the Tenasserum coast until they could meet a more demanding set of safety and operating rules.

The Council's activities in technical fields are significant but are greatly overshadowed by Ne Win's personal strategy on how to stimulate progress in Burma. The Chairman anticipated that the greatest barrier to rapid change would be the attitude in the professions, the press, and especially the civil service that "we cannot change Burma by ourselves." At publicized conferences with leading members from most branches of public life, he lashed out with sweeping denunciations of past efforts. Concurrently with these meetings, Ne Win initiated a series of private conferences with representatives from the three major political parties. His objective was to encourage their reconciliation and eventually to form a single national party, somewhat in the image of Aung San's League of 1945. Whereas Aung San captured the loyalty of all but the communists, Ne Win has failed as yet to win over either the top AFPFL and Pyidaungsu leaders, or the two underground communist groups who still have an estimated 1,500 men fighting the government. Only a Marxist league, the National United Front, has pledged its complete support to such a national party. Revolutionary Council members encouraged this decision several weeks before the coup by inviting three or four leftist politicians to their homes to serve as unofficial advisors.

The association of the military with the NUF, when combined with the continued confinement of U Nu and other esteemed leaders, and the astringent conferences with non-military leaders, have shaken some of the complacency that followed the coup initially. The Soviet press has hailed the new government as one "truly imbued with the spirit of socialist revolution," while many in the Western community are wondering if the domestic policy of the military leaders will eventually move Burma from her now famous position of positive neutrality.

The Council's foreign policy remains unaltered as yet. In the United Nations Committees and in the General Assembly, Burma's voting record follows the pattern of the past decade. The representatives at the Geneva disarmament conference suggest, if anything, more sympathy for the proposals of the Western powers than for those of the Soviet Union. With respect to the Laotian problem, American military intervention in Vietnam and Thailand, and nuclear tests in the Pacific, the government has been concerned, but less vocal in opposition than certain Western groups far removed from the scene, e.g. the British Labour Party. On colonial issues, there is no indication that Burma's moderate counsel within the Afro-Asian orbit will be changed. Foreign economic policy continues in the same pattern, with most trade flowing between neutral or Western-oriented countries. There is a new Chinese loan, negotiated by U Nu last year, bringing $80 million U.S. worth of capital and technical aid. However, increased reparations from Japan are likely to be agreed upon early next year, and fresh aid from West Germany, plus existing governmental contracts with the United States, will combine to equalize the amount and type of development aid that Burma is receiving from East and West.

III

Yet one dimension of Ne Win's domestic policy, his determination to simplify administration and encourage Burmese to greater self-reliance, has radically altered the status of private aid programs. One month after the coup, the American ambassador was advised to suspend non-governmental aid from the United States. For a third time, Americans have been placed in the position of appearing to be over-zealous aid givers in Burma. In 1953, all government assistance was cancelled due to the KMT issue. Again in 1958, the contracts with private economic and technical firms were hastily terminated by the Caretaker regime because of their expense and "excessive influence over economic policy." This time the Ford and Asia Foundations were given six months to conclude their operations. The portions of the Fulbright and British Council programs, which brought in American and British teachers, were also curtailed, the former being completely suspended for the coming year. A Rockefeller museum project at Pagan was cancelled, as was a partially completed W.H.O. malaria eradication program.

Since 1953, these private and semi-governmental aid groups have played an ever greater role in educational and welfare activities. The Ford Foundation has expended $9,000,000, the Asia Foundation over $1,200,000, and the combined Fulbright-British Council programs have brought in more than 300 lecturers and teachers during this period. At this point, probably a thousand Burmese have returned from abroad with higher degrees or specialized training through these and other state scholarship, Colombo Plan, or United Nations programs. Many of these individuals have been satisfactorily placed in the fields of their training, but an increasing number are being shunted into minor and insignificant posts. Only a most drastic measure, a $10,000 deposit or guarantee by the family of a government grantee, has prevented a higher rate of return to the West on the part of these frustrated young people.

The same problem of over-training or misplaced training has involved far larger numbers of youth within Burma itself. And foreign Foundations could not escape association with this failure of the Burmese education system, however much their efforts may have been directed toward certain alterations. Now public education, from primary schooling through graduate training abroad, has come under heavy criticism with the encouragement of the Revolutionary Council. The *Guardian* newspaper, in which editorial opinion closely reflects Council policy, initiated the attack through a series of critical editorials. Shortly thereafter, Ne Win met with education officials and university faculty, at which time he advised them either to solve the problem or "have us solve it for you." Suggested remedies published in the press differed radically, with the systems of education in China, the USSR, Britain, and the United States serving as models.

Burma's fundamental problem in education is similar to that of other modernizing states with predominantly agrarian populations. Most parents regard their children's high school and college training as a route to higher incomes and improved social status, and a means to escape the drudgery and confinement of village life. The system itself encourages this motive by offering little vocational, agricultural, or mechanical training, and until now, neither the government nor the society has offered incentives to the student of manual arts. Ne Win is aiming directly at this problem by reducing college enrollments and revising secondary education to include a far greater amount of craft and agriculture training. It is ironic that the Ford Foundation should have been asked to leave Burma, because this type of approach has been a major pillar of their program. That the new government regards it as one of their central needs underlines the validity of Ford Foundation efforts, but it also suggests that the Council is right in wanting to handle the education problem itself. If there is to be a thorough revolution in the system, it will have to be administered by Burmese, not a foreign aid group.

IV

On balance, what has happened in Burma since the coup, is a thorough upbraiding of officialdom and educators, no significant change in foreign policy, and an overt sympathy expressed for the Marxists who support the Revolutionary Council. How can one explain this curious identification of the military group with Marxist socialism?

The Council, of course, has given no official reason for its political inclinations, and its motives may well remain a conjecture for months. There are several explanations that deserve consideration. The most simple is that the Army has long harbored a core of communists who are finally unmasking themselves. Such a thesis, however, is as unlikely as it is simple. The Council is controlled by former commanders and staff officers who rose to their present ranks while fighting communist insurgents. It is inconceivable that, after gaining political power, these same men would submit themselves to the ideological domination of their former enemies. It is relevant that the two major communist leaders, Thakin Soe and Thakin Than Tun, have remained underground and have published their reasons for opposing the regime.

A more plausible explanation for the Council's Marxist sympathies is the assertion that they desire to win over the rank and file of the communists and fellow-travelers, thus terminating the fifteen-year insurrection. Once communist remnants had surrendered and were disarmed, the Council could proceed with a non-ideological development program. The communist insurrection, though it involves relatively small numbers of men, is very costly to the government both in money and in time. That the present leaders are capable of such political shrewdness, is indicated by their treatment of the Shan politicians. The military staged their coup when U Nu's conference on federal problems was being held in Rangoon. That meeting drew the entire political elite from the Shan States, including a former President of Burma and the long-time Foreign Minister, Sao Hkun Hkio. Thus the Shan leaders could be confined at that time with a great economy of effort and little or no violence. At any other time, many would have been abroad or scattered throughout the Shan States with their own police protection. Although it is unlikely that the top communists would attend any such conference, it is conceivable that lesser leaders and their men would accept amnesty if the government could convince them that the insurrec-

tion was not only hopeless but was delaying the socialist revolution. In a sense, of course, this has long been the U Nu policy,
and thus the military are building on a policy that they inherited.

A third explanation emphasizes practical politics. It has
been pointed out that the military has no political base through
which to persuade, or be persuaded by, public leaders in the
districts. Neither the AFPFL nor the Pyidaungsu party has been
willing to play a role; yet over the long run, some form of mass
contact is essential. The various parties of the NUF have strong
urban and rural organizations with a large number of loyal
workers in several key districts. Also, through an alignment with
the NUF, the military has cleansed itself in the public mind of its
past close association with the AFPFL, which has now lost public
support and has weak organizations in many rural sections. In
brief, the military group has sought to achieve the dual objective
of cutting itself loose from the past and, at the same time,
establishing a secure political base throughout the country.

Finally, "socialism" is deeply implanted in the recent Burmese tradition as the best approach to modernization. It is very
likely that most of the Council sincerely believes that socialism
with its publicly controlled institutions is a better approach to
rapid development than either "capitalism" or "communism."
The idea of socialism has won nearly universal approval among
Burma's politicians over the past thirty years; hence any regime
seeking popular support could scarcely avoid its endorsement.

V

In this analysis of Revolutionary Council actions and attitudes, we have thus far omitted a discussion of personalities and
also certain natural human instincts—the penchant for power
and the desire for revenge against those in public life who "had
made a mess of things." At present, the idea of revolution is the
dominant theme of the Ne Win government, but this idea could
very easily be coupled with a mood of repression and totalitarianism. It is here that the issue of personality is crucial, and
Ne Win will be the key personality until he is deposed, falls ill

(he has not been well) , or retires. Ne Win does not seem to enjoy public life or the glory to be gained as a national leader. However, he obviously does enjoy playing the role of strategist, employing his excellent sense of timing and making crucial decisions more or less behind the scenes. Here is the strong, silent type of leader. He has confidence in few men, but those who do enjoy his respect are playing key roles in the present government. The most important are Brigadier Aung Gyi, Colonel Kyaw Soe, Colonel Tin Pei, and Colonel Khin Nyo. They are physically active men who, like Ne Win, live rather anonymous "managerial" lives. They are not prone to military solutions on all occasions, as evidenced by the army's "wait-and-persuade" strategy in connection with the insurrection and as suggested by the coup itself. Ne Win enjoys immense respect within the army, and those senior officers, who may have challenged his authority earlier, have been retired or sent abroad as ambassadors over the past decade. There are strong personalities within the Council, but their energies are bent to the will of the Chairman. Discipline is their training and their habit. Rumours of factions are rampant, and some may well be founded on fact, but to remove Ne Win within the near future would cost any single faction more than it would possibly gain.

The sense of discipline and mission is the Revolutionary Council's greatest asset as a political force. Its supreme weakness is the reverse of this quality; that is, a fear of opposition and distrust of the non-conforming but creative leaders in political, business, and intellectual life. However valid or rational the military policies may have been up to date, the methods of this group have been crude in dealing with non-military leaders. This suggests slight understanding of the role that journalists, politicians, or academicians play in the modern state. Spontaneous criticism is probably more muted in Burma today than at any time since the Japanese occupation. No member of the Council would claim to be an intellectual and probably none of them are; therefore, it is difficult for them to perceive clearly the function of roles other than their own. There is little rapport between Burma's formally educated civilians and the military leadership.

This situation might well change should the Council members succeed in mounting a more effective development program and become more secure in their positions as public leaders.

*   *   *   *

It is apparent that the military has marked out a unique path to be followed by Burma, and that they intend to push the country along that path with their own enthusiasm and will. Their success would represent a long stride across the gulf that presently separates traditional Burma from modernity. If the military exercises patience and forebearance in utilizing their tremendous assets of power and organizational experience, there can certainly be significant change. But should factions break the Council apart, or fail to agree on Ne Win's successor if he falls ill, the sense of mission would not only be immediately lost, but the country could well plunge into another civil war. Such a conflict would be very likely to involve Burma's giant neighbors, as well as the Western powers. This is, therefore, a crucial test of the ability of Burma to survive as an independent nation.

Parliamentary Government
and Military Autocracy
in the Middle East

1960

H. B. SHARABI

*or fair - smce maybe
held The mil. is a
'moderating' force*

Until the end of the First World War, Muslim society in the
Middle East knew only two forms of sovereignty: that of the
Caliph and that of the Sultan. The Sultanate was simply a
military autocracy established *de facto* and defended in terms of
the medieval Islamic principle which maintained that "tyranny
is preferable to anarchy" and that "any effective ruler must be
obeyed"; the Caliphate disintegrated at a relatively early stage in
Muslim history (by the end of the tenth century A.D.) and was
absorbed by the military autocracy.[1]

The transformation of the political map of the Middle East
after 1918 and the rise of modern nation-states from the ruins of

[1] See Bernard Lewis, "The Concept of an Islamic Republic," *Die Welt des
Islams*, NS IV (1955), pp. 4–6. The last Ottoman Sultan-Caliph to use
effectively the prerogatives of the Caliphate was Abdul-Hamid II (1876–
1902); the Sultanate was abolished by Mustafa Kemal in 1922, the Caliphate
in 1924; the last Caliph was Mehmed VI (Vahiduddin). In 1924 King Hussein
of Hijaz proclaimed himself Caliph, but was not acknowledged by the Islamic
community. In 1949 shortly before he was assassinated, Hassan al-Banna, the
founder and Supreme Guide of the Muslim Brothers, also declared himself
Caliph. See Ishaq Musa al-Husseini, *al-ikhwan al-muslimun* [*The Moslem
Brethren*] (2nd ed., Beirut, 1955), p. 69.

Reprinted by permission from Orbis, *a quarterly journal of world affairs,
published by the Foreign Policy Research Institute of the University of
Pennsylvania, 4 (Fall 1960), 338–355.*

the Ottoman Empire and Persia led to the gradual emergence of
Western-type parliamentary regimes of the Middle East.[2] Yet, in
none of these states did the introduction of universal suffrage and
the administrative machinery of the democratic system bring
about a genuinely popular democracy on the Western model. On
the whole, the transplantation of the parliamentary form of
government, with its pluralistic system of political parties, to
archaic social and political structures served only to maintain the
power and prestige of the traditional Middle Eastern aristocracy
and perhaps even to retard the development of true democracy.[3]
The protectorate system, the mandatory regimes, and the "treaty
relationship" applied by Great Britain and France to most of the
Arab world between 1920 and 1955 have contributed to the
gradual paralysis of parliamentary government.[4] Elections were,
and in certain Middle Eastern countries still are, merely rituals
devoid of any profound political significance. Yet, there can be
no doubt that the very process of going through the mechanics of
democratic procedure may be educational in the long run: in
Turkey, for example, such a process was definitely instrumental
in bringing about, in 1950, the peaceful transition from the
dictatorship of Kemal's single party to the democracy of the
two-party system. It remains to be seen whether this pattern can
be repeated in other countries in the Middle East.

Bloc Parties

The first stage of modern political organization under the parliamentary system in the Middle East is the *parliamentary bloc*
formed as a political party. A parliamentary "bloc party" in the
Middle East is usually composed of notables and politicians
joined by social, economic and political interests. These groups
are not bound by any formal system of membership or allegiance

---

[2] Excluding the patriarchal states of Saudi Arabia and Yemen and the
principalities and sheikhdoms of the Persian Gulf and South Arabia. Israel is
here excluded because it does not constitute part of the political pattern that
has characterized the development of the Muslim states of the Middle East
during the last 30 years.

[3] Charles Issawi, "Economic and Social Foundations of Democracy in the
Middle East," *International Affairs,* XXXII (January, 1956), p. 28.

[4] *Ibid.,* p. 27.

to ideology or party doctrine, but rather by personal loyalties. In parliament, bloc parties maneuver against one another over issues that relate rarely to the real problems of the country but often to the struggle for distribution of government offices and positions of power.[5] Attempts by professional parliamentary politicians to establish popular political movements generally end in the formation not of parties, but of factions with a limited professional following and no genuine representation of mass sentiment. In such attempts, even before programs and goals are thought out and presented, the question of leadership usually becomes the overruling consideration, so that in most cases the so-called political parties of the traditional type are in reality no more than names given to small groups headed by "known" personalities.[6] The bloc party system in this sense may be characterized by its political conservatism, social and sectarian rigidity, and by the sharp cleavage that divides the "ins" and the "outs," the "haves" and the "have-nots," the rich ruling minority and the poor oppressed majority. This system, which we may call the "multibloc-party system," predominates in Iran, Jordan, Lebanon and Libya.[7]

Three of the four states in this category are conservative monarchies, deeply rooted in the social and political *status quo;* the fourth, Lebanon, though republic in structure, shares the same attributes by reason of the peculiar religious and denominational composition of its population.[8] These inorganic and un-

[5] In Iran, for example, between 1941 and 1948 about 300 positions in some 24 cabinets were filled, with few exceptions, from a group of 70 to 80 traditional politicians. See P. Elwell-Sutton, "Political Parties in Iran," *Middle East Journal*, III (January, 1949), p. 46.

[6] See Marcel Colombe, "Réflexions sur les origines et le fonctionnement du régime représentatif et parlementaire en Turqie et dans les Etats arabes du Moyen-Orient," *Die Welt des Islams*, NS/II (1953), pp. 256–257. "Avant de se donner des programmes, ils se donnérent des chefs qui furent élus à vie à leur présidence. Chacun d'eux se fit passer pour le seul représentant de la nation." *Ibid.*

[7] Egypt belonged to this group of states before the revolution of July, 1952, as did Syria before its amalgamation with Egypt in February, 1958, and Iraq before the *coup d'état* of July, 1958.

[8] See Clyde G. Hess, Jr., and Herbert D. Bodman, Jr., "Confessionalism and Feudality in Lebanese Politics," *Middle East Journal*, VIII (Winter, 1954), pp. 10–26. Lebanon's five major denominations are the Maronite

stable formations are by their very structure intermediate and overlapping, and represent a transitory phase of political development in the Middle East.

Under the monarchic form of government, suppression of all attempts at the formation of opposition parties has been in some cases more severe even than under single-party dictatorship. This was particularly true after times of crisis when monarchic institutions and the entire regime were threatened, as happened in Iraq in 1941, in Iran in 1953, and in Jordan in 1957.

Many of the bloc parties, especially in Iraq and Iran, were never able to transcend the narrow limits of the ruling class by reaching out to the masses. The National Bloc Party, founded in Syria in 1929 on a "personality group" basis, led the national movement for independence for almost twenty years; when independence was attained in 1946, the party split into the National Party and the People's Party, which dominated Syrian parliamentary life until 1951—but again without being able to organize a mass following.[9] The Egyptian Wafd Party is perhaps the only bloc party in the modern history of the Middle East which maintained for over thirty years (1919–1952), even after independence had been attained, a truly popular backing while preserving the organization and character of a personality-group party.[10] Significantly, the Wafd, despite its popular support, did not further the development of parliamentary democracy in Egypt; on the contrary, it served to maintain and strengthen the almost exclusive monopoly of power in the hands of Egypt's

Christians, the Sunni Muslims, the Greek Orthodox Christians, the Shi'a Muslims, and the Druzes.

[9] Cf. Nicola A. Ziadeh, *Syria and Lebanon* (New York, 1957), pp. 192–193, 203.

[10] As in the National Bloc, serious splits took place within the Wafd, the most important of which occurred in 1938 with the formation of the Sa'dist Party under Ahmad Maher and in 1942 when Makram Ubaid formed his own Wafd Bloc; both of these factions were typical parliamentary bloc parties without a clear political program or an organized mass following. See J. Heyworth-Dunne, *Religious and Political Trends in Modern Egypt* (Washington, 1950), p. 24. For a general survey of the development of the Wafd, see Bruno Aglietti, "Il Partito Wafdista egiziano dalle sue origini (1918) ad oggi," *Oriente Moderno*, XXIII (October, 1943), pp. 407–427.

pasha class, whose control could not be effectively challenged except by total revolution.[11]

Single-Party Dictatorship

The single-party regime is as integral a part of modern parliamentary government in the Middle East as the conservative bloc party system. The introduction of one-party rule, first in Turkey and more recently in Egypt and Syria, was aimed primarily at destroying the "corrupt and backward" socio-political monopoly of the old ruling class—the feudal lords, the pashas, the rich merchants, the religious hierarchy—and establishing a new regime of "modernism, progress, and reform."

The Kemalist as well as the Nasserite dictatorship does not base itself on the *doctrine* of the single party; in both cases, the dictatorship phase is viewed as a temporary but unavoidable necessity.

The *de facto* monopoly of power wielded by Kemal's People's Republican Party was never sanctified by official doctrine; rather, it was the result of unique political circumstances.[12] Kemal's attempts, in 1924–1925 and in 1930, to establish an opposition party[13] reflected his preference for the European type of pluralist system. Moreover, the party's organization had nothing in common with that of the totalitarian parties of Nazi Germany, Fascist Italy and Communist Russia; it derived its power from

[11] Describing Egypt's political parties in 1950, veteran Egyptian politician and former prime minister Isma'il Sidqi writes: "Our parties are [composed] of persons bound by similar circumstances, friendship or common recollections, or they are factions that broke away from another party because of some disagreement. . . . I do not see any benefit in all this, except that which affords these persons the means whereby to assume power. If you review all Egyptian parties and examine their general trends, you can distinguish no difference between them." *Mudhakkarati* [Memoirs] (Cairo, 1950), p. 57.

[12] See Ettore Rossi, "Dall'impero Ottomano alla Republica di Turchia: Origine e svippi del Nazionalismo turco sotto l'aspetto politico-culturale," *Oriente Moderno*, XXIII (September, 1943), pp. 381–386.

[13] The Republican Progressive Party, dissolved in 1925 during the Kurdish uprising; the Free Party, led by Fethi Okyar, former prime minister, dissolved in 1930.

neither the militia nor a cell structure.[14] Although the election of party leaders invariably was by manipulation, the electoral principle was always present, and ideological and doctrinal differences did not result in purges, nor did factions representing dissenting views run the risk of being eventually liquidated. The fact that elections were based on single candidates, and independents were restricted to a government-instigated formula of parliamentary "opposition," actually marked a point on the road to political democracy, even though the spirit of true democracy may have been violated in the process.[15]

Orderly evolution toward a genuine parliamentary democracy in Turkey was made possible not only by Kemal's radical political reforms but also by the revolutionary social and economic changes which he introduced during the first ten years of his regime. By the 1950's a new generation had arisen in Turkey, dominated by a new liberal middle class and an educated public opinion which, though limited in comparison to its Western prototype, constituted a new phenomenon in the Muslim society of the Middle East. That "Kemal Ataturk was a dictator in order that there might never again be a dictator in Turkey" may now be accepted as general justification for the temporary phase of single-party dictatorship.

To a certain extent, the Egyptian revolution follows the pattern of the Kemalist revolution. The abolition of all political parties in Egypt was followed, at least formally, by the establishment of a single party, the so-called National Union, which is to remain the uncontested political organization in the country until the "transition phase" is completed and "normal" political life again becomes possible.

Although both the Kemalist and the Egyptian revolutions

[14] Nevertheless, Kemal's party was the first Western-type political party in the Middle East. It was based on a nation-wide constituency organization with branches in every rural center of Anatolia; the pre-republican domination of the countryside by the Aghas was destroyed, and the peasantry which constituted over 80 per cent of the population was gradually infiltrated by the new spirit of Kemalism. See Bernard Lewis, "Recent Developments in Turkey," *International Relations,* XXVI (July, 1951), p. 320.

[15] Cf. Maurice Duverger, *Political Parties,* translated by Barbara and Robert North (London, 1955), pp. 276–278.

were pragmatic and generally nondoctrinal in structure, they differ in their basic motivation and goals. Kemal frankly utilized the state to effect a total "Westernization" of all aspects of life, positing Western parliamentary democracy as the goal of the revolution. Nasser, on the other hand, has sought to carry the revolution beyond the frontiers of Egypt, replacing at least temporarily the primacy of internal political and social objectives of the revolution by the nationalist ideal of Pan-Arab unity.

Two-Party System

The emergence of a genuine two-party system in Turkey after the 1950 elections did not constitute a departure from the basic political and social principles of Kemalism.[16] The Democrat Party, which won a landslide victory in 1950, originated as a splinter group within the People's Republican Party and was headed by Celal Bayar, a former prime minister and close associate of Kemal. This bloodless revolution, which was no less important than the establishment of the Republic itself in 1923, was not exclusively the work of the Democrats; at least in part, it was the result of the Republicans' decision in 1945 to end their monopoly of political life and to allow the formation of a genuine opposition.[17]

Until 1960, the two-party system in Turkey was the only such system in the Middle East. Yet, developments in the Sudan until the military *coup* of 1958 presaged the rise of the two-party system along lines that were sufficiently clear to allow the classification of the Sudan in this category. Since the first Sudanese elections in December 1953, parliament was dominated by the two major parties, the National Unionist Party and the Umma

[16] The Democrat Party's program differed little from that of the Republicans', except for a more liberal economic policy; the six fundamental principles of Kemalism were emphatically reaffirmed: "Turkey is nationalist, democratic, etatist, secular, republican and reformist."

[17] In November, 1945, Ismet Inonu, Kemal's successor to the presidency of the Republic and to the leadership of the Party, recommended a change in the electoral system from the two-degree ballot based on the Ottoman electoral law of 1876 to the direct single-ballot system; another amendment was introduced in February 1950, which transferred the supervisory authority of elections from the executive power to the judiciary. See G. L. Lewis, *Turkey* (New York, 1955), p. 127.

(Nation) Party.[18] But long before the organization of political parties, political life in the Sudan was dominated by two religious schools, the Mahdiyya and the Khatimiyya, whose political conflict turned on the question as to whether the Sudan was to be united with Egypt or be independent. Since their foundation in 1942, both the Umma and the Unionist parties had been organized around this issue. The Umma was backed by the Mahdists, who favored independence from Egypt, and the Unionists by the Khatimists, who stood for union with Egypt.[19]

Contributing to the liberal character of Sudan's political life before the *coup* of 1958 was the socio-economic structure of Sudanese society—its equitable distribution of wealth and almost complete lack of the feudal control common to other countries of the Arab Middle East. Moreover, fifty years of direct rule by the British have left their stamp on the administrative and judicial institutions of the country, which are still among the most advanced in the Middle East.

It may be added that in all the countries of the Middle East which have parliamentary governments, the parties' representation in parliament does not reflect accurately their political strength or actual influence. Nor, for that matter, is there any other numerical yardstick for measuring their strength and degree of participation in the political life of their particular countries. This is especially true of those countries in which the multibloc party system still predominates.

Dominant-Party System

The fourth type of system in the political evolution of the Middle East—or more broadly, the Muslim world—is what we might call the "dominant" party system, which is characteristic of

---

[18] Of 97 seats in the House of Representatives, the Unionists occupied 51 seats and the Umma 22; the remainder went to minor groups and independents. In 1958 the Umma occupied 68 seats as against 47 won by the Unionists.

[19] The political maturity of Sudan's two-party system represents one of the many paradoxes of political life in the Middle East. Sudan is one of the most economically underdeveloped and culturally backward countries in the region. For a survey of Sudan's political development, see P. M. Holt, "Sudanese Nationalism and Self-Determination," *Middle East Journal*, X (Spring, Summer 1956), pp. 239–247; 368–378.

Tunisia and Morocco. Unlike the single party, the dominant party does not rest on the principle of a deliberately instituted temporary dictatorship, because it does not explicitly prohibit opposition or the formation of other parties. In essence, the dominant party is liberal and democratic in organization and leadership, and its monopoly of power is conditional upon internal developments over which it wields no direct or complete control. As such, its predominance is truly temporary. There is every likelihood that the dominant-party system, as it exists in Tunisia and Morocco, will be replaced eventually by a dual- or multi-party system.

The accession to power of the Neo-Destour and Istiqlal [20] Parties in Tunisia and Morocco capped a long national struggle in which each of the two parties became the symbol and spokesman of the national movement, assimilating all other political factions and groups or relegating them to the background.[21] Despite some differences in political orientation and experience, the two parties are united by the cultural bonds of the Maghreb (North African) society which embraces Morocco, Algeria and Tunisia. The Neo-Destour Party is probably the political organization in the Arab world which resembles most closely the European prototype of a party. Perhaps its most distinctive characteristic is a genuine secularized view of the state in which the idea of the nation is altogether dissociated from that of the religious or linguistic community; [22] its liberal ideology is fused

[20] The Choura Party was included in the first Moroccan cabinet for internal political reasons that have little to do with the Choura's political standing; equally, the acceptance of Bakai, an independent, as the first prime minister was motivated by considerations other than the Istiqlal's power to install its own president as premier, had it wished to do so.

[21] This was also true of the Wafd Party in Egypt. After 1918 and during the Egyptian revolution of 1919, the Wafd acquired the same status of leadership in the national movement and emerged in the period of independence as the dominant party. Although it maintained its dominant position until 1952, it surrendered its monopoly of power after 1928, and the system of dominant party may be said to have given way to the multi-party system on a personality-group basis.

[22] Cf. Hedi Nouira, "Le Neo-Destour," *Politique Etrangere*, XIX (June-July, 1954), p. 322. Also see Benjamin Rivlin, "The Tunisian Nationalist Movement: Four Decades of Evolution," *Middle East Journal*, VI (Spring, 1952), pp. 167–193; Felix Garas, *Bourguiba et la Naissance d'une Nation*

to an unrestricted though tightly knit administrative structure. Founded in 1934, the Neo-Destour represents the beginning of a new phase of political development in the Arab world, for it marked the first significant transition of national leadership from the old traditional nationalists to the intelligentsia of the younger generation, which in many Arab countries is still excluded generally from political power and responsibility. Though exposed to the same cultural influences and confronted with the same political problem as its Tunisian counterpart, the Istiqlal Party was influenced in form by Islam and in ideology by Arabism.[23] Its political doctrine and organization follow on the whole the same pattern as that of the Neo-Destour.

Sectarian and Doctrinal Parties

Finally, there has arisen in the Middle East a separate class of parties which we might call "minority parties." They are divided into two main categories, the sectarian and the doctrinal. Sectarian parties correspond to those sections of the population that are differentiated on religious, racial, or linguistic grounds and express the interests, ambitions and fears of these minority groups. Political organizations in such groups are not too common: for example, the Kurds and Assyrians in Iraq, Turkey, and Iran and the Druzes, the Jews, and Shi'a Muslims in Syria and Lebanon are not politically organized. Nevertheless, they play an important role on the electoral, if not on the parliamentary, plane and very frequently tip the scale of votes.[24] Other sectarian

---

(Paris, 1956) , pp. 91–102; Lorna Hahn, *North Africa: Nationalism to Nationhood* (Washington, 1960) .

[23] Alal al-Fassi, leader of the Istiqlal, is a devout Muslim steeped in Muslim learning. Balafrej, a prominent leader in the party and at the time of this writing the foreign minister of Morocco, is a Hajj (i.e., he made the pilgrimage to Mecca) . In an address given at the first general convention of the party since independence, he emphasized the party's Islamic foundations. See the "General Conference of the Istiqlal Party held in Rabat, December 2–4, 1955," [in Arabic] (Rabat, 1955) . Also cf. Abdelaziz Benabdellah, *Les Grands Courants de la Civilization du Maghreb* (Casablanca, 1957) . For a brief sketch of Moroccan nationalist leaders, see Rom Landau, "Moroccan Profiles: A Nationalist View," *Middle East Journal*, VII (Winter, 1953) , p. 48 ff.

[24] An interesting example is the Jewish and Armenian vote in Beirut which in the Lebanese elections of 1957 and 1960 was decisive in defeating the Opposition.

groups, especially in Lebanon, are politically well organized.[25] Whether or not they have parliamentary representation, such parties are very strong locally and in most cases control political attitudes in their communities.

Doctrinal parties are, on the other hand, minority parties only in the ideological sense, not in the religious, racial, or linguistic sense, for they all aim at mass recruitment and the eventual seizure of power in the state. The role and significance of doctrinal parties in the political life of the Middle East vary from country to country and are determined largely by circumstance and events. The Muslim Brotherhood, for example, though ideologically a minority party, is one of the two mass movements in the Middle East whose fates have been determined more by particular developments after the Second World War than by their actual strength and appeal to the mass of the population. The same is true of the Tudeh Party in Iran, the other mass movement of the Middle East, which was dissolved in Iran at the very moment when its political victory was almost assured. Its relegation since 1954 to the status of an ineffective minority group is due to factors and developments that have slight bearing on its political stature and strength. Likewise, the unexpected intrusion of the army into politics in Syria in 1949 suddenly made possible the active participation in political affairs of the country's three major doctrinal parties, the Syrian Social National Party, the Socialist Arab Resurrection (Ba'th) Party and the Syrian Communist Party.

The formation of doctrinal parties constitutes an important landmark in the political development of the Middle East. To a greater or lesser degree, all these parties strive to elucidate a comprehensive view of man and society and to base their doctrines on all-embracing philosophies that explain and justify their strivings and goals. They all share in the same type of rigid party organization, the same militancy of spirit, the same Jacobin extremism, and they are all masters of clandestine activity, not only because they have generally been the object of suppression and persecution, but also because they have inherited the conspiratorial tradition of secret societies from the old-generation

[25] E.g., the Phalanges (Maronite) and the Najjadah (Sunni Muslim) parties, which are very active in Lebanon's politics.

nationalists. It must be added that the general totalitarian character of these parties should be attributed less to their deliberate espousal of the principles of totalitarianism than to their bitter and frustrating experience with parliamentary democracy as the Middle East has known it. When the principles of elections and parliamentary procedures are emptied of meaning, all effort to influence or persuade the electorate becomes futile, and when the habit of continuous suppression of political opposition renders ineffective all means and practice of democratic action, recourse to force and violence becomes inevitable.

Significance of Doctrinal Parties

Membership in doctrinal parties, unlike that in all other parties in the Middle East, is based on vigorous, wholehearted participation and recruitment. Both membership and active backing generally come from the three most politically active groups in the Middle East: the students, the clergy and the army. It is perhaps a characteristic of the Middle East in its present stage of development that its class of intellectuals is the least politically stable element, tending toward either total withdrawal or total commitment in public life.[26]

Leadership in the doctrinal as well as in other types of parties in the Middle East, even under the most elaborate elective systems, is usually oligarchic. Yet the real power of leadership depends more on the degree of party centralization of power and regimentation of members than on the theoretical function assigned to the leader or executive group.

The centralized organization of doctrinal parties is based on the hierarchical system which is best suited for unity of command and for secret and underground activity. Of course, the most tightly knit form of organization is commanded by the communist parties, based on the cell structure and organized along occupational and geographic lines.[27] In Iran, Iraq and Syria, the

[26] See Hisham Sharabi, "The Crisis of the Intelligentsia in the Middle East," *The Muslim World*, XLVII (July, 1957), pp. 187–193.

[27] Little data is available on communist organization and activity in the Middle East. For general desultory information, see Evron M. Kirkpatrick (ed.), *Year of Crisis* (New York, 1957), pp. 127–146, 193–206. W. Z. Laqueur, *Communism and Nationalism in the Middle East* (New York, 1956), offers

communists have succeeded best in establishing indigenous organizations attuned to local conditions, yet in harmony with the principles of international communism.[28] While other doctrinal parties, such as the Muslim Brotherhood, the Ba'th and the Syrian Social National Party, rely chiefly on the branch and regional type of organization, they also turn to the cell system, especially in times of persecution and intensive underground work. All command some kind of militia organization, and all actively strive to acquire and store firearms.

The future of doctrinal parties, especially that of the communist movement, hinges in large part on the development of the rising Middle Eastern proletariat—the peasant and labor classes which have emerged as a potent political force in the Middle East only since the Second World War. In this respect, the present state of flux in the Middle East bears a remarkable resemblance to that prevailing in China before its communization in 1949. If in the nationalist, tradition-bound peasant society of China the family could be destroyed, traditional values displaced, and a proletarian state established, there seems to be no reason why the same transformation could not take place in the Muslim, nationalist and predominantly peasant society of the Middle East. In this sense, a communist triumph in the Middle East is not only conceivable but, given the requisite circumstances, quite in the realm of the possible.

Significantly, the labor organization movement in the Middle East, except in Tunisia, is still in its first stages of development. In many countries trade unions and peasant cooperatives have been extremely limited in size and number and almost totally ineffective as a force of social and political change. In Tunisia, the labor movement traces its origins to the early twen-

---

fragmentary information and omits Iran, which has the largest communist movement in the Middle East. For a brief survey of the Iranian Tudeh, see George Lenczowski, "The Communist Movement in Iran," *Middle East Journal,* I (January, 1947) , pp. 29–45.

[28] Theirs is the only movement in the Middle East to have made effective use of the front organization. In the Fertile Crescent states the idea of the class struggle is subordinated to the ideals of nationalism. Infiltration into the armed forces and the Palestinian refugees takes precedence over the penetration of all other groups, including the peasants and the workers.

ties; [29] and the first workers' union, the Confédération Général des Travailleurs Tunisiens, came into being in 1936. In the late thirties, the C.G.T.T. was subjected to severe repression by the French at the same time that Tunisian nationalists were being persecuted; by the time Tunisia was liberated by the Allies in 1943 the union had all but disappeared from the scene.[30] In 1944, the best organized and most powerful labor union ever formed in the Middle East, L'Union Général des Travailleurs de Tunisie, was founded by the well-known Tunisian leader, Ferhat Hached.[31] Tunisia's independence is as much the result of the U.G.T.T.'s struggle as it was of the Neo-Destour's. This solidarity between the working masses and the nationalists, more than any other single factor, provides the clue to Tunisia's social and political stability and strength after independence.

Ideology vs. Actuality

The general process of democratization of Middle Eastern society since World War II has not followed the Turkish or Tunisian example. The overflow of the Egyptian revolution beyond Egypt's boundaries demonstrates that not only has the attempt at the "institutionalization" of the democratic form of government in the Middle East been partially destroyed but a new process of "personalization" of authority and power has set in. For the first time in the modern Middle East, mass leadership, in Max Weber's charismatic sense, has become possible.

It is now clear that this social upheaval has already almost completely transformed the closed-in Muslim community of the Middle East into a new kind of twentieth-century collectivity in which the aspirations and demands of the downtrodden masses and not the traditional rights and privileges of the feudal aristocracy are the prime movers of social, economic and political

---

[29] Started by the Tunisian patriot M'hamed Ali, who was exiled by the French before his movement fully matured; he died in obscurity in the mid-thirties after being run down by a car in Jiddah. See Habib Bourguiba, *La Tunisie et la France* (Paris, 1954), pp. 378–382.

[30] Cf. *Ibid.*, p. 383.

[31] *Ibid.*, pp. 385–391. The assassination of Hached by a French terrorist organization in Tunis on December 5, 1952 marks the beginning of the North African rebellion in Morocco.

action. If the Middle Eastern masses have not yet chosen the path of revolution to redress the injustices and inequalities to which they have so long been subjected, it is only because their awakening has not yet been translated into the self-consciousness of an articulate proletariat. Both articulation and leadership are still the monopoly of the middle-class intelligentsia. On the one hand, the docility of the awakened but still illiterate masses feeds the rise and power of the new leadership. On the other hand, however, it holds the leadership captive, and both leader and led remain bound by a reciprocal relationship in which alone the identity and self-recognition of each can be attained.

Perhaps the most salient feature of political life in the Middle East today is the dichotomy between the traditional nationalism of the old-guard nationalists and the new post-World War II revolutionary brand of nationalism. It might seem artificial to apply the arbitrary terms "right" and "left" to Middle Eastern political forces. Yet, it is nevertheless true that the traditional school of thought, with its emphasis on evolutionary democracy and its instinctive reliance on legal processes, constitutes the conservative right, while the new revolutionary school, with its conception of the welfare state and its pragmatic socialist activism, forms the liberal left. In the latter category are the communists, the independent socialists, and the Arab nationalist socialists.[32]

The dilemma of the leftist Arab intellectual consists in a growing political alienation from the West on the one hand, and an increasing intellectual and cultural attraction to it on the

[32] In this general sense one might include in the rightist category all parties, from the bloc type to some of the doctrinal type. After World War II and the emergence of the Soviet Union as a world power, the political doctrine of socialism in its various shades began to penetrate the Middle East so rapidly that in a few years socialist parties were formed in practically every Middle Eastern country. The Arab Ba'th Party, for instance, became the "Socialist Arab Ba'th" Party in the early fifties. The Egyptian revolution, after a strictly nationalist beginning, began gradually to absorb socialist ideas (". . . a free socialist society under a nationalist government." Anwar as-Sadat, *qisat ath-thawra kamila* [The Complete Story of the Revolution], Cairo, 1957, p. 11) . The postwar left-wing nationalists propounded a new definition of Arab nationalism: "Arab nationalism . . . is democratic, socialist, popular and cooperative." Abd ar-Rahman al-Bazzaz, "Islam and Arab Nationalism," *Die Welt des Islams,* NS III (1954) , p. 214.

other. For while socialism—which, after all, is a European impor-
tation to the Middle East—may serve to draw him toward the
communist political orbit, at the same time it ties him to the
European sources of his intellectual creed. This psychological
polarity has given rise in recent years to an impassioned movement of political and cultural emancipation from both East and
West expressed in the idea of positive neutralism in the East-
West conflict and in the theory of a self-sufficient national culture
based on Arab history and Islam.

In the practical realm, however, this dilemma is pushed into
the background, and political action is guided by considerations
that have little or no relation to ideology. All "imagination and
effort [become] concentrated upon an immediate objective—the
removal of something that can no longer be borne. What is to
follow is left to the future to decide." [33] This dilemma can be
attributed partly to the intellectuals' failure to grasp the limits
that action always sets upon thought and partly to the common
man's incapacity to face facts and always to surrender to rhetorical exaggerations and the literary imagination.[34]

De Facto Military Control

In the Middle East today, the principle of the distribution of
power guides only those regimes which are based on the two-
party and dominant-party systems, e.g., in Turkey, Tunisia and
Morocco. Without radical and speedy adjustment from *within,*
the remaining multibloc party regimes (Iran, Jordan, Lebanon,
Libya) are likely to fall under the vicious onslaught of the social
and political revolution sweeping the Middle East. The political
triumph of the Egyptian revolution and its adoption of the
Damascus brand of Arab nationalism has introduced a new factor into the political life of the Middle East—namely, the rein-

---

[33] H. A. R. Gibb, *Modern Trends in Islam* (Chicago, 1947), p. 113.
[34] E.g., the Lebanese Progressive Socialist Party promises that "every
citizen shall be a property owner . . . the worker shall be partner with his
employer . . . there will be no unemployment for intellectuals and men of
the free professions." *Bulletin of the Progressive Socialist Party* (Beirut,
1950). In the Lebanese crisis of 1958, Kamal Jumblat, the leader of the party
who is also a Druze chief, took to the mountains to fight the government at
the head of his Druze villagers, not of his socialist followers.

troduction of the old principle of *de facto* control of the state by
military autocracy.

The tendency in the Middle East toward military autocracy,
whether in the form of personal or oligarchic dictatorships, is not
difficult to explain. In the first place, in all the countries of the
Middle East that have recently experienced military *coups,* the
shift has not been from a democratic form of government to a
dictatorship, but simply from one form of non-democratic rule to
another. In Iraq, for example, the government of Nuri as-Sa'id
could not be described as democratic by the farthest stretch of the
imagination, although in structure it was based on the Western
type of parliamentary system. Nuri's civilian autocracy was
merely replaced by a military one. The real issue at hand, therefore, is not whether freedom and representative government have
been destroyed by Brigadier Kassim, but to what extent the
present military regime will affect the precarious balance between East and West in the Middle East. In the Sudan, where the
two-party system seemed to have the best chance for development
in the Arab world, the political balance suddenly snapped, and a
military government emerged overnight.

In the course of the last hundred years or so, the entire non-
Western world has been transformed under the impact of the
technology and institutions of the West. The consequence of
Westernization in all of these countries has been the deterioration and breakdown of the traditional way of life and social
and political structures. The one institution that was preserved—
and, indeed, invigorated—in some non-Western nations was the
army.

The impact of Westernization always manifested itself first
in the military establishment. The very first instance of modernization along Western lines in the non-Western world occurred in
Turkey in 1789, when Sultan Selim III, having been defeated by
Catherine the Great of Russia, decided to introduce what he
called the *new order,* which consisted of reorganizing the military
establishment with the help of European instructors and re-equip-
ping it with Western armaments. Again it was the modernized
military forces of Japan which, over a century later (1905),
proved to the world that an Asian nation could defeat a major

Western power by adopting Western ideas and techniques. It is worth noting here that, both in launching the movement of Westernization in Asia and in bringing about the beginning of the end of Asian inferiority vis-à-vis the West, it was Russia that represented the West, first as a formidable foe for non-Western peoples to emulate and later as an equal to challenge and overcome.

The Significance of the *Coup d'Etat*

During the last half-century (or more precisely since the Young Turks' *coup d'état* of 1908), it has become increasingly evident in the Middle East that the only effective agency of internal political change is not the political party but the physical might of the military establishment. Even now, neither the weight of religious or moral censure nor the pressure of public opinion can hope to match the force and political effectiveness of the coercive arm of the state. Since that first successful military *coup d'état* of 1908, Middle Eastern politics have never been free of violence, and the basic tactic adopted by all parties or groups aspiring to power has become: "Infiltrate the army!" From the dozen or so major military *coups d'état* that took place in the Middle East during the half century between 1908 and 1960—the Turkish in 1908 and 1960, the Persian in 1921, the Iraqi in 1936, 1941 and 1958, the Syrian in 1949 and 1951, the Egyptian in 1952, the Sudanese and Pakistani in 1958—a clear pattern has emerged which may be summarized in the following formula of action:

1. When infiltrating the military, concentrate on the officer corps, choosing those officers who fit at least three of the following five criteria: a) dissatisfied with the political state of affairs; b) personally ambitious; c) young; d) in sensitive posts (e.g., in command of mechanized units stationed in or near the capital) ; e) nationalistic.

2. Organize officer membership in secret societies, making sure that the identity of members and that of the leadership circle is not known.

3. Wait until the political situation deteriorates; if the situa-

tion permits (as it did in Egypt and Syria), incite mass chaos, precipitating crisis, or else await the opportune moment to strike.

4. In a few hours, three objectives must be attained: a) the government and members of the opposition must be arrested; b) government offices, centers of communications, and key installations must be occupied; c) announcements must be broadcast that the *peaceful* and *bloodless* change of government in the people's name has been made, assuring the nation and the world that complete control now rests firmly in the hands of the new regime.

5. Establish a provisional (front) government including, if possible, known and respected political figures; declare martial law and announce objectives of radical social, economic and political reforms; complete the rounding up of known and suspected enemies of the regime.

6. Obtain international recognition abroad and proceed firmly to stabilize the regime at home by a) dissolving or suppressing all political parties, b) initiating long public trials of leading members of the former regime, c) reshuffling major commands in the army, and d) purging the civil and diplomatic services.

This in simplified form is the technique of the *coup d'état* in the Middle East. But a *coup d'état* may not be judged successful merely by its seizure of power. Inherent in usurpation is the real task not simply of grasping power, but of consolidating and strengthening it. With the stabilization of external control, and after the first flush of victory and excitement have abated somewhat, there follows a phase of silent but deadly struggle within the ranks of the new leadership which usually results (if the regime does not collapse) in (1) the defeat of the civilian political members of the new leadership and their subordination to the military; (2) the emergence of the leader of the winning faction as the head of state. It is only after this post-*coup* "palace" revolution has taken its course and the locus of absolute power in the new regime has been unmistakably determined that the stability and security of the new government are established.

The fact that the last few years in the Middle East have witnessed a reversion to the autocratic form of government should not be surprising. For, apart from the autocratic tradition of Islam, dictatorship in the Middle East today is bolstered by so-called democratic and parliamentary procedures, by the use of plebiscites, "democratic" constitutions and the establishment of Western-type judicial and executive systems. These forms are but a facade for the real power—dictatorial power.

One fact is certain: once a *coup d'état* is successfully executed and sustained for a time, the old order is a thing of the past. It can never be resurrected. This is especially true of the Middle East, where social action today is almost synonymous with revolutionary action.

It is futile to argue against the valid claim that the new revolutionary dictatorships are more effective and more efficient than the "parliamentary" governments they replaced. In a sense, they do command more genuine popular backing and represent more accurately than their predecessors the people's hopes and fears. Yet, it is equally futile to hope that the present military autocracies will eventually lead, after a period of transition, to the gradual establishment of democratic institutions. The dominant political regimes in the Middle East must be assessed for what they are: genuine military autocracies which, while bent on protecting their absolute independence and achieving the nationalistic welfare state, are at the same time desperately determined not only to maintain their power, but to consolidate and strengthen it.

The Military Elite
and Social Change in Egypt

1960

MORROE BERGER

If we were willing to stretch the evidence a bit to achieve order and symmetry, we could construct a continuum of the resort to military leadership in both the economically advanced and the underdeveloped world. At one end we should place those countries, in Africa for example, which are achieving independence without benefit of a native professional military elite. They are authoritarian in a traditional sense, but they have not yet been able to build a military class because their defense was until recently conducted by their European rulers. Nearer to the middle of the scale we might place those countries which have enjoyed independence for a longer period. Several Arab states, for example, with more modernized institutions, have reasserted their authoritarian tradition by becoming military republics as the European powers, which built up their armies in the first place, have declined in influence. On the other side of the center of the spectrum we should place those slightly more developed countries, such as several in Latin America, which have recently banished their military dictators. Farther along would come such Western countries as . . . France, which are now guided by military father-figures, gentle or stern. And at the end we should

Reprinted from Morroe Berger, Military Elite and Social Change: Egypt Since Napoleon *(Princeton, N.J.: Center of International Studies, Princeton University, Research Monograph No. 6, 1960)*, *pp. 1–3, 18–35, by permission of the Center of International Studies.*

place those old-fashioned Western nations which have kept the military elite in its traditional place in a civil society.

In both economically advanced and underdeveloped countries, the military elites assume increasing importance as wars and the preparation for them engage more and more of a nation's resources, and as newly independent states impatiently strive to achieve national power and a higher standard of living. Though Western society has been profoundly affected by wars and their scientific-technological requirements, they have with few exceptions retained civilian control over military affairs; the military elites have not played an independent or major role in introducing social change. In the contemporary Moslem Arab world, however, the situation has been almost the reverse. There, technological backwardness has dulled even the impact of war upon a loosely organized society whose social and geographical constituents have been somewhat isolated from one another. This backwardness has survived even the painful realization that political independence requires military strength, which in turn requires technological advance. Yet the military elites in the Near East have been more important in introducing social change than their Western counterparts have been. One reason comes quickly to mind: in the effort to increase their national strength these countries have had to rely more upon their military than upon their native political and industrial elites, which have been weak and timid in an area that has known little democracy and technological-industrial growth but much subservience to foreign rule. The impotence of other elites, such as have reached dominance in the West, has placed the Arab military elites in a strong position to introduce change.

The military elites of Western countries have been conservative or reactionary in outlook, especially in politics but even in economic and social policy. The military elites in the newly independent Near Eastern and Asian states are not notably democratic or liberal in political outlook. They too criticize parliamentary democracy as a failure, inefficient and corrupt, and claim to be pursuing national greatness through discipline, sacrifice and hard work. But they are rather more willing to abide changes in economic and social policy. Particularly in the Moslem Arab states, both this "revolutionary" character of the military elite and their accession to political power in Egypt, Syria and Iraq stem from foreign rule and its recent decline. Drawn from the urban and peasant middle classes, the native officers felt no traditional loyalty to such conservative classes as the large landowners or the commercial interests—the former with strong Ottoman ties, the latter chiefly Western or Arab Christians. Western power, supplanting Ottoman rule, for a time firmly controlled the native military elite. The nationalist movement, in its political as well as violent phases, was led by absentee landowners, career politicians, lawyers and journalists, not by the military. Army officers, whatever their sentiments, were too close to the means of violence to be permitted freedom of political action. But when the nationalists were victorious and the Western power no longer controlled domestic politics, the inherent strength of the military could be expressed. Cohesive, relatively modern in outlook, not bound to conservative interests, and controlling the means of violence, officers were able to overcome the weak, confused, and inexperienced civilian regimes which succeeded foreign rule.

Egypt since Napoleon provides a good example of the introduction of social change under the impetus of a military elite's intention to increase the nation's power in the international arena. Since we are interested in the sources and patterns of social changes, we shall select certain periods rather than try to cover the entire historical sequence. We can distinguish two main eras and their "incubation" stages, so to speak, in which military considerations have dominated in the introduction of change.

The first era is that of Muhammad Ali, roughly the first half of the nineteenth century. Its preparatory period was the Napoleonic invasion and occupation of Egypt at the turn of that century. The second era we shall discuss is the current one beginning in 1952 with the army officers' *coup d'état* and continuing under Nasser's leadership. Its preparatory period was the previous British occupation. Between these two eras there was an abortive revolt of army officers led by Colonel Ahmad Arabi.

Lasting only a few months, it nevertheless had an impact upon the national consciousness of Egyptians, although it did not in itself generate social change.

The Napoleonic adventure introduced some new ideas, techniques and products, but these could hardly take hold in the short time the French army occupied Egypt. The main effect, in retrospect and from our viewpoint, was that it forced Egypt into renewed contact with the West. When, soon after the French were driven out, Muhammad Ali rose to power within the Ottoman social and political framework, there lay before him the vistas opened by Napoleon and by those Frenchmen who remained or came anew after the military expedition had failed. Muhammad Ali's goal was to make Cairo the center of an empire. Aiming at dynastic rather than national greatness, he nevertheless understood that he needed a modern army both to conquer other Ottoman territories and to defeat further European adventures in Egypt and the empire he sought to build. He clearly saw that to create a modern military force he had to introduce a range of techniques on several levels of society and touching many other institutions besides the military. He made the army his instrument for modernization, but this elite did not play an autonomous role in which it introduced social change deliberately.

Even before the death of Muhammad Ali in 1849 the pace of social change in Egypt had waned. Soon afterward, European power began to penetrate Egyptian society on European terms and not, as under Muhammad Ali, in ways determined and controlled by the rulers of Egypt. The dual process of Western exploitation and tutelage led to an early nationalist revolt, the high point of which was the movement led by Colonel Arabi in 1881, and which culminated in the British occupation. This marked a new era in Western influence: it became steadier, more systematic and wider-ranging, though perhaps less immediately shocking. Under British control the Egyptian army was not an agency of social change but was itself an object of change. Since the British had contact with other Egyptian urban elites, the native army was only one of several which felt the Western impact. Because the Egyptian officers had intimate and enduring tutelage under the British both in Egypt and in England, and because they formed a disciplined, cohesive unit by the nature of their calling and professional education, they became the strongest and most solid native elite familiar with Western patterns of the rationalized application of violence.

As British power declined after World War I, the autonomous influence of the Egyptian military elite grew until a new group of officers were able, in 1952, to depose the government, dismiss the king, eradicate the monarchy and embark upon a calculated course of change embracing all major aspects of Egyptian social life. In the current era, therefore, the army is a conscious, independent agent of social change. . . .

In assessing the role of the army in the current period of social change, we are aided by the articulateness and public-relations sense of three important leaders, General Naguib, Colonel Nasser, and Colonel Sadat, all of whom have written revealing books about the army's relation to politics.

Sadat's book, *Revolt on the Nile,* is especially useful in its expression of the army's discontent with affairs before the 1952 *coup d'état* and its consequent embroilment in various political and ideological movements. One of the "leading themes" of Egyptian developments in the last twenty years, he says, has been "the Army's discontent at the decay of the State." The "squabbles" of the Egyptian political parties while the British "ruled by a hidden hand" gave the army "a right to intervene." According to Sadat, it was in early 1939 that several young officers, recent graduates of the Military Academy, formed a "secret revolutionary society dedicated to the task of liberation" of Egypt from its social and political ills. This group, he adds, "was the embryo of the Council of the Revolution which assumed power after the *coup d'état* of July 23, 1952." [1]

Ideologically, the discontented officers had no firm roots except in the nationalistic passion to rid Egypt of British power and to make the nation strong. In 1941, therefore, they reached an agreement with German headquarters in Libya and sought a "junction . . . between Egyptian insurgents and Axis troops."

[1] Anwar El Sadat, *Revolt on the Nile* (Wingate, London, 1957), pp. ix, 13–15.

The plan was to "carry out a military *coup d'état* in Cairo, . . . harry the British forces . . . , join up with the Axis troops, and the fate of the British Empire would be sealed." The failure of these efforts did not prevent the officers from spreading their influence within the army. They entered politics openly, it would appear from Sadat's comments: "We organized lectures and public debates for the discussion of current problems. These meetings attracted a large number of young people anxious to learn and to make their own ideas known. Previously, the Army officer's life had been a daily routine of mathematics, military history, ballistics, theory of strategy, field exercises. The study of social reform gave their lives new meaning." [2]

Nationalism, and political and social reform—in a word, modernization: this was the main preoccupation of many of the younger officers reared in a period of British imperial decline. Colonel Sadat's own criterion of the good officer is, at least inferentially, the degree of his familiarity with the West. Speaking favorably of the military capacities and the patriotism of the Egyptian chief of staff in World War II, Sadat adds as one of his good qualities: "He was receptive to modern ideas, having travelled in France, England and Germany." [3] For several years, therefore, the army included an active, influential core of young officers whose model of national political life was Western and who had justified to themselves their plans to seize power. Colonel Nasser remarks that the young officers saw it as their "duty" to turn against the regime: "If we did not perform it would betray the sacred trust in our charge." And they were convinced that no other group would perform the necessary act. "If the army does not move," Nasser says the officers told themselves, "who else will?" [4]

We are accustomed in Western European and Latin American history to the army in politics playing a conservative role, upholding established social institutions even when it uses unorthodox political methods. (General Perón in Argentina is an

---

[2] Sadat, *op. cit.*, pp. 34–35, 42–43, 86.
[3] *Ibid.*, p. 31.
[4] Gamal Abdel Nasser, *The Philosophy of the Revolution* (Dar Al-Maaref, Cairo, 1954) , p. 18.

exception to which we shall briefly return later.) But the Egyptian army (and the Syrian as well as some elements of the Jordanian) has not played a conservative or stabilizing role, for it is composed of a different social class and acts in a different social situation from those we have been familiar with in European history. In the West, army officers have usually exercised a stable if not reactionary political influence, for they have been connected to the upper governing classes by ties of family, education, and common interests in political stability. As Naguib has himself pointed out, however, the social origin of Egyptian officers gave them little stake in existing social and political arrangements. "Except for the royal family," he says, "there was no aristocracy, and the landowners' and traders' sons who might have led the Armed Forces were too busy enjoying their wealth to be bothered with military service. The officers' corps in consequence was largely composed of the sons of civil servants and soldiers and the grandsons of peasants." [5] In their attitudes toward foreign rule and the influence of foreigners in Egypt, young Egyptian officers resembled other young men who went from the villages or from urban middle-class homes to fill the secondary schools and universities supported with public funds. The military school and the university were alike the avenue to social ascent: a secure post in the military or civilian service of the state. Khadduri aptly points to the easy passage between military and non-military pursuits after higher education; Naguib thus had had legal training before he became an officer and hundreds of other officers in Arab armies entered upon military careers after teaching in public schools. "Not infrequently," Khadduri says, "high school teachers and lawyers, dissatisfied with their professions, or believing their ambitions can better be attained in the army, enter military schools and resume their public careers in the military service." [6]

Of all the native elite groups, the army probably has held

[5] Mohammed Naguib, *Egypt's Destiny* (Doubleday, N.Y., 1955), pp. 14–15.

[6] Majid Khadduri, "The Role of the Military in Middle East Politics," *American Political Science Review* (1953), Vol. 47, p. 517. See also, A. V. Sherman, "Intellectual Ferment in the Middle East," *Soviet Survey* (London) (1957), No. 16–17, pp. 22–26.

the most rationally calculating, secular, and unromantic approach to the problems which Egypt has faced. In this sense, it has been the most "Western" of the elites. Socially, however, the army officers have not transcended their conservative middle-class origins and upbringing. Their wives and families, for example, especially those of the few officers most prominent in the military regime, are seldom seen in public. Here intense nationalism combines with social conventionalism to discourage Western patterns in their private lives. There is also among these leaders a certain tendency toward puritanical attitudes which is compounded of the sexual modesty enjoined by Islamic doctrine and their passion for work to transform their country.

The fact that Egyptian officers do not follow a native aristocratic military tradition has probably facilitated their integration into the civilian government since 1952. Several officers who were members of the Revolution Command Council, which ruled Egypt in the early years of the regime, are still cabinet ministers. Others who were less prominent hold important positions. Among those whom this writer has personally seen at work, one was charged with revising the structure of the civil service, another is minister of culture and national guidance and emphasizes the former as much as the latter, a third is a novelist and secretary-general of the official council of arts and letters, a fourth is in charge of cultural exchanges in the ministry of foreign affairs. Other officers are ministers and ambassadors to foreign countries, and still others are in important administrative posts in privately-owned enterprises in which the government holds shares. Indeed, some young officers now think of their military careers as good training for high administrative posts in governmental and private enterprises. Whatever the regime's political motive may be in placing these dozens of officers in high posts, their performance of these civilian functions has not been "militaristic" or unresponsive to non-military requirements. It is entirely possible, moreover, that such power and responsibility has already made the upper reaches of this elite much less responsive to adventurous policies in foreign or domestic affairs. Professional tradition and present self-interest can combine quickly to make them conservative despite their own social origin.

The military elite's rationalistic, secular outlook and temper are best revealed in its relationship to such a fundamentalist religious group as the Moslem Brotherhood. Naguib summarized the attitude of the leaders of the military revolt when he said that though they sympathized with the "desire to apply the teachings of Mohammed to modern life," they also "were convinced that to do so blindly would spell disaster." Intent upon increasing Egypt's influence in the modern world, he added: "The rebirth of Egypt, in our opinion, depended on the continued modernization of its social, political, and economic institutions." [7]

Colonel Sadat provides some details of the relations between the army officers and the Moslem Brotherhood which reveal the attitude of the former irrespective of the reinterpretations the author may be presenting in the light of subsequent events. Pointing out that the Brotherhood "rose to a position of power with extraordinary rapidity," it seemed, he says, at least "in its early days," a "useful ally to our revolutionary movement." Sadat himself was the liaison between the officers and the Brotherhood's Supreme Guide, from whom he learned that "the dogmas of Islam must be inculcated in all branches of the Army." Unsure of its own political direction but certain that it wanted power, the officers "hoped to use our association with the Brotherhood as a lever to achieve our own ends." As Sadat states, "we were deceived in our calculations." In those ideologically confused times, many officers, Sadat states, were sympathetic to the Brotherhood. He himself believed that "great things" would follow their cooperation, but even long before the officers had seized and were exercising state power, clashes between them and the Brotherhood were frequent. From Sadat's brief account, it is clear that the officers were secular and looked to a modernization of Egypt along Western technological lines whereas the Brotherhood was of course fundamentalist before anything else. The mystery, the rough egalitarianism, the ignoring of civil-military status distinctions, the inconsistency and weakness of the program, the vagueness of the top leaders as to the program, and the emphasis upon unquestioning faith in the Supreme Guide—all of these irra-

[7] Naguib, *op. cit.*, p. 134.

tional, semi-charismatic and mysterious qualities of the Brotherhood repelled the army officers.[8]

It is not that the latter were ideologically consistent, but that
they were a secularized group within the context of Egyptian
social and political life. As individuals, the officers may have been
no less superstitious or emotional or extremist than the members
of other organizations then forming and dissolving and reform-
ing in Egypt. Yet their leadership had an image of the secular
Egypt they wanted, and moved with as much directness as possible toward that goal and with no more secrecy, mystery and
conspiratorial ceremony than was necessary. . . .

As an advanced elite, the army has been aware of its own
place in Egyptian life and can look back upon a tradition of
nationalism and social change going back several generations.
Nasser himself plainly expounded the role of the army in social
change in a speech in 1954 celebrating the second anniversary of
the revolution which it led. The army, he said then, "is not
merely barracks separated from the people by a high wall, but a
university with open doors to all classes of the people, teaching
them, strengthening their bodies and raising their morale. . . .
We assure our soldiers that armies can never gain a victory
except by the aid of scientists behind their microscopes and test
tubes and by the aid of every individual member of the nation." [9]

When the young officers took power they found it necessary,
if they were to succeed in changing Egypt, to retain their hold
rather than to share it for long with the older political elite. To
protect both their goals and their new position, they had to
unfold a program, mobilize support for their acts, and prevent
the deposed forces from reasserting themselves. A few months
after the 1954 internal crisis as a result of which his leadership
was consolidated and made formal, Nasser described for an
American audience the goals of the revolution: "to end the
exploitation of people, to realize national aspirations and to
develop the mature political consciousness that is an indispen-

[8] Sadat, *op. cit.*, pp. 28–30, 79–81.
[9] Reprinted in *Goals of the Egyptian Revolution* (pamphlet distributed
by Republic of Egypt but indicating no publisher or date) , p. 73.

sable preliminary for a sound democracy." In order to attain these goals, he continued, "the standard of living of the masses must be raised, education expanded and social consciousness developed." [10]

In this deliberate attempt to introduce social change, the officers have intensified two main tendencies begun long before their advent: nationalism and industrialization. By a propaganda program which depends heavily upon the mass media of communication, they seek to weld all Egyptians into a conscious national unit and to make them leaders among the Arabs, Moslems and Africans who are undergoing the same kind of transformation. They have made reforms in education and encouraged certain types of interpersonal relations to conform to the goals of nationalism and industrialization. Egypt has thus experienced increasing governmental direction of economic and social life as well as of political affairs. This is a more serious matter today than in previous eras in which Near Eastern governments have made such claims because today the state apparatus, with its monopoly of new weapons and of the means of mass communication, cannot be challenged as could a regime in the looser social structure of the past. There are many programs and acts which are part of this trend: abolition of political parties; reconstitution of an elected parliament under the regime's own conditions; control of press and radio and greater surveillance of all literary, artistic, and religious expression; encouragement of science and technology; shift of the acts of formerly somewhat independent associations (trade unions and professional bodies) into closer alignment with the government's programs; more direct government role in economic life; mobilization of military forces and their equipment with more advanced weapons; heightening of national consciousness through many acts in regional and world politics.

The officers display in their own service journals the sentiments, attitudes and intentions appropriate to the goals and policies just summarized. Some are technical journals for officers only. Others, more general and popular in tone, are apparently

[10] Gamal Abdel Nasser, "The Egyptian Revolution," *Foreign Affairs* (1955), Vol. 33, pp. 208–9.

meant for enlisted men too. And one or two seem to be edited for the reading public at large. They contain articles on politics, nationalism, economic reform, culture, personal problems, and so on, as well as the more strictly military discussions. Though virtually all of the articles are written by officers, a few of the non-military ones are by civilians, such as one by a professor of journalism at Cairo University which severely criticized American policy in sending troops to Lebanon in the summer of 1958.[11] An examination of some of these articles reveals the military elite's conception of their own role and of the nation they want to build.

An article published in 1958 discusses "Military Education and Character Training."[12] Pointing out the place of military training in the development of nationalism and individual excellence, the author says: "Military life is the school of the people; it is an advanced school in public, social and national aspects of life, for the first lesson that a young soldier learns is self-denial and to exert all his efforts towards a noble cause. It is the repudiation of personal interests in favor of the public interest. Then the individual becomes a sound, ideal citizen." The importance of creating a new type of individual to conform to the national goals is stressed in two other articles. One of them,[13] concerned with the fact that population is growing faster than food resources, warns that a powerful nation in peace or war needs healthy, properly-nourished citizens. The other[14] emphasizes that the individual human being is the basis of a strong economy, which in turn is needed to make a nation militarily

[11] *Air Force Magazine* (*Majallat al-Quwwāt al-Jawwīyah*) (Cairo) (1958), No. 33, p. 5.

[12] By Capt. Sharaf al-Dīn Za 'balāwi, *Military Magazine* (*al-Majallat al-'Askarīyah*, pub. at Damascus by GHQ, 3d Div., Syrian Army) (1958), Vol. 8, pp. 49–54, esp. p. 50.

[13] "Agricultural and Food Resources and Their Effect on the War Effort," by Col. 'Alī Munīr Murād, *Army Magazine* (*Majallat al-Jaysh*, pub. in Cairo at the al-'Abbāsīyah Barracks) (1955), No. 68, pp. 30–35.

[14] "Material and Moral Mobilization of Human Resources for War," by Major Ibrāhīm Khūrī, *Military Magazine* (*al-Majallat al-'Askarīyah*, pub. at Damascus by GHQ, 3d Div., Syrian Army) (1958), Vol. 8, pp. 26–34, esp. pp. 26–28.

powerful. A sound military program is thus said to require the participation of the entire nation, direction by a central authority, equality of sacrifice, a high level of health and education especially among the youth, and an intimate relationship between the people and their military forces.

Some articles are designed to instruct the readers as to the new values which the regime seeks to inculcate. Thus an officer writes [15] a general article on the nature of nationalism, defining such terms as nation and patriotism, because these concepts will be influential in the Arab world. In a more popular journal, an unsigned article [16] glorifies the industrial worker as intelligent and patriotic, sacrificing to contribute to his country's welfare. Describing the Egyptian workers in heavy industry, the writer asserts that they are well educated, endure great hardships, and are as skilled as foreigners. In the old days, the reader is told, a few years of formal education made a man aspire only to a clerical job, but now things have changed. "So," the reader is encouraged, "if you hold a general secondary school certificate, do not hesitate. You have a good job waiting for you and a secure future. But you must have the capacity for endurance to become one of the pioneers, the pioneers in the heavy industry of Egypt." An article in another magazine [17] reverts to the question of living standards and reviews the steps taken to increase industrial production so that the population may become healthy and well educated. An editorial in a more technical journal [18] summarizes not only these actions of the government but also praises the effort at land reform, improvement in water supply and roads, housing, sewage, and so on. In a naval magazine an officer discusses insurance schemes as a means of improving health stand-

[15] "Nationalism," by Capt. Muhammad Anwar 'Abd al-Salām Ahmad, *Artillery Magazine* (*Majallat al-Madfa'īyah*) (1958), No. 44, pp. 90–95.

[16] "This Worker Lives Under 1650 Degrees of Heat," unsigned, *Armed Forces* (*al-Quwwāt al-Musallahah*, pub. by Department of Public Affairs, Egyptian Armed Forces) (1958), No. 332, pp. 22–23.

[17] "Our Social Revolution," by Col. 'Abd al-Tawwāb Hadīb, *Army Magazine* (*Majallat al-Jaysh*, pub. in Cairo at the al-'Abbāsīyah Barracks) (1956), No. 72, pp. 132–38.

[18] "This Revolution," editorial, *Military Engineers' Journal* (*al-Muhandisūn al-'Askarīyūn*) (Jan. 1956), pp. 3–6.

ards.[19] He contends that "nationalization" of medical care, as in England, requires a high civic sense, an educated public with a high standard of living, and a medical profession dedicated to service rather than its own interests. He therefore concludes that for Egypt it would be more appropriate to introduce health insurance based upon premiums. . . .

This is the image of the country which the military elite would like to build—industrialized, militarily powerful, respected in the world community, and composed of educated, healthy citizens loyal to the nation-state. Nasser has often summarized this goal as socialism, cooperation, and democracy. Late in 1959 he gave this goal characteristic expression while insisting, perhaps in response to Western critics of the "negativism" of Arab nationalism, that this ideology can be constructive. "Arab nationalism," he told a mass audience at Port Said, ". . . is a deep-seated constructive idea, a progressive and changing idea. It represents the social revolution as well as the political revolution. . . . We want to achieve a socialist, democratic, cooperative society. . . . The time has come for Arab nationalism to prove that it has a progressive creed." Veering toward a kind of humanistic optimism seldom expressed by Arab leaders even in oratory, he went on: "Human progress opens vistas before us which are without limits and our backwardness in the past will not impede our progress in the present." [20] Because of the traditional weakness of civic spirit and the suspicion of government, it has been easier to use the state machine as the engine of movement and change. The regime has tried, nevertheless, to galvanize the nation into voluntary action, though always in strict accordance with official goals and without permitting the growth of competing centers of political power.

What is the relationship of the military regime to democracy and freedom? In common with elites in other societies undergoing modernization, the Egyptian military elite has looked upon democracy and freedom in national rather than individual terms.

[19] "Health Insurance," by Major 'Abd al-Shakūr Sālih al-Shihābī, *Fleet Magazine (Majallat al-Ustūl,* pub. by Naval Forces in Egypt) (1955), Vol. 3, pp. 29–32.
[20] *al-Jumhūrīyah* (Cairo), December 24, 1959, p. 5.

These goals are equated with self-government, that is, government by a native rather than a foreign elite. The freedom of the individual to challenge such native rule is not accepted as a mode of political life, though differences of opinion are expressed as to the means by which the goals laid down by the regime may be attained. The regime does not feel free to permit an opposition in the traditional Western sense because it fears that, given wide public apathy, such an arrangement might enable deposed elites to return to power and reverse the trend toward modernization. What the modernizers want to do might thus be frustrated in a democratic system by those who oppose land reform, secularization, the inculcation of political attitudes among the sections of the population which really lay outside the political community until now, and the emphasis upon national power in the world arena. Not bound to the past, as were the elites they deposed and the masses they seek to arouse, the military elite feels it must impose change—and must therefore retain control of the state machinery to help in this effort and to prevent interference with it. For this reason it has destroyed or transformed those political and professional associations which have challenged its program or its authority.

For all its suppression of political dissent, the military regime has enlarged other kinds of freedom for the individual. Though it rejects Western parliamentary democracy (for the present only, it insists), it has not only permitted but even promoted liberalism in non-political realms. It has broadened educational opportunity, supported efforts to overcome learning by rote, tried to develop education in science (traditionally neglected), and encouraged methods of education which permit freer expression of individuality. In public administration it has tried to encourage greater individual responsibility as part of a broad program to increase efficiency as well as to develop a spirit of public service. In family life it allows the growth of liberal ideas of child-rearing and above all the emancipation of women from seclusion through education and employment outside the home. In art and literature, the regime has encouraged new forms of expression and has not interfered with the growth of various schools so long as immediate political issues are avoided or, if touched at all, are treated in accordance with the official position. All of these tendencies in education, position of women, interpersonal relations, joined to the effects of a more politically alert population, urbanization, creation of articulate social groups of workers and executives in an industrializing economy, may be setting up pressures for increased personal freedom in the political realm as well. The weakening of old authorities may prompt the questioning of new authorities, too. Though perhaps not directly intending to promote democracy as a purely political arrangement, the military regime is, by its colossal effort to introduce social change, willy-nilly creating some of the socio-economic and attitudinal bases conducive to democracy.[21]

We have examined several stages in the introduction of social change in Egypt by a military elite. In the Napoleonic invasion the military elite was foreign and did little to instruct or develop a native elite. It transported to Egypt the products of Western science and technology and some aspects of Western ideologies, and shocked the native elites into recognition of Western achievements. In the Muhammad Ali era, covering almost the first half of the nineteenth century, an "Oriental despot" sought military strength to establish a dynastic empire at the expense of both Europe and the Ottoman empire. In the process of creating a modern army and navy he forced many changes upon the country without developing in the general population a will and a desire to match the passion which impelled him in that unfamiliar direction. The effect was to develop at least the beginnings of a native elite and, especially, to make the army officers more familiar with Western science, technology, and habits of mind than any other important, cohesive elite near the seat of political power. During the following decades Western influences were diffuse and varied but the British occupation, in 1882, began a long era of sustained, extensive spread of Western techniques and values. A really native Egyptian military elite developed which, rather than introducing social change, itself

---

[21] On these socio-economic conditions characteristic of the democracies and the degree to which they may be found in the Arab countries, see Charles Issawi, "Economic and Social Foundations of Democracy in the Middle East," *International Affairs* (1956), Vol. 32, pp. 27–42, reprinted in Walter Z. Laqueur, ed., *The Middle East in Transition* (Praeger, N.Y., 1958), pp. 33–51.

underwent considerable modernization in technical capacity and ideology. Becoming aware of itself as a cohesive group, drawn from the middle and lower middle classes, the army officers had little stake in the existing political and social system. Seizing power in 1952, a group of them introduced a new period of conscious, deliberate, planned modernization in all realms of Egyptian life; having changed, the officers now proposed to change Egypt.

The extent of the change which the military elite introduces is in part conditioned by the level of technological and social development of the whole society. Muhammad Ali, for example, did not find it so important to convince the nation that his course was right or beneficial to them, nor did he need to create a political movement. The army officers under Nasser, however, coming after a period of parliamentary government, and during the era of mass communication resulting from vast technological innovations, realize that sheer force is not enough. So they find it possible and advisable to use these technological developments to create some degree of consensus in the nation, almost, one could say, consciously to create a class with a stake in the regime's program. And they find it advisable, also, to seek to awaken the national consciousness of sections of the population, mainly the peasants and the urban workers, which had previously lain outside the political community. They have thus instituted agrarian reform as more than a purely economic measure and have sponsored cooperative experiments as a demonstration of the direction in which planned social change may go. For the entire nation, moreover, the regime has had to adjust to recent political experience by seeking to substitute for the outlawed political parties first the Liberation Rally and now the National Union, conducting a plebiscite in the absence of elections, and introducing a new constitution and parliament in place of those which were abolished. The military elite today must, to realize its goals, cover a much broader area of the nation's life than did Muhammad Ali a century ago. Because he must obtain some degree of consensus, Nasser must move into virtually every fastness of social and personal relations.

The differences between two regimes more than a century

apart are instructive. Muhammad Ali wanted an efficient military force and modern technology. In the process of attaining these ends he had to begin to modernize other institutions such as medical care, education, and administration, though he was not interested in the latter as ends in themselves; and he created a military elite as a consequence of building an advanced military machine. Under Nasser an existing, already Westernized military elite consciously undertook to infuse a new spirit into the nation, to modernize social relations directly and not merely the economy and the technology of the society. Nasser wants a strong military force and a modern technology too, of course, but he also knows that he must create a modern nation to achieve such goals. The present military elite is itself the human engine of change, pushing the community onward, seeking modernization in all realms as an end in itself.

Both the Muhammad Ali and the Nasser eras exemplify the persistent influence of secular military authoritarian regimes in Egypt. Military authoritarianism had been combined with religious claims of leadership under the Ottomans and the Mamluks. That type of regime was deposed by the Napoleonic venture, and thereafter secular influences pervaded the military elite to an increasing extent. When Napoleon was ousted from Egypt through the combination of local resistance and British power, Muhammad Ali arose in the wake of this foreign power and imposed his military dynastic regime. With his defeat and the subsequent penetration of Egypt by Western Europeans culminating in the long British occupation, military authoritarianism receded. But as British and Western power itself waned, the current military authoritarian regime came to power. It would seem, therefore, that there is a strong drift in Egypt toward this kind of political control except when foreign powers occupy or otherwise dominate the country. When foreign influence weakens, native military authoritarian regimes rise.

These secular military elites differ, of course, from the pre-Napoleonic Egyptian military-political-religious elites, who combined these various forms of power and prestige in the traditional Islamic way. Perhaps because of the Napoleonic shock, Egypt seems to be one of the first Islamic Ottoman territories to have experienced this separation of military from religious power; Muhammad Ali's conquests, for example, were by an army not imbued with nationalism or religious fervor. Muhammad Ali thus institutionalized and consolidated the tendency, introduced by the Napoleonic conquest and persisting in increasing extent down to the present regime, to separate military from religious power. In recent years the religious elite has not challenged the secular authorities in Egypt, and this is especially so in the present regime. The effort of the Moslem Brotherhood to revive the unity of political, religious and military power has failed repeatedly.

Historically the army in Egypt has not always been the most technologically advanced elite or the one least attached to the prevailing political and social system. Ayalon, for example, has shown [22] that the failure of the Mamluks to adopt gunpowder and artillery in the field against the conquering Ottomans in the sixteenth century was the result of Mamluk social organization and the conservatism of its military-political elite; adjusting to the new mode of warfare would have required changes in social status and functions which they were unwilling to abide. It is only since the advent of Western influence, the separation of the military from political and religious elites, and the recruitment of officers from classes other than those at or near the top of the social hierarchy, that the military elite has become at once highly Westernized in a technological-ideological sense and alienated from the political and economic interest of the upper classes.

This Egyptian pattern of social change introduced out of military considerations and along lines set by a military elite is related to, though not necessarily the same as, other patterns elsewhere. . . . Perhaps the closest parallel to the Near East pattern may be found in Latin America where, in some countries, the army has not only ruled but has sought to modernize the society. Argentina's course from 1943 in some important ways presaged that of Egypt from 1952. The army there had looked with disfavor upon the growth of political parties and sympathized with popular distrust of national regeneration. Those who

[22] David Ayalon, *Gunpowder and Firearms in the Mamluk Kingdom* (Valentine, Mitchell, London, 1956), pp. ix, 46–48, 62–63, 97–99, 102, 108.

overthrew the government announced that they planned to make Argentina dominant in Latin America, a goal which would require the nation to "work, make sacrifices, and obey." Following the *coup d'état,* three army officers rapidly succeeded each other in the presidency and then Perón emerged as the real wielder of power, backed by a group of officers. Under Perón the army and the government-controlled trade unions were the two pillars of the regime. Egypt's course parallels this in some essentials. In 1954, moreover, when the officers in the ruling Revolution Command Council used the trade unions to help depose Naguib, it looked as though they too were going to rely on the army and organized labor as the twin bases of their power. But subsequent events did not follow this lead.

This review of social change introduced through military needs or by a military elite raises two general questions concerning social change originating in this way. We can discuss each only briefly.

First, in what order is change diffused by borrowing or imposition? It is clear that generally a change in modes of transportation will be more easily diffused than a change in religious belief. Changes in military technique, too, will be readily adopted by a conquered people who want to resist further conquest. In Egypt, then, as perhaps elsewhere too, if the military elite becomes imbued with a will to change its style in order to become more effective, other elites that are determined to preserve the nation's other values will not be likely to resist. Thus no one in Egypt attacks military modernization as an undesirable imitation of the West, although many groups have resisted the introduction of Western political forms on two grounds: first, simply that they are Western and hence undesirable; and second, because such new political forms may threaten the power of established groups and classes or interfere with other goals sought by important and powerful elements of the society. Military change, or at least readiness for adoption of new military techniques, is a type of innovation which is not resisted very much. The implications of the desire for military change, however, such as improved technology, educational changes, industrial development, and so on may not be so welcome or may be difficult to impose upon a nation.

One of the oldest questions in the theory of cultural diffusion is whether material things are more quickly adopted than beliefs, ideas, tastes, and attitudes. In recent years it is coming to be realized that "ideas" and "things" are both involved in many instances of borrowing. Thus diffusion of modern military weapons involves a capacity to use them, that is, a certain technological facility which in turn requires an attitude of mind receptive to a particular kind of rationalism. Generally, of course, a culture will borrow most readily those "things" or artifacts which will permit it to realize its existing values and goals; this, too, makes it clear why Western military technology is attractive to nations already imbued with the goal of increasing their power in international relations. Indeed, it may be argued that "ideas" diffuse before "things," if we broadly interpret "ideas" to include tastes, desires, and attitudes. Thus the modern Western idea of nationalism diffused to the Arab world long before Western technology. The desire for automobiles and radios, too, diffuses before the capacity to build them. So, too, Egypt's desire for tanks, planes and submarines is highly developed but not so its capacity to produce them. Strictly speaking, the desire for a thing and the capacity to produce it are both complexes of non-material culture. Irrespective, then, of which diffuse first, those ideas *and* things are most readily borrowed which are most easily adapted to the existing institutions and goals.

Another facet of cultural diffusion is the agent through which change is introduced. Innovations may be the result chiefly of indigenous needs and inventions, such as most of the communications media have been in modern Western society, or they may result from imitation of foreign models, as in the case of industrial and technological change in the contemporary Arab world. Military change in Egypt has been in the latter class, of course, but it leads to further change of local origin, as we have seen in the sections on social change under Muhammad Ali and the present regime.

The second general question is: How enduring are these

social changes introduced through military channels of any kind? This involves an even broader issue: How thoroughgoing can planned social change be, whatever its origin or motive power?

To help us understand planned social change in Egypt, especially in the present era, we can look at the experience of the Soviet Union and Turkey, where similar efforts have been made by a strong, authoritarian, centralized oligarchy. "In the Soviet case," Inkeles aptly points out, "we have the distinctive combination of planned social change instituted from above, centrally directed and executed by a body whose occupational role is that of effecting change, backed by the power and all the economic and political force which a totalitarian regime can muster, guided by a central theory or ideology, carried out at a relatively unprecedented rate, and extending into every dimension of social life." Yet even in these surely unprecedented circumstances in modern history, Inkeles continues, there are many areas of social relations which the Bolsheviks found they could not change directly and, indeed, in which they had to retreat in their effort to remold the nation. "It appears," Inkeles concludes, "that despite the massive destruction of the main formal elements of the old social structure and the extensive elaboration of new social forms, a large number of basic attitudes, values, and senti- ments, and of traditional modes of orientation, expression, and reaction tend to be markedly persistent." He refers to the popu- lar attitudes toward authority, conceptions of private property, kinship structure and interpersonal relations within the family as features of Russian life resisting change.[23]

Social change in the Turkey of Ataturk was in some realms directly aimed at even more personal aspects of life than in the Soviet Union. Thus the equalization of women's status, the re- forms in dress, the alphabet change, the secularization of law, education and personal relations, and the weakening of the reli- gious elite and the diminution of the place of religion—all these probably sought to upset traditional Turkish life more than the Bolshevik innovations did traditional Russian life. In other re-

[23] Alex Inkeles, "Social Change in Soviet Russia," in *Freedom and Control in Modern Society*, ed. by Morroe Berger, Theodore Abel and Charles H. Page (Van Nostrand, N.Y., 1954) , pp. 244, 253.

spects, however, such as in the distribution of political and economic power, Turkish reform has not gone so far as the Soviet. Yet the Turkey of Ataturk's successors has also had to retreat, especially in the area of religion.

The Russian and Turkish examples indicate the limitations of planned social change imposed by any means, for some realms of life cannot be directly affected in an enduring way through the machinery of government. Moreover, we could expect even less social change in Egypt in the several periods we have reviewed because in none, including the present one, have the rulers enjoyed the degree of control and the explicit, detailed program and ideology of the Bolsheviks or the fierce intention to force rapid modernization that moved Ataturk. Yet, Egyptian changes in education, encouragement of industry, development of a national spirit, and spread of the network of communications may bring about, indirectly, the changed family relations, the secular outlook, and the general complex of tastes and attitudes which we associate with an industrial, urban, technologically advanced society. Egypt has not decreed full equality for women, but if the primary and higher education of girls continues to grow, there will be a slower but perhaps irreversible trend toward equality in and outside the home. What is happening, therefore, is that the present regime is encouraging those developments in the economy which stimulate the growth of attitudes and tastes that cannot be directly induced by law or decree—that is, the change from a personality-type which is undisciplined, unaccustomed to the time-rhythm of an industrial society, oriented to local and family loyalties exclusively, and not anxious for self-advancement in modern terms, to a personality-type which displays wider loyalties, adjusts to the tempo of an industrial-urban society, is more oriented toward the future, strives for economic and educational advancement and is an active part of the national community.

The Nasser regime has already accomplished the easiest type of change; it has shifted political power from the combination of foreign interests, the monarchy, large landholders, and a small business and professional class, to the military elite and its mass organizations. The more fundamental economic changes have only been touched—land reform, redistribution of economic functions and wealth, quickening of industrialization, educational expansion, Egyptianization, and changes in occupational distribution. The implicit goals of modernization of personality and interpersonal relations are only beginning to appear—national orientation, new relations within the family, loyalties appropriate to an industrial nation.

How enduring are the social changes imposed through military channels of any kind? There have been few, perhaps no, studies of Western history designed to help answer this question, and certainly none with respect to the Egyptian experience. . . . One hypothesis that suggests itself concerning the influence of the military channel of social change which we have reviewed is that this mode may be an effective way to introduce new ideas and techniques which, left to other and less direct means of diffusion, would spread less systematically and rapidly. Social change through military considerations or by a military elite shocks a society into awareness of new things. The deep penetration of this awareness, its transformation into spontaneous, free desires and tastes and attitudes, may require a longer process of consolidation through means that are less arbitrary and authoritarian.

Politics, Social Structure and Military Intervention in Latin America

1961

GINO GERMANI AND KALMAN SILVERT

. . . Most Latin American countries have reached their first century and a half of independent existence. However, their social development into national states lagged behind formal independence and it is only now that a few of them are reaching a stage of full nationhood. While in some countries the breakdown of the traditional structure began in the last quarter of the nineteenth century, in many others a similar process of structural change did not start until the last two or three decades of the present century. Furthermore, one must remember that nowhere, not even in the most "advanced" Latin American nations, may it be said that the transition is complete.

In this transitional process we shall distinguish a series of successive "stages" so that the degree of development reached by any single Latin American country can then be described and compared to others. It is hardly necessary to emphasize the intrinsic limitations of such a procedure: nevertheless, it seems the most convenient one to yield a short-hand description of the present situation, while at the same time retaining a clear awareness of the total dynamics of the process. . . .

A tentative simple typology of the social structure of the twenty republics has been summarized in Table I. In construct-

Reprinted by permission from the European Journal of Sociology, *II (1961)*, *62–81.*

TABLE I   (1950 circa)

COUNTRIES	% middle and upper strata	% in primary activities	% in cities of 20,000 and more inhabitants	% middle and upper urban strata	% literates	university students per 1,000 inhabitants

Group A: (a) *Middle strata: 20% and more;* (b) *cultural, psychological and political existence of a middle class;* (c) *ethnic and cultural homogeneity; national identification and considerable level of participation in different spheres;* (d) *urban/rural differences and geographical discontinuity exist, but to a lesser extent than in other Latin American countries.*

Argentina ⎫	36	25	48	28	87	7.7
Uruguay ⎬ urban predominance	...	22	50	...	95	5.2
Chile ⎭	22	35	43	21	80	3.9
Costa Rica rural predominance	22	57	18	14	80	3.9

Group B: (a) *Middle strata: between 15 and 20% (approx.) heavily concentrated in some areas of the country;* (b) *cultural, psychological and political existence of a middle class;* (c) *ethnic and cultural heterogeneity; pronounced inequalities in the degree of participation in national society and in other aspects;* (d) *strong regional inequalities with concentration of urbanization and industrialization in certain areas and rural predominance in the greater part of the country.*

| Mexico lesser survival of traditional pattern | 17 * | 56 | 24 | ... | 59 | 0.9 |
| Brazil greater survival of traditional pattern | 15 | 62 | 20 | 13 | 49 | 1.2 |

Group C: (a) *Middle strata between 15 and 20% (approx.);* (b) *emerging middle class (but there is no agreement as to its degree of auto-identification);* (c) *ethnic and cultural heterogeneity, pronounced inequalities in the degree of participation in national society and other aspects;* (d) *pronounced discontinuity between rural/urban areas and strong regional inequalities.*

Cuba ⎫ urban predominance	22	44	37	21	76	3.9
Venezuela ⎭	18	44	31	16	52	1.3
Colombia rural predominance	22	58	22	12	62	1.0

Group D: (a) *Middle strata: less than 15%; emergent middle strata in some countries, but clear persistence in all, in varying degrees, of the traditional pattern;* (b) *ethnic and cultural heterogeneity in almost all;* (c) *vast sectors of the population still marginal;* (d) *rural predominance in general; regional inequalities.*

Panama	15	55	22	15	70	2.6
Paraguay	14	54	15	12	66	1.3
Peru	...	60	14	...	42	1.6
Ecuador	10	51	18	10	56	1.4
El Salvador	10	64	13	9	57	0.5
Bolivia	8	68	20	7	32	2.0
Guatemala	8	75	11	6	29	0.1
Nicaragua	...	71	15	...	38	0.7
Dominican Republic	...	70	11	...	43	1.2
Honduras	4	76	7	4	35	0.7
Haïti	3	77	5	2	11	"

[...] *No data.*   *1940.*

ing it we have taken into account those traits which we consider most relevant to the problem at hand: namely, the economic structure; the social stratification system (especially the existence of a self-identifying middle stratum) ; the degree of economic and cultural homogeneity and participation in a common culture and in national life; the degree of national identification; and geographical discontinuities in the socio-economic level of the various regions within the country [1]. While we do not identify the successive "stages" of the historical scheme with the different "types" of social structure described in the Table, we suggest that various degrees of 'delayed development' may have resulted in situations similar to those indicated in the typology.

STAGES 1 AND 2. Predominance of the Traditional Social Structure; Formal National Independence and Civil Wars

The common trait of these first two stages of Latin American development is the persistence of the "traditional" society which maintained its essential features throughout the political upheaval and radical changes in formal political organization.

STAGE 1. Revolutions and Wars for National Independence

At the time when they gained their independence (in most cases *circa* 1810) the Latin American countries may be said to have approximated the "ideal type" of the "traditional society": subsistence economy marginal to the world market and a two strata system characterized by little or no mobility and caste-like relationships. The Spaniards and Portuguese were the ruling group, and immediately below them we find the small élite of the *créoles,* of European descent and mainly urban, who while de-

---

[1] The table appeared in a slightly modified form in Gino Germani, "The strategy of fostering social mobility", paper prepared for the Seminar on *The Social Impact of Economic Development in Latin America* (Proceedings published by UNESCO . . .). Only part of the basic data are shown in the table. For the main concepts used in formulating the scheme, see G. GERMANI, *Integración política de las masas* (Buenos Aires, CLES, 1956 . . . K. SILVERT, "Nationalism in Latin America" in *The Annals of the American Academy of Political and Social Science,* 334 (1961), pp. 1–9. . . .

prived of political power still belonged (subjectively as well as objectively) to the higher stratum and retained a dominant position from the economic and cultural point of view. It was this creole élite who brought about the revolutions and achieved national independence with support of the lower strata, including the *Mestizos* and even part of the outcast group of the Negroes and the Indians who filled the armies of the independence wars. The creoles were inspired mainly by the American model, the French revolution and seventeenth century illuminism. They attempted to establish modern democratic states with their corresponding symbols: the 'constitution', the 'parliament', the elected rulers, and so on. There were, however, two basic limitations to their action. The first may be found in the creole elite itself: it was the expression of a traditional structure and in spite of its ideology, it still perceived itself as an aristocracy widely separated from the popular strata. The democracy they dreamed of was the "limited" democracy of the wealthy, the educated, the well-bred of proper descent. On the other hand, the prevailing state of the society was scarcely adequate to the establishment of a representative democracy: powerful geographical as well as ethnic, cultural and economic factors made such an undertaking simply utopian.

STAGE 2. Anarchy, "Caudillismo" and Civil Wars

The outcome of such a situation was simply that, even before the end of the long and cruel wars of independence against the Spaniards, the constitutional "fictions" created by the urban élites broke down. The political and institutional vacuum resulting from the disappearance of the colonial administration and the failure of the "constitutional fictions" resulted in the geographical fragmentation of political power: the rise of local "caudillos" often of *mestizo* or even Indian origin, frequent local wars, and a rapid succession of military coups.

The army of the "caudillos" was seldom anything more than an armed band, under the leadership of a self-appointed "general". At this stage we do not find in Latin America any professional army, but the political rule of the caudillos often adopted some symbols both of the army and of the democratic regimes:

the geographical fragmentation took the form of a "federal" state, the absolute rule of the caudillo that of the "president" and, at the same time, "general" of the army. During this stage the social structure remained very much the same. This was especially true of the primitive state of the economy, the stratification system, and the isolation, both economic and social, of most of the population.

STAGES 3 TO 6. Transition of the Social Structure from the "Traditional" to the "Industrial" Pattern

While some countries show a clear succession of these four stages, in the majority of the cases there is much overlapping. Nevertheless the scheme is useful as a conceptualization of the transition towards a mature national state: that is, toward political unification and organization, attainment of certain preconditions of economic growth, changes in the social structure and progressive enlargement of social participation (including political participation).

There is one very important and well known feature of this process which must be emphasized here; the unevenness of the transition, the fact that some groups within the society and some areas within each country remained unchanged and underdeveloped while others underwent great changes. This is a familiar fact in most countries, but in Latin America (as in other underdeveloped areas) it acquired a particular intensity. The typical *dual* character of the countries both from the *social* and the *geographical* points of view is expressed in the contrasts between the socially "developed" higher and middle strata and the "backward", more primitive, lower strata; the cleavage between certain areas in which most of the urban population, industrial production, educated people, wealth and political power are concentrated, and the rest of the country, predominantly rural, with a subsistence economy, illiterate, and politically inactive and powerless. The transition, in Latin America, cannot be understood without taking into full account the repercussions of this dual structure.

Social development involves first the extension of the modern way of life to a growing proportion of the people living in the most favored areas (the emergence of an urban middle class and a modern industrial proletariat in the "central" sector of a country), and second the incorporation—by way of massive internal migration or by geographical diffusion of industrialization and modernization—of the marginal population living in "peripheral" areas. The circumstances of the process, and especially its speed, are of the utmost importance for the political equilibrium of the country.

STAGE 3. Unifying Dictatorships

The struggle between the caudillos within a given country was eventually replaced by the hegemony of one among them. The unity of the state was restored and a degree of order and stability achieved. However, the character of these "unifying dictatorships" differed very widely. For our present purpose they may perhaps be classified into two main categories: "regressive" dictatorships, which maintained completely intact the traditional pattern, and "enlightened" dictatorships, which introduced at least some modernizing measures. The most important difference between the two lies in the economic sphere. While the former maintained their countries isolated from the world market, and the old subsistence economy continued to predominate, the latter fostered at least a minimum degree of economic development, through the construction of means of transport and communication, some modernization of agriculture, some educational measures, organization of the public bureaucracy, and so forth.

Generally it was these relatively more enlightened authoritarian regimes, as well as the "limited democracies", which marked the beginning of the transformation of the Latin American countries into producers of raw materials and their integration into the world market. Foreign capital was introduced, the beginnings of industrialization took place, and these changes began to produce some impact on the social structure. While they left untouched the main features of the traditional pattern—the concentration of land ownership, the two class system, the isolation of the great majority of the population—they created certain dynamic factors which in time produced further changes making for transition. The integration of the country into the world market and the degree of economic modernization often fostered the emergence of new urban middle occupational strata. While they remained a relatively small proportion of the total population, and significantly, continued to be identified with the traditional upper class, these urban strata also represented an essential precondition for further changes.

One important feature of the enlightened dictatorships is the attempt at a "professionalization" of the army and the fact that while the dictators were often military men they tried to control the army itself, submitting the unruly military caudillos to the central political authority of the state.

well of course

STAGE 4. "Representative Democracy with Limited Participation"

The changes in the social structure under a "limited democracy" were often only slightly more pronounced than those induced by the "enlightened" dictatorships. In other cases, however, the modification was more substantial. This happened chiefly when the modernizing attitudes of the elites were bolder and the resulting economic and cultural changes more profound. In some cases the contribution of massive immigration from Europe—a part of the modernizing policy of the elite—was a decisive element in the transformation of the social structure.

The most significant feature of this stage is the formal functioning of democracy, the existence of a party system, the periodical replacement of the government through elections, freedom of the press and other "constitutional" guarantees. Another and no less essential feature is the "limitation" of democracy to only a fraction of the total population. This limitation is twofold. On the one hand the existing deep cleavage between developed and backward areas within a given country involved the almost complete exclusion of a substantial proportion of the population, practically all those living in the "peripheral" areas. On the other hand, a similar cleavage existed within the "central" areas, between the elites and the emerging middle strata, on the one side, and the lower groups on the other. Often the cleavage had also an ethnic basis even if we cannot speak of "racial" discrimination in Latin America. Both kinds of cleavage—geographical and social—meant the lack of a common basis for a real national identification on the part of a substantial proportion of the population, and of course a lack of cultural and economic participation. In consequence, the functioning of democracy was really limited in the sense that only the higher strata and the small newly formed middle groups (which identified themselves with the elite) living in the "central areas" did participate in one way or another in the political process (even at the lowest level of simple voting).

However, in those countries where the middle occupational strata could expand to a higher proportion of the total population, and because of their immigrant origin, or their economic and cultural significance or some other causes, were able to acquire a greater psychological and social autonomy, strong political movements appeared which strove for a more real and enlarged democracy. In general such a situation was reached only in the most advanced areas of the country.

STAGE 5. "Representative Democracy with Enlarged Participation"

The typical structure corresponding to this stage is still that of the dual society referred to previously, involving the geographical juxtaposition of a modern "central region" and "backward" peripheral regions. The former comprising most of the urban population, the industry, the literates, the middle strata and the modern urban proletariat, including, of course, the industrial workers. This region would contrast sharply with other regions which still remained—even though to a lesser degree—outside this development. Democracy, social, cultural and political participation, as well as national identification, included mostly people residing in the "advanced" areas. The difference from the previous stage of "limited" democracy is that now not only the middle strata would usually participate directly in the government or even control it, but the urban proletariat of the "central" region would also be included through the unions and political parties. The spread of nationalism—right and left—and of different "ideologies of industrialization" are characteristic of this phase.

STAGE 6 (A). "Representative Democracy with Total Participation"

With the growing integration of previously marginal social groups and geographical areas into the cultural, economic and political life of the nation as a whole, with the acquisition of national loyalties and identification by all the inhabitants, and with the resulting higher degree of cultural and economic homogeneity of the various groups in society, we reach a new stage which we may call, for lack of a better term, that of "full nationhood". A high degree of urbanization, total literacy and a high average education, a high degree of occupational differentiation and a high proportion of the urban occupational middle strata which may now well be nearly 50% of the active urban employed population, are the other well known traits which characterize such a stage.

While in older nations, cultural homogeneity and national loyalty may not be accompanied by a high degree of economic development, in most instances "mass consumption"—that is, mass participation in the material culture of the industrial society—may also be regarded as one of the traits of the phase of "total participation democracy". From the political point of view it means effective full citizenship for the entire population, irrespective of area of residence or of socio-economic or ethnic affiliation. As a result, an important indicator of this stage is that of political participation at the level of voting of a substantial majority of the adult population of both sexes [2].

STAGE 6 (B). Total Participation through "National-Popular" Revolutions

This pattern, which is increasingly typical of many underdeveloped countries—either under the form of communist totalitarianism or under the form of nationalistic authoritarianism—has also appeared in Latin America. It is obvious that the kind of

---

[2] The phenomenon of 'non-voting' and 'political apathy' which appear in some developed countries (as the U.S.A. for instance) has a different meaning from the non-participation of the marginal and isolated sectors in underdeveloped countries.

"political participation" which takes place in the framework of such "national-popular" regimes is quite different from that of "representative democracy". However, it would be a mistake not to recognize the tremendous change involved for the marginal strata of the "dual" underdeveloped society.

While the national popular regime negates the very values which are the basis of participation in "representative democracy"—such as civil liberties—it does incorporate the marginal strata into the economic, cultural and political life of the nation. It induces their forceful "nationalization", and results in a change from passive acceptance (through internalized norms) to "compulsory participation". In Latin America, perhaps more than in other countries, "national-popular" regimes appear to be the outcome of the failure to develop into a full "representative democracy". From this point of view such an outcome appears to be connected with the failure in the formation of adequate channels of political expression for the social groups which successively emerge from the isolation and marginality in which they lived within the traditional social structure.

Such seems to have been the role of both "limited" and "enlarged" democracy: to prepare the institutional means and adequate outlets for the political pressure of the emerging larger strata of the population, within the framework of "representative democracy". Obviously, this is not only a political problem. The successful integration into such a framework also requires an expanding and modernizing economy, at least sufficient to give, even at a very modest level, an increasing degree of participation in the material culture of the industrial civilisation, and this latter requirement is certainly more acute today than it was in the countries of Europe in which development occurred earlier.

If "limited democracy" is to succeed in the role we have mentioned, at least two conditions must be met. Firstly, the regime must be stable enough and last long enough to allow the establishment of a party system adequate for the expression of the increasing popular participation. Secondly, the "revolution in aspiration" must be to a certain extent synchronous with the economic and technical possibility of raising the level of living of the population. If both conditions are not satisfied, the chances are very high that political participation will be reached through one kind or another of "national-popular" revolutions. The marginality or the complete isolation of these larger strata of the population explains the greater stability achieved in the past by "limited" democracy both in Latin America and elsewhere. The chances of such stability are decreasing very sharply today and for a country whose socio-economic development has been retarded for one reason or another, political participation is more likely to take the form of a "national-popular revolution" than that of a "limited" or even "enlarged" democracy.

Considering now the present situation of the 20 Latin American Republics we find examples of most of the "stages" just described, with the obvious exception of the first, and (perhaps) the second, stage. The "contemporaneity of the non-contemporaneous" certainly does apply to present Latin America, even if qualifications must be made for the peculiar historical circumstances of each country; and for the fact that certain changes would affect every country irrespective of their general socio-economic conditions. It is true, furthermore, that we do not find here a strict correlation between the political and the total social structure, or, as was pointed out earlier, with the type and extent of military intervention. But let us insist on the purely descriptive character of our typologies. They are no more than devices for introducing some order in a rather confusing and contradictory picture.

There can be little doubt that while "representative democracy" did reach—at least during certain periods of their history—a fairly high degree of stability in the countries we have classified at the top of Table I (Groups *A* and *B*), it never appeared or else it failed to attain a comparable duration and stability in the other two groups (*C* and *D*). But, of course, many inconsistencies both apparent and real appear all along the continuum from minimum to maximum national and socio-economic development as defined according to the criteria adopted.

With the possible exception of Colombia, and to a lesser degree and more recently, of Venezuela, Peru and Ecuador, it can be safely stated that most of the 14 countries included in the two

lower groups have failed to escape the vicious circle of dictatorships, brief attempts (or none at all) at "limited" democracy,
succession crises (in general under the form of military "coups"),
even if at one time or another some more "enlightened" autocracy may have introduced a certain degree of "modernization",
at least in opening the country to foreign capital and enterprises
to exploit the local resources in raw materials. These combinations have often proved to be stable enough—small groups of big
landowners, mainly military autocrats, and foreign investors.
Such is clearly the case of the Dominican Republic, Haiti, Nicaragua, Honduras, El Salvador, Paraguay, and we may note that
their present social structure is fairly consistent with their political history and actual situation. Of the other countries, Colombia
—with a relatively high proportion of middle occupational strata
—has managed to maintain for a longer time a more stable
"limited democracy", but even so gravely perturbed by the
chronic civil wars between political factions. Venezuela showed
the first symptom of changes towards representative democracy
after the long dictatorship of Gomez. Its first freely elected government (1946) had a short duration and only in recent years a
new attempt at a "representative democracy" is being made.
Similar processes can be seen in the other countries.

It is not surprising that it is precisely in this area that in the
last decade there have been at least three "national-popular"
revolutions (Bolivia, Cuba and Guatemala), and that presently
the attempts at "representative democracy" of the new civilian
regimes of Peru, Ecuador, Venezuela and Colombia encounter
such great difficulties in the face of the growing pressure of the
previously marginal strata, which the rapid urbanization and the
growth in communication media are so swiftly displacing from a
passive to an active role. While the ruling class may perhaps be
ready to accept the functioning of a "limited" democracy, they
are certainly not disposed or prepared to accept an enlarged
participation with all its economic and social implications. The
chances of incorporating the new strata—statistically the great
majority of the population—into the framework of a representative democracy are greatly impaired not only by this opposition,
but also by the relatively politically "anomic" situation in which

these vast social groups find themselves because of the lack of adequate channels of expression of their political aims within the existing party system. The legitimacy of the regime is frequently at stake and its stability greatly diminished.

The six countries of the first two groups fit rather closely into our scheme of the transition. All of them had their period of anarchy, centralizing autocracies, limited democracies and, now, enlarged democracies. The modern urban proletariat and the urban middle strata form the human basis of such regimes. In Mexico and Brazil, while both groups only constitute a relatively low proportion of the total population, their heavy concentration in the cities and in certain regions within each country explains their dominant role in political life. But although with many peculiarities "representative democracy" can be said to function at present in these countries, they do offer contrasts as to the degree of stability and degree of interference of the military in civilian affairs.

Perhaps the contrast between Argentina and the other countries is the most disturbing fact. While Argentina may be considered as the most "advanced" as a national state on the basis of the usual indicators, it is also the most unstable and disturbed. After more than 60 years of continued functioning of a representative democracy, and having passed from a limited to an enlarged level without major troubles, it has relapsed in the last three decades into military revolutions, a decennial dictatorship and the very uneasy democracy of the post-Peronian period. There is, however, a difference. While most of these countries are certainly to be considered as "enlarged" democracies, the situation of Argentina can be better described as one of recent transition into a—as yet unstable—"total participation" democracy. Its very instability as compared with the greater stability of the other countries can be interpreted, at least partially, as one effect of this difficult transition. The level of voting is certainly suggestive of such an interpretation. If we consider the proportion of voters in the total adult population we find a sharp contrast between Argentina on the one hand and Mexico, Chile and Brazil on the other. While in Argentina the percentage of voters in the total adult population (20 years and more) is over 80%

(and if we take, according to the legal definition, persons of 18 years and older it is still 75%), in Mexico (1958) it is 48%, in Brazil (1960) 40%, in Chile (1958) 34%. We must also remember that if we discount the foreign residents, who in Argentina are around 15% (adult age groups), the proportion of participants would be even higher. In the remaining countries the foreign residents are a very low proportion and would not make any significant difference.

We are not assuming that the proportion of voters is a cause of instability; we are using it as an indicator of the level of functioning of democracy and of integration into national society: here it is sufficient to mention countries such as England (80%, 1951), Australia (86%, 1949) or Canada (74%, 1949). We have used as a uniform basis for comparison: percentage of voters on total population of 20 years and more. It cannot be denied that the low proportion of voters in countries such as Brazil, Mexico and Chile simply means that a considerable sector of the adult population is not yet integrated into the national body. The rural dweller, the peasant isolated in his small community, is certainly less politically relevant than the industrial worker in the cities, and his role continues to be more a passive than an active one. This integration is certainly a fact in contemporary Argentina and here we must take into account the historical circumstances which caused the partial failure of the "enlarged" democracy to create an institutional framework for the smooth functioning of a representative regime at a total level of participation, in order to understand the apparent "paradox" of this country, relatively so advanced (within the Latin American continent) and still in the grip of continuous military intervention.

While it would not be safe to make any prediction, it is reasonable to think that the greater stability enjoyed by both "limited" and, later on, "enlarged" representative democracy in Chile, the strong traditions which have been formed through its long political experience and the more firmly established party system (in comparison with Argentina) will be great assets in the transition from the present "enlarged" participation, to the coming level of "total" participation. But, in any case, in all the five countries, with their rapid rate of urbanization and the even more rapid spread of communication, the incorporation of the still marginal groups is imminent. It will involve a great strain on the present institutions and, as the cases of Vargas and Peron show very clearly, they will not be immune from the possibility of "national-popular" solutions.

The role of the military in Latin America must be understood in this rather complex picture. If we conceive it as related both to the kind of political system and to its *degree* of stability, then we must expect everywhere in Latin America and at all levels of socio-economic and national development the possibility of some intromission of the military into civilian affairs. In fact, some degree of stability can be reached in most of the transition stages, even at the "backward" one of centralizing autocracy; and conversely instability may appear even at the most "advanced" level of "enlarged" democracy if its corresponding social and political requirements are not adequately satisfied.

Let us formulate now a typology of institutional civil-military relations and relate them to the different particular situations of the Latin American countries [3].

1. *The classical military garrison state.* This form develops typically in response to real or imagined external factors. No example of such Spartan organization is to be found in Latin America, where cases of truly serious and devastating wars of sufficient duration to work fundamental institutional change are extremely scarce. The major exception is the Paraguayan War of the last century, but social conditions in that country were insufficiently advanced to permit of the establishment of a truly centralized garrison state, despite the devastating nature of the armed conflict itself.

[3] For a narrower version of this typology and other suggested categorizations of Latin American politics, see K. H. Silvert, Political Change in Latin America, *in* Herbert MATTHEWS, ed., *The United States and Latin America* (New York, The American Assembly, 1959). Also refer to the March 1961 issue of *The Annals of the American Academy of Political and Social Science,* entitled *Latin America's Nationalist Revolutions,* for other pertinent and recent information.

2. *The modern totalitarian garrison state*. This phenomenon is still, fortunately, an evil dream of imaginative writers, for
no historical examples are to be found anywhere. The low state
of the technological arts everywhere in Latin America makes this
development at present impossible for these republics.

3. *The totalitarian politico-military relations*. This pattern
of relationships inextricably intertwines political and military
functions within a monolithic public organization, as in Nazi Germany. Once again the insufficiencies of Latin America's technological state have to date prevented the formation of modern,
totalitarian states, although such a country as Argentina is beginning to approach at least the material ability to include such a
solution within its array of social possibilities. The "national-
popular" revolutions have not attained so far this politico-military structure and one reason may be the technical underdevelopment of their bureaucratic organization. On the other
hand, the rapid extension of radio, television, and other media of
mass communication heightens this possibility as the unilateral
dependence on weapons alone for social control in extreme cases
thus becomes less necessary.

4. *The military as institutionalized governors*. This kind of
authoritarianism is very common in Latin America, and is a
persistent form from the earliest days of independence to the
present day. The existence of the armed forces as an organized
and ostensibly efficacious group in administrative affairs has
tempted to the simple transposition of personnel from military to
governmental functions and to subsequent rule as *de facto* and
eventually *de jure* governors. Given the long-standing tradition
of military privileges (from the colonial period) and military
participation (from independence wars) in Latin America, such
a pattern is likely to appear whenever the political instability
reaches a point at which the social legitimacy of a regime or a
government is no longer accepted by the major relevant groups
within the society. Such a situation may happen, as we noted
earlier, at every level of the transitional process. It is obvious why
it would predominate during the early days of independence and
the years of confusion and anarchy which followed the failure in

establishing modern states in the liberated colonial territories. And it still predominates in the more retarded countries such as the Dominican Republic, Honduras, Haiti and Nicaragua, in all of which the structure of traditional society has changed very little. But it is small wonder that relatively more advanced countries such as Argentina from the early thirties and, in very recent years, Colombia and Venezuela have experienced the same phenomenon. Here the instability must be related, as we indicated before, to a different underlying situation. The crucial common ground of all these cases is an irreconcilable division among the various politically relevant groups, and the lack of shared norms regarding political activity. The military, clearly and loyally, has usually worked in conjunction with important civilian elements, serving as an arm for the maintenance of group interest. History belies the simplistic belief that such alliances have always been between the most conservative groups and the military. On many important occasions organized military might has been brought to bear to promote the interests of new industrial agglomerations against the pretensions of landed Conservatives and sometimes even the Church. During certain periods of Mexico's growth, for example, the military in combination with civilians contributed heavily to the social experimentation characterizing that country from 1917 until 1940 at least. This important category of events needs, thus, to be subdivided in accordance with the civilian allegiances and ideological orientations of the military, and the resultant effects on the total socio-economic and political structures.

5. *The military as trustee governors.* As naked military intervention becomes increasingly viewed as shameful, this phenomenon has increased in incidence. There are two notable recent cases, that of the Provisional Government of General Pedro Eugenio Aramburu in Argentina (1955–1958), and that of Admiral Wolfgang Larrazabal in Venezuela (1958–1959). Both governments arose after the fall of dictators, both of whom had risen out of the ranks of the military and subsequently were deposed by the military in combination with civilian groups. Aramburu and Larrazabal committed themselves to "cushion"

governments, *interregna* permitting the formation of parties, the holding of legal elections, and the installation of civilian authorities.

6. *The military as orienters of national policy.* This very subtle manifestation involves the exercise of power not on the immediately visible scene but rather in the fashion of a grey eminence. The military in this situation attempt to establish the broad policy limits within which civilian activity may express itself, the sanction for disobedience obviously being deposition of the legally constituted authorities. The significant Mexican developments mentioned above are, in all their real complexity, a combination of this category with the two immediately preceding. Whether or not the Mexican armed forces still effectively limit the freedom of the Mexican Government is a matter of some debate, especially given the strength of the single official party of Mexico and the very wide distribution of the civilian sectors supporting this party system and the incumbent governors [4]. Perhaps the clearest, most evident case of tutelary military behavior can be seen now in Argentina, where the military overtly acts to contain the policies of the Government, openly threatens coups, publicly debates political policies, and on occasion even moves troops to back its demands on the civilian governors. Military budgets are holy, and officers of the armed forces in a limited retirement occupy many important administrative positions in the civil service.

7. *The military as pressure group with veto power.* This rather standard manifestation of military power in many devel-

---

[4] Oscar Lewis, in his "Mexico Since Cardenas", *in* Lyman BRYSON, ed., *Social Change in Latin America Today* (New York, Harper, 1960), pp. 301–302, writes:

"A comparison of the allocations of federal funds to the various departments over the four presidential administrations from Cardenas to Ruiz Cortines reveals [. . .] some highly significant trends. Especially marked is the sharp decrease in the proportion of funds allocated to national defense, reflecting the demise of *caudillismo* as a serious factor in Mexican life. Adolfo Ruiz Cortines was the first president since the 1920's who did not depend heavily on either the national or a private army to maintain his control."

Professor Lewis then points out that between 1935 and 1940 defense expenditures absorbed 17.3 percent of the national budget, dropping to 8.1 percent in the period 1953–1956.

oped countries is still little seen in Latin America, except possibly in the case of Chile. In this situation the military institution has the power to prevent antagonistic civilian action undertaken against it, but cannot initiate independent action or policy in fields outside of its range of professional interest.

8. *The military as simple pressure group*. This stage, the last before the military fades away into complete subordination to the civil authorities, is probably the status of the armed forces of Uruguay alone among the Latin American republics. The very special circumstances of Uruguay's past offer some apparently reasonable explanations of this phenomenon. A buffer state lying between two relatively powerful neighbors, Brazil and Argentina, Uruguay has never been able realistically to dream of armed exploits. Further, the country is politically a city-state, a fact which has contributed to the early development of what can truly be called a "bourgeois" society (in the primitive sense of the term). Moreover, a high degree of political involvement of the citizenry has created areas of civil power not conducive to military adventures.

9. *The military as simple police force in complete subordination to the government*. Costa Rica prides itself on having this kind of civil-military pattern, and is even wont to deny the existence of an army altogether, stating that the civil force is in truth merely a police agency. If the situation is not really such a pure subordination of the armed forces to the civil authorities, still the case offers a reasonable approximation. Once more circumstances unique for Latin America have brought about this situation. Costa Rica was unattractive to early Spanish colonizers, for it had a small indigenous population and no readily available minerals. As a result the Costa Rican central valley was an area of slow and secondary settlement, peopled by persons who had to work the land themselves. This emergence of a landed peasantry permitted the development of a type of "bourgeoisie" (in the figurative sense of the word) which, as in the case of Uruguay, has had long experience in the organization and application of its power to the detriment of armed pretenders.

10. *The military as political arm of the state*. This pattern, obviously closely related to the idealized versions of the functions

of the Red Army of the USSR and of the various "People's Armies" invariably tends to emerge from revolutionary situations of the left. The Arevalo-Arbenz Governments of Guatemala (1945–1954) and the present Governments of Cuba and Bolivia are the only three cases in Latin America of frankly leftist politics, albeit of different colors. In the Guatemalan case no serious attempts were made to turn the military into an active arm of the government; instead, especially during the interrupted term of President (and Lt. Col.) Jacobo Arbenz Guzman, the design was to keep the army small and the officer corps highly contented. According to available report, the Castro Government has broken the professional army by investing civilian militias with great power and by politicizing the officer corps of the regular forces. This procedure was also used in Bolivia with the establishment some eight years ago of an armed civilian militia whose primary function was to counterbalance the regular army.

what about
11. Military – professional role, subord. to pol. policy
U.S.

Military intervention in civilian affairs, as is suggested by this typology, clearly does not occur either in an ideational vacuum or in the absence of a sometimes very wide range of interests and pressures. Military politics inevitably and invariably involve identification with wider social interests and ideologies. The patterning of these identifications depends in important measure on the social origins of the officer corps and the social mobility functions which the military institution may serve. Unfortunately there are almost no reliable data available on these questions. From subjective evaluations and informal observation, however, one may suspect a considerable variation in the social origins of officer groups from country to country, and a consequent variation in the political identification of the military. It is also entirely evident that there must be great variation in the opportunities for upward social mobility offered by differing armed forces. Wide differences in budgets and in the sizes of the military establishments must affect mobility, of course, as do generalized social attitudes concerning the prestige of the military [5].

A relatively safe generalization is that throughout Latin America the sons of middle class families are more attracted to the military than are the sons of the upper groups. The result often has been to split the ideological unity of the military, to create inter-service rivalries as well as intra-service discord. This growing fragmentation must be projected against the increasing complexity of Latin American society itself, affected as it is by economic development, changing world ideological currents, and rapidly growing industrial urbanization. Because nowhere in Latin America—even in famed Uruguay and Costa Rica—are the institutional patterns of secular and impersonal representative democracy fully established, many civilian groups are innately revolutionary in their attitudes and predisposed to the use of force as an inherent and thus desirable part of the social pattern. Both military schisms and military adventures are encouraged by the civilian groups soliciting armed aid for their political ambitions. Even though the following quotation concerns the Spain of the 1930's, it is valid for the Latin American arena as well:

[5] *The Statistical Abstract of Latin America 1960* (Center of Latin American Studies, University of California in Los Angeles), p. 32, offers some partial and tentative figures on the percentage of Latin American budgets devoted to defense expenditures. The data are incomplete for all countries.

Country	Percentage of National Budget	Year
Mexico	11,3	1958
Costa Rica	3,8	1958
El Salvador	10,2	1958
Guatemala	8,8	1958
Honduras	11,7	1957
Haïti	19,1	1957
Argentina	21,1	1958
Brazil	27,6	1958
Chile	21,9	1958
Colombia	5,7	1958
Ecuador	21,6	1957
Peru	23,2	1958
Venezuela	9,5	1959

These figures are admittedly tenuous, and probably err on the low side, of course.

No doubt the generals in 1936 thought they were saving Spain [. . .] The State must be capable of embodying and responding to what Maura called the vital forces of the community. Otherwise, as he warned repeatedly, the army will claim to embody the national will in order to enforce changes which political institutions are impotent to encompass. Above all, no democrat, repeating the follies of the progressive and moderate minorities, can appeal to the sword rather than to conviction, however slow the educative process may be. Though the Republic of 1931 came in on a vote, many Republicans were willing to see it come in through the army. Repeating the tactics of Ruiz Zorrilla, they systematically undermined the loyalty of the army. Some saw the danger. 'I would prefer no Republic to a Republic conceived in the womb of the army.' Many did not. How could they complain when other forces tampered with the loyalty of the army in 1936 [6]?

The military will be reduced to their barracks and their professional functions alone only when Latin American countries develop sufficiently complicated power structures and a society sufficiently flexible and integrated; when social and geographical discontinuities have been greatly lessened and isolated or marginal masses incorporated into the national body; when economic and social conflicts have found institutionalized expression within a common framework of shared norms.

[6] A. R. M. Carr, "Spain", in Michael HOWARD, ed., Soldiers and Governments: Nine Studies in Civil-Military Relations (London, Eyre and Spottiswoode, 1957) , pp. 145–146.

Peru: The Politics
of Structured Violence *– gap. from labor unions*

1965

JAMES PAYNE

At first glance Peruvian politics presents a chaotic scene to the political analyst. Demonstrations, riots, rebellions, electoral irregularities, *coups* and dictatorships: the political panorama unfolds so rapidly that there seems to be nothing permanent on which to base an analysis.

The recent political history of Peru has been kaleidoscopic. From 1939 to 1945 the country experienced a repressive government under Manuel Prado. In 1945 elections were held and a period of free government under Jose Luis Bustamante y Rivero ensued. In 1948 Bustamante was removed through a military *coup* and General Manuel Odria headed a dictatorship which lasted until 1956. Elections were held and Manuel Prado took office as President of a free regime once again. In 1962 his term was ended a few days short of the constitutional six-year period by another military *coup* which grew out of the election crisis. A military government—which observed political freedoms—ruled for one year, elections were held again, and Fernando Belaunde Terry emerged as President of a free regime in 1963.

It might seem, after gazing at this record, that the pattern of Peruvian politics is simply incoherent, that there are no regularities. The problem lies, however, in defining the system to be analyzed. An American, familiar with the regular constitutional

Reprinted from The Journal of Politics, 27 *(May 1965)*, *362–374, by permission of the author and the publisher.*

procedures of the United States, tends to look at the same institutions in Peru. Finding these practices atrophied or abused, he would become discouraged, concluding lamely that the *system* is 'unstable' or 'perverted.' But his discouragement and his lame conclusions are simply the result of adopting an inadequate theoretical perspective.

Analytically it is impractical to view Peruvian politics in a constitutional framework, for constitutionalism is not the modal pattern of interaction. To treat violence and the military *coup* as aberrations places one in the awkward position of insisting that practically all significant political events of the past half-century are deviations. Demonstrations, clashes with the police, military take-overs: these are *normal* in a purely descriptive sense. They happen frequently and they are significant.

Consequently, we must identify as a system for analysis the pattern of interaction characterized by violence and other extra-constitutional practices. In the same way that elections are central components of a constitutional democracy the military *coup* is considered essential to the functioning of the system in Peru. Riots are fully a part of the Peruvian pattern, not merely distasteful, peripheral incidents—as they are considered in the United States. When we make violence the focal point of analysis the behavior of the participants becomes understandable and—over a certain range—predictable.

In treating Peruvian politics in a short essay we must narrow down our scope of concern. Two explicit restrictions are placed on our analysis. First we shall deal with patterns of decision-making in which violence plays an immediate, critical role. Such issues include: most labor disputes, both specific wage demands and many general laws on such subjects as discharge and length of the working day; some university student-administration (or faculty) conflicts; numerous specific agrarian conflicts (land occupation by peasants, strikes of plantation workers) ; occasional conflicts over the cost-of-living in general or over prices of specific commodities (cement, meat, gasoline) ; and certain positions involving foreign policy which organizations of journalists and lawyers as well as workers and students might seek to defend violently in a particular case.

Deciding such violence-connected issues is a substantial part of the activity of government, and as such these cases merit study. In addition, an understanding of these cases is extremely useful in analyzing most of the other decisions of government, since decisions on most non-violent issues are made with the possibility of future violence in mind. For example, the decision made in late 1961 to raise the export tax on fishmeal—opposed by both the producers and the longshoremen's union—was not accompanied by violence. But decision-makers were influenced by the knowledge that to disappoint the longshoremen would engender their animosity and make future violence more probable. By analyzing the decision-making process on issues of violence we thereby gain insights into many other decisions as well. However, we make no attempt to give a complete account of all patterns of conflict resolution.

We shall further limit our analysis to a discussion of interaction during a free regime. A "free regime" may be defined as characterized by the actual freedom of all major political parties and interest groups to exist and operate, and the actual observance of freedoms of speech, press and public protest. Naturally, as in the United States, these freedoms are not absolute; nevertheless there is a wide difference in the degree to which these freedoms are observed in a free regime and in what may be termed a "dictatorship." It should be pointed out that our conception of a "free regime" does not include the idea of permanence. It is simply one phase of a global pattern.

Under a free regime groups may organize and communicate. They may mobilize opinion and gain adherents. Under a free regime groups are able to develop and stage violent attacks upon the government.

The violence to which we refer is not random or isolated; it is politically-structured violence, violence which is meaningful in the political context. In the Peruvian context politically significant violence must have the following characteristics: 1) it must be directed against significant political leaders and/or parties. In nearly all cases the object of the attack will be the President; 2) it must involve a prominent political issue on which there is wide disagreement. A simple murder, for example, does not have these properties and consequently it is not politically relevant.

In its ultimate form structured violence involves a physical attack upon agents of the government over some issue of political concern. An illustration is provided by the assault of the Congressional building in October, 1961 which occurred during the strike of the public school teachers. A group of about 300 demonstrators rushed at the entrance, the guards fired, the demonstrators fled, but one lay behind, killed by a bullet. Were this event isolated it would have been generally condemned as either silly or repugnant. But because it was structured within the political context it had highly significant repercussions.

The teachers' strike—during which this episode occurred—had become a national issue. Opposition parties and newspapers, along with the left-extremists (Communists, Trotskyites, and others) had condemned the government for its stinginess. When the demonstrator was killed it was taken as proof of the cruelty of the government. In spite of the decree suspending Constitutional guarantees (which formally prohibited all public gatherings) a gigantic funeral demonstration was held. Striking teachers joined opposition forces and gathered in the Parque Universitario. The situation was explosive. The slightest incident would have led to a massacre of serious proportions. The army troops carefully kept their distance, waiting in side streets away from the crowd. On this occasion the demonstration ended peacefully. But it could easily have been otherwise.

Uncertainty, as the reader can see from this example, is a feature of this structured violence. No one knows exactly when violence will take place. But all the participants are acutely aware of the relative probabilities of violence occurring at any particular moment. In this sense the violence is structured. Each event bears a relationship to the next so that we must speak of a pattern and not of isolated events. The congressional attack had serious overtones because it led to an even more explosive situation. But the attack in turn had its antecedents in earlier demonstrations, in newspaper invective, in opposition party meetings, in extremist activity on the issue, in the hunger strikes of some teachers, and so on. Structured violence, then, is an entire pattern of interaction, the end product of which is significant physical violence directed against the government.

Why does this pattern exist? How does violence fit into the

processes of decision-making and leadership change? These are the questions which we shall attempt to answer. Our discussion will center around five propositions about political interaction during a period of free government:

1. The conflict for control of the Presidency is intense.

2. Opposition forces are disposed to employ extreme methods to destroy an incumbent President—including the use of physical violence.

3. The armed forces will remove a President when widespread "dissatisfaction" exists and incidents of violence become frequent.

4. The President, when his tenure is threatened by the use of violence, will attempt to prevent violence by making concessions to those groups which threaten its use.

5. Therefore politically structured violence is a highly effective weapon for those groups which can employ it.

The underlying drive for the Peruvian system—the mainspring, as it were—is the intensity of the conflict between the opposition and the President. Opposition forces do not view politics as a gentleman's game played for moderate stakes in an atmosphere of restraint. They see it as a struggle of overwhelming significance. The intensity of conflict explains, in large part, the frequent use of violence. Opposition forces see the outcome of this struggle against the executive as *more significant* than constitutional norms, moral injunctions or physical safety. We have in American history occasional examples of conflict so intense that it transcended the usual moral and constitutional norms—the Civil War, for example. But in Peru such intense conflict is not occasional; it is the permanent condition of political society.

We may briefly suggest certain conditions which produce this high level of conflict intensity between opposition forces and the President.

1. The Peruvian government is, and has been since colonial times, highly centralized. At the apex of the system is the President. State and municipal governments, Congress and the courts are, in practice, subordinate to him. The chief executive can and does issue authoritative decrees on almost every conceivable subject. As a consequence of this centralization the President

is considered omni-competent and hence, omni-responsible. From the price of meat to the backwardness of agriculture; from holes in streets of a provincial town to the profit rate in the mining industry: when anything goes wrong the executive is considered to have committed a sin of commission or omission.

Needless to say things do go wrong, many things. And the affected groups hold the incumbent President responsible. In a free environment the dissatisfied sectors will organize and concentrate their opposition on a single point: the executive. Whereas in most of the established Western democracies opposition is directed at diverse points in the various decision-making matrices, in Peru the President and his immediate subordinates, being the only decision-makers of consequence, receive its full impact.[1]

In addition to broadening the responsibility for policies, a dispersal of the decision-making processes also serves in countries like the United States to mitigate the opposition to the existing regime. Because opposition forces have, in one way or another, a foothold in the existing system, because they are contained within the government, their hostility to it is never total. In the United States a Southerner may be disappointed with the incumbent President, but he knows that he can make his views felt in the Senate as well as in local decision-making and administration. But in Peru a group excluded from the executive has no other arena in which to exercise influence. Consequently such a group finds its only practicable alternative is that of attempting to unseat the President.

Groups which formed a permanent opposition during the

---

[1] It is interesting to note that Alexis de Tocqueville, in discussing the causes of the French Revolution, noted a similar centralization under the *ancien regime:* "In times of dearth—and these were frequent in the eighteenth century—everyone expected the Intendant to come to the rescue as a matter of course. For the government was held responsible for all the misfortunes befalling the community; even when these were 'acts of God' such as floods or droughts, the powers-that-be were blamed for them." *The Old Regime and the French Revolution* (Doubleday, 1955), p. 71. In discussing the stability of the American system, de Tocqueville praised the federal arrangement which insured that "political passion, instead of spreading over the land like a fire on the prairies, spends its strength against the interests and individual passions of every State." *Democracy in America* (Mentor, 1956), p. 85.

Prado government (1956–62) included the Popular Action Party of Belaunde, the Odria Party, the Christian Democratic Party, seven left-extremist groups—Communists, two Trotskyite factions, the APRA Rebelde, the Progressive Socialists, the Leninist Committee and the Socialists—as well as interest groups in which these parties had a controlling position: the Federation of Students of San Marcos University, the Federation of Bank Clerks, the Lima Union of Construction Workers and a number of others. Consistent with their position of isolation these groups maintained a posture of total opposition to the President.

2. The large amount of patronage which the President dispenses is another factor contributing to the isolation and intensity of the opposition. Whereas in a country like Sweden or Switzerland few posts go to political appointees, in Peru the civil service is based largely on the spoils system. Job hunters (and their friends and relatives) are numerous. In the above-named countries a change of government leaves public employees practically unaffected; in Peru it creates a horde of angered ex-office holders who see the new President as directly responsible for their loss of employment.

3. Another condition which contributes to the intense conflict found in Peruvian society is the existence of exclusive, partisan communication patterns. Holders of different political views tend to locate themselves in the communication channel which reinforces their position. This phenomenon is most clearly seen in the case of the Aprista party organization. The Apristas have their own cafeteria and barber shop, their own medical assistance staff, soccer teams, and party newspaper, *La Tribuna*. In addition there are numerous secondary groups within the party: university students, workers, high school students, artists, lawyers, and so on. Hence an Aprista may live within the party's world and never have his party loyalty weakened by contradictory communications. The other parties, to varying degrees, tend to provide their adherents with similar unified opinion environments.[2]

[2] The analysis here draws upon the general theory of cross-pressures and attitude formation. For specific reference to the problem of political conflict see: David B. Truman, *The Governmental Process* (New York, 1960), pp. 157 ff., 507 ff.; Sigmund Neumann, *Modern Political Parties* (Chicago, 1956), p. 404; Seymour Martin Lipset, *Political Man*, (Anchor, 1963), pp. 74–79.

Two of the three major Lima newspapers, *La Prensa* and *El Comercio,* are part of the partisan channels of communication. The former supported the government in the period 1959–1962, the latter attacked it with skill and venom. Those individuals who sided with the opposition found in *El Comercio* a copious supply of criticism and invective which served to reinforce their dissatisfaction with the Prado government.[3]

Political conflict in Peru, then, is intense and bi-polar: between the In's and the Out's. Those groups which are excluded from the executive become intensely opposed to the incumbent President and are willing to take extreme measures to depose him. Centralization places in the hands of the President practically all formal decision-making power; consequently he is a significant target. Excluded from this pin-point of power opposition forces have no alternative but to work for his downfall. Deprived of patronage and reinforced in their animosity by partisan channels of communication, opposition groups see the destruction of the President as a noble and necessary task.

The visitor to Peru does not pass many days in the country before grasping the polarized nature of political conflict and the intensity of the opposition to the executive. A chat with a taxi driver, a newspaper headline: the American soon realizes that politics is a serious, even deadly, business. The desire to destroy the incumbent President is of paramount significance. The intensity with which this objective is pursued results not only in the use of violence, as we have suggested, but also in the formation of seemingly incongruent alliances. The Christian Democratic Party (in the opposition in 1961) had a peasant affairs bureau which worked closely with members of the Trotskyite and Rebel APRA parties who were attempting to foment a revolution through rural violence. That the Pope's sworn enemies should walk hand-

[3] The third Lima daily, *La Cronica,* was more mass consumption-oriented and tended to avoid partisan political issues. The television stations were also relatively nonpolitical, again apparently because they were attempting to reach the largest possible audience and thus realize the greatest return on their investment. One might expect that *El Comercio* and *La Prensa* may also be forced by economic necessity to 'tone down' partisan politics. For a discussion of the relationship between political cleavage, economic variables and the mass media the reader should consult Otto Kirchheimer, "The Waning of Opposition in Parliamentary Regimes," *Social Research,* Vol. 24, No. 2 (1956), pp. 149–150.

in-hand with his disciples testifies to the overwhelming importance of the struggle against the executive in the eyes of these
participants.

The picture, as far as we have presented it, leaves out an
important component: the armed forces. They maintain the chief
executive in office; they protect him from the enraged opposition.
The guards one finds outside the homes of most high officials are
mute testimony to the military's role. And when demonstrations
and riots reach excessive proportions, it is the Army which contains and disperses the mobs.

Although the armed forces tend to establish broad limits to
the actions of the executive, they are characteristically uninter-
ested in details of policy. What they are interested in is peace. It
is incorrect to suppose that the military is the enemy of peaceful
free government. Direct military intervention in politics has
taken place only in times of acute crisis, in times when civilian
political conflict threatened to lead to dangerous extremes. The
military *coup* of July, 1962, is a case in point. None of the three
major presidential candidates—Odria, Haya de la Torre, and
Belaunde—obtained the requisite one-third of the ballots for
election. Belaunde, seeing his position was weakest, agitated for
annulment of the elections on the grounds of fraud. He was
joined by the extremists and *El Comercio*. The other two candidates could not agree—until it was too late—on a coalition. After
civilian politicians had struggled for nearly a month and produced only greater uncertainty, the armed forces stepped in and
put an end to the chaotic scene.

The logic of the situation dictates that intervention should
occur at such times of crisis. The armed forces, composed of
different factions holding conflicting ideological and political
sympathies, can act unanimously only if the civilian government
has demonstrated its inability to keep order. When things are
going along smoothly an attempted *coup* by one faction would be
opposed by other factions of the armed forces which sympathized
with the incumbent regime. A *coup* attempted in times of peace,
when the armed forces are divided in their opinions, would be
very dangerous. At best it could mean a court martial for the
losers; at worst, internecine war.

Consequently, as long as the executive manages to keep

unrest at a minimum the military tends to support the incumbent regime. But if the armed forces are repeatedly engaged in clashes with agitated mobs and armed demonstrators, they will come to believe that the wisest course is to depose the object of civilian dissatisfaction, the President. When civil war threatens, the armed forces become united in their disapproval of the existing government and a bloodless *coup* can be quickly executed.

The President of a free regime, then, while all-responsible, is by no means all-powerful. He is situated between a ravenous opposition on one side and an ambivalent military on the other. As the political temperature rises—strikes, solidarity strikes, demonstrations, clashes, deaths, protest demonstrations—the tenure of the chief executive becomes increasingly uncertain. Since the first object of the chief executive is to stay in office, the manner in which he must behave is quite clear: he must attempt to pacify, undermine or at least contain the groups employing violence against him. The most obvious manner in which he can forestall violence is to give those who threaten it a part of what they want.

This leads us to consideration of the dynamic impulse given to the system by interest groups. We have identified three actors with interrelated roles: the opposition, the President, and the military. But what sets these participants in motion? We have shown how violence cannot be random if it is to be politically effective. A group of political party members cannot simply rush out onto the street and attack a policeman. Successful violence must be structured; it must be meaningful. The opposition political parties require substantive issues of conflict on which to construct their attack upon the government.

Interest groups, particularly labor unions, provide these issues. These organizations, through their specific, substantive demands, provide opposition forces with a cause around which violence may be structured—as well as an additional supply of agitators. Once a conflict has been initiated by worker organizations—or less frequently by groups of students or peasants—the opposition forces may swing into action. It follows therefore that if these interest groups are relatively quiet or if the President meets their demands rapidly with adequate concessions, violence has little opportunity to build. The crucial, "violence-initiating" position of interest groups under a free regime explains why, first of all, they are successful if they are able to initiate violence and, secondly, why control of these organizations is so important to political parties.

Opposition forces wish to control these groups in order to initiate and extend violence. In the case of labor unions opposition party (or left-extremist) control results in exorbitant demands, prolonged strikes and the frequent use of the solidarity strike for a wide range of political issues. Government-supporting parties (e.g., the APRA party during the Prado regime) wish to control interest groups to prevent their use against the executive. Worker organizations influenced by these forces tend to make their demands moderate, to avoid or curtail strikes whenever possible and to refrain from solidarity strikes except when such strikes clearly involve limited worker objectives.

In practically all major political crises worker organizations play a key role. The June 1961 strike of the construction workers provides a typical example. Called by the Communist-controlled Federation of Construction Workers, the strike was immediately given full and sympathetic coverage by *El Comercio*. The issue began to build. One worker was killed when a group of strikers attacked two policemen guarding non-striking workers. In the Chamber of Deputies members of the Popular Action and Progressive Socialist parties presented a motion to censure the Minister of Interior. The opposition-extremist Federation of Bank Clerks held a one-day sympathy strike. The extremist-led regional federations of workers in Callao and Arequipa threatened to strike. University students, under the leadership of a member of the Christian Democratic Party, staged a 48-hour protest strike.

In view of the agitated political atmosphere the Ministry of Labor issued a decree granting a 12 to 15 percent (depending on the category) wage increase for construction workers. Interest waned. The construction workers had received substantial gains and were uninclined to remain on strike. Extremist leaders of other unions, although they might have wished to add to the tension, realized that rank and file workers would not obey a solidarity strike order in support of the already successful construction workers. So opposition forces withdrew to wait for the next opportunity which a worker organization conflict would provoke.

The support of political parties which have strength in the labor movement is an important asset for a President since these parties will attempt to moderate the violence which worker organizations will use. One of the major reasons for the 1948 *coup* against Jose Luis Bustamante y Rivero (President from 1945 to 1948) was the 1947 shift of the APRA party, and the many labor organizations it controlled, from support to opposition of Bustamante. The repeated use of violence-oriented strikes and demonstrations by these APRA-led unions greatly added to the political tension which finally resulted in a military *coup*. The support of the APRA party and its labor leaders provides one explanation for the relatively long term of Manuel Prado (1956–1962). This is not to say that APRA labor leaders did not threaten or use violence. But they were careful to circumscribe overt union activity so that their threatened crises seldom materialized.

Through his control over the timing and content of conflict-resolving decrees, the President has another important asset. As we pointed out above, the limits on presidential action are broad. He is not bound by constitutional constraints or similar legal trappings. He (or his ministers with his authority) may issue any decree, which has the force of law, on almost every conceivable subject. By carefully adjusting each decree to a series of variables —preference intensity of the interest groups involved, cohesiveness of these organizations, the possibility of solidarity strikes, the popularity of the cause, and the general political temperature— he can carefully circumscribe violence while not making extravagant, and eventually dangerous, concessions.

In dealing with labor conflicts, the executive has a highly institutionalized procedure to accomplish this dual objective of low violence and sound economics. When a local union voices a demand, it bargains first with management. When it fails to receive satisfactory concessions from the employer it appeals to the Ministry of Labor for a decree and, at about the same time, begins a strike. The Ministry allows time to elapse (3–10 days) in order to gauge the severity of the threat. If violence seems unlikely, the Ministry issues a modest sub-directoral resolution which awards the workers about as much as, perhaps slightly more than, the employer was willing to grant. If violence becomes imminent—solidarity strikes, newspaper agitation, opposition party rallies, university student parades—then a second (directoral) resolution is issued, usually on the eve of a solidarity strike or proposed mass demonstration.

This two-step process makes it possible to allow the assaulting union to expend most of its resources so that it might be disposed to accept a relatively low offer. At the same time the executive has a second, more generous resolution ready which may be used if the situation moves to the brink of full-scale agitation.

In order to absolve itself of the enormous responsibility inherent in 'dictating' employer-employee relations throughout the country, the Ministry attempts to maintain that it employs objective criteria for its decisions: cost of living index, comparable wages, "subsistence level." But of course this is mere verbiage. Wage increases are each carved out to fit particular conflict situations, generosity being proportional to the violence potential.

For example, a tiny group of workers for the small shop Ciurlizza Maurer struck in December 1961 for higher wages. The Ministry of Labor granted a 4.26 percent increase (the rise in the cost of living index for that year). The workers were not satisfied and continued striking. After nearly thirty days of strike the Ministry made a second offer of 6 percent which the workers eventually accepted. Although there were minor instances of local violence (fist fights, for example), there was no major incident. The group of workers was very small, they belonged to no higher organization which would carry out a solidarity strike and the issue was virtually unknown to the public.

In the case of the strike of the San Miguel factory textile workers the situation was quite different. This relatively large union belonged to the Federation of Textile Workers which can muster nearly 20,000 workers into the streets in a solidarity strike in support of a member union. And behind the Federation stood the Confederation of Peruvian Workers, the national labor center. The general secretary of the Confederation was a past officer of the Federation and ties between the two organizations were quite close. When the San Miguel workers went on strike in August 1961 the Ministry of Labor granted an 11 percent wage increase, which the workers would not accept. Then, two and one-half weeks after the strike began, during a meeting of the Federation of Textile Workers where a solidarity strike was being discussed, a messenger arrived from the Ministry with a decree granting a 14 percent increase. This the workers accepted. Only by taking into account the political environment can we explain the difference between the outcomes in the case of these two unions.

Violence which is structured into the political context, then, is an eminently successful political weapon in the Peruvian free regime. A President threatened by its use will make generous concessions to the assaulting groups. And it must be thus. Many Americans fail to understand the role of the executive. They complain about his supposedly "unconstitutional," "unnatural" intervention in such affairs as labor disputes. But he must intervene to survive. It is suicidal for a President (and his Labor Minister) to "stand aloof" from such conflicts for the ever-widening circles of violence would quickly engulf him. He could, of course, attempt repression, but the road to and through dictatorship also has its dangers, not the least of which is the problem of military disunity.

The President acts as he must, as do the workers in employing violence. For them violence is a highly successful weapon. The alternative of collective bargaining, a tactic of economic coercion, offers little promise. Successful use of collective bargaining requires that numerous economic variables be favorable, particularly that the supply of unemployed labor be small. In Peru where migration has created severe unemployment, economic strikes would, in most cases, be undermined by replacements. To ask Peruvian unionists to use collective bargaining and refrain from violence is tantamount to urging dissolution of the labor movement.

The leverage of these interest groups comes, in turn, from the intense, bi-polar conflict between the opposition and the

President. The role which the military plays as arbitrator must also be interpreted in light of this conflict. Were Peruvian political society characterized by friendship and tranquility, the military would not find itself encouraged, even forced, to effect *coups*.

The intense conflict between the President and his opponents, then, we identify as the force which structures the entire pattern of interaction. We have briefly discussed some of the institutional and social variables which contribute to this conflict, but the problem is clearly one which invites further analysis.

The Military in Sub-Saharan Africa

1965

HERBERT J. SPIRO

The most important feature of the role of the military in sub-Saharan Africa is that their role has generally been insignificant. The insignificance of that role has been a truly significant contributory factor to the comparatively smooth and comparatively rapid development of politics in the newly independent countries of Black Africa. Yet the significance of their insignificance has not often been recognized by outside observers, including both scholars and those charged with responsibility for the African policies of the United States government.

The reasons for our failure to recognize the significance of the insignificant role of the military in Africa are multiple and varied and present an interesting problem for the sociology of (political) knowledge. Let me suggest only one reason: the very concept of "developing" countries or areas. At least since publication of Almond and Coleman's *The Politics of the Developing Areas*,[1] there has been a strong tendency among scholars, even when they have been engaged in explicitly comparative work, to assume from the outset that the developing countries shared in common certain peculiarities *beyond* the process of development itself, which distinguishes them from countries not described as developing (because, presumably, they had already developed or had not yet begun the process). In this context, use of the term "development" is not crucial, as is indicated, for example, by the title of Lucian Pye's influential paper on "The *Non-Western*

[1] Gabriel Almond and James Coleman, eds., *The Politics of the Developing Areas*, Princeton: Princeton University Press, 1960.

Presented to the Conference on the Military in Developing Nations, sponsored by the Oberlin College student International Affairs Committee, March, 1965.

Political Process." [2] For purposes of encouraging and organizing research, the assumption of common peculiarities (which may be more or less marked from one political system to the next) is useful, and the studies on political development published under auspices of the Social Science Research Council illustrate the utility of the assumption. However, if we let ourselves be carried away by the assumption to the conclusion, e.g., that the role of the military is similar in most or all developing countries, then we are likely to make a mess of both scholarship and policy.

Let me illustrate this danger with one of the very few and, in this case, temporary exceptions to the general insignificance of the military in Black Africa, the Belgian Congo in 1960, and expectations of, as well as public policies toward it then. I was in Southern Rhodesia when the Belgian Government announced that it would grant full independence to the Congo on June 30, 1960. The then Prime Minister, Sir Edgar Whitehead, publicly stated his expectation that the Congo would turn out to be one of the most stable independent African states because of the size and the reputed efficiency of the *Force Publique*. Before the final dissolution of the Federation of Rhodesia and Nyasaland and achievement of independence by Malawi and Zambia, it was fashionable among "White Settlers" to assert that "the only thing Africans understand is force." If the White Settlers, or the European colonial powers, simply asserted their overwhelming force, along with their readiness to apply it, they would *never* have to leave Africa. If, on the other hand, a European colonial power suffered from a "loss of nerve"—and this was the prevalent diagnosis of Belgium's malady—then it still had the opportunity of leaving a legacy of stability to its former dependency in the form of a sizable and efficient military force.

We now know how wrong this interpretation was. Far from becoming the Congo's sheet anchor of stability, the *Force Publique* not only disintegrated immediately after independence, but also, in the course of its disintegration, set off most of the new

[2] Presented to the American Political Science Association, Sept. 1957; see also George Mc T. Kahin, Guy Pauker and Lucian Pye, "Comparative Politics of Non-Western Countries," *American Political Science Review*, vol. XLIX, 1955, pp. 1022–1041.

state's major troubles. The interesting thing today, three and a half years later, is that no Congolese military or police force of similar proportions or of any degree of reliability has been brought into being. Nor can this fact be explained in terms of any reluctance on the part of outsiders, including the United States, to provide military supplies and training to the Congo. On the contrary, various Western countries, acting on their own initiative, though usually trying to funnel their military assistance through the United Nations, have repeatedly tried to "beef up" and to stabilize the Congolese National Army. These outside states, and especially the United States, have often based their policies of military assistance on a cluster of three assumptions concerning the role of the military in all developing countries . . . .

First, there is the assumption that the military can provide stability in the face of the collapse of other social and, especially, political structures. Second, there is the related assumption, which is particularly relevant to the focus upon development, that the military can act as a major agent of modernization. And third, these two assumptions are tied together in a third one, to the effect that popular support can be mobilized on behalf of the goals of modernization by the military who are playing their role of political stabilization.

In Black Africa, none of these assumptions has been proved correct. They have not been proved correct in a single country south of the Sahara. I used to follow the general academic (and State Department) practice of classifying the Sudan as part of the Middle East, but nowadays I need not even do that in order to back up my point. The military have played neither stabilizing, nor modernizing, nor political mobilizing roles in the Black African countries. In fact, as I suggested at the outset, they have been simply insignificant. Morris Janowitz, in *The Military in the Political Development of the New Nations,*[3] cites only one sub-Saharan country with a high level of military expenditure: Ethiopia, with 27 per cent—and Ethiopia, whatever else it may be, is not a very new nation. All the others, for which informa-

<hr>

[3] Morris Janowitz, *The Military in the Political Development of the New Nations,* Chicago: University of Chicago, 1964.

tion is available, range from 3 per cent for Tanganyika to 12 for the Sudan (while it was still described as a military dictatorship) . And we can assume that the percentages were closer to 3 per cent than to 12 for those countries about which the relevant information was not available.

What can explain this relative insignificance of the military in Black Africa? What implications does it have for policy?

The explanation seems relatively simple to me. None of the sub-Saharan colonies that has achieved its independence did achieve it by means of massive organized violence. All of them gained independence as a result of other factors which varied from one colony to the next, and from one European colonial power to the next. I want to stress the importance of this non-violent path to independence, because some of the literature puts the emphasis on the importance of the military in the colonial regime. The case of the Congo suggests that this emphasis is mistaken. So do the formerly French West African states, many of which contain large groups of veterans of the French Army, but in none of which the military, as a self-conscious group, have played a political role of sustained significance. I think this statement requires no qualifications; in the case of the assassination of President Olympio of Togo, for example, the soldiers responsible for it soon returned leadership into the hands of politicians.

Of course, simply because the military have been insignificant so far does not mean that they will not become more significant in the future in some of the countries in this area. But such a trend seems unlikely to me, for several reasons. To begin with, independence was achieved under genuinely *political* leadership, except in the Congo where it was "non-achieved" under no leadership, because the Belgians had not permitted politics and "divided and quit." The career ladders of the Black African elites had no rungs on which military expertise could be acquired, or from which lateral sympathies with the generally small military establishment were likely to be engendered. In the few countries which today assign high priority to enlargement of their armed forces, this enlargement is taking place on the initia-

tive of the non-military political leaders. In most of the new
states, the leaders are keenly aware of the incompatibility of
massive military spending with their more important goals of
modernization. They also realize that achievement of none of the
goals to which they assign high priority can be promoted by
means of a sizable military establishment.

This last assertion could be questioned: Could not African
countries with territorial claims against their neighbors put their
chips on an enlarged army and air force? And, on the continental
plane, is the Organization of African Unity not likely to try to
marshal a large military force in its projected attacks upon the
Republic of South Africa? These two questions point to another
remarkable feature of the role of the military in Black Africa,
and that is how early the political leadership recognized their
unreliability. I think this speed of recognition of unreliability is
more important than the facts of unreliability themselves. For
example, the mutinies in the three East African countries occurred before their governments had taken any steps towards
augmenting their military strength. After the experience of the
mutinies they are unlikely to pursue policies requiring a strong
military establishment, at least if it is to be organized along
conventional lines. And even Ghana had a similar experience,
when a mutiny occurred in one of its battalions on duty with the
United Nations in the Congo. In other words, even if one lends
credence to those of President Nkrumah's critics who charge him
with "irredentist" ambitions against Togo, one need not expect
him to seek to realize these ambitions by military means.

Why have Black African military units so often proved
unreliable? A complete answer to this question would require too
many comparisons with military units elsewhere to be possible
here. Let me, therefore, mention only one possible factor: the
African soldier's unwillingness to take ultimate risks of life on
behalf of his state, because it does not—at least not yet—engender ultimate loyalties, except conceivably in the struggle
against "neo-colonialism." But such feelings of ultimate loyalty
are necessary for the kind of discipline required for fighting
modern wars, including guerrilla wars. One interesting aspect of
events in the Congo during the past four and a half years has

been the general unwillingness of Congolese troops of all camps, with the apparent temporary exception of the "Zimbas" during the most recent rebellion, to take major personal risks. The lack of discipline and the unreliability has often been lamented by Western observers, who have called for programs of military training and other assistance to correct these short-comings. But that is precisely where, in my opinion, they are making a mistake. Instead of trying to push the Congolese in particular and the Africans in general into the same overall pattern of development through which many now developed countries have passed in the course of their history, we should ask ourselves whether the circumstances surrounding the African achievement of independence do not suggest the possibility of other patterns of development that are more likely to bring those results which the Africans are after—and which may be quite different from the results that the United States Government, with its often short and narrow perspective, would like to see them pursue. With particular regard to our focus upon the role of the military, the fact that in the independence period of, say, the United States and the Latin American Republics the military did play a "style setting" role; or the fact that this military tradition and other factors made possible a highly disciplined Civil War in this country; or finally the fact that Europeans have had such efficient military establishments and such loyally committed and disciplined populations that they have been able to slaughter each other by the millions roughly once every generation in the past century; do these facts suggest that the Africans should model their new military establishments and the role to be played by them on the conventional pattern with which we happen to be historically familiar?

My own answer, obviously, is No. But there are many competent persons, not just journalists or members of the "Tshombe lobby," who deny the possibility of either a permanently insignificant role or a markedly different role for the military in this last major geographical region to achieve self-government. Not all of these persons, certainly not all of the scholars among them, are wedded to the idea of eternally repetitive identical patterns of development. But most of them—with very few exceptions like Professor Hans Daalder—are disinclined to envisage an insignificant role for the military in the process of development and modernization.[4] And it is here, when they lump together development and modernization, that they commit their fundamental error, an error which tends to distort their understanding of events in Black Africa.

The identification of development with (substantive) modernization was built into the study of the "Politics of the Developing Areas" from its beginning. "The impact on politics of various factors making for change" was the focus of inquiry, according to James Coleman, in the book co-edited by him and Gabriel Almond. Ever since, most scholars have asked: How does modernization affect politics? What are the substantive prerequisites of democracy, i.e., how much wealth, urbanization, industrialization, and literacy are required before politics can develop toward democracy (usually understood rather ethnocentrically)? These questions are based—no doubt quite unintentionally—upon a neo-vulgar Marxian approach which assumes that politics is a third-hand reflection of economic processes and economic-power processes. In fact, of course, and especially during the last one hundred years or so, industrial, social, and cultural development has been the result of political action and of political development, not the other way around. To cite only two cases, this was true of Germany, after national unification, in the nineteenth century, and of Russia, after the Bolshevik Revolution, in the twentieth. In these two otherwise quite different cases, politics was deliberately used in order to forge new goals, to popularize them, and then to mobilize the population on behalf of the new goals. Massive industrialization and modernization, and the build-up of vast military establishments, were among the major goals. In other words, the direction of flow in the causal sequence was more from the development of politics to modernization, than from modernization to the development of politics.

The major difference between the German, Soviet, and many if not most recent cases of development outside of Black Africa, on the one hand, and the development of politics in

[4] Hans Daalder, *The Role of the Military in the Emerging Countries,* The Hague: Mouton, 1962.

Africa, on the other, is the degree to which organized violence was used during the period straddling independence. Because of the very low incidence of violence in the new African states, and as a result of the nature of the so-called independence "struggles" where they took place (i.e., again excluding the Belgian Congo), the political style of the new states has developed along non-violent lines—not in the sense of a *comparative* lack of awareness of what adherents of the school of *Realpolitik* like to call the "realities of power." Moreover, because of the generally procedural bias in sources of authority in most traditional African societies, African leaders and the populations to whom they appealed have tended to assign higher priority to the development of politics than to the development of anything else, including industry, schools, and cities. This tendency is stated clearly in Nkrumah's motto, "Seek ye first the political kingdom . . . ," which has been acted upon even by those leaders who are otherwise at odds with President Nkrumah.

By "development of politics" I mean that expansion of the capacity of the political system to process a heavier volume of problems, to discuss a greater range of issues, to forge new goals as old ones are being approached, and to make more people conscious of the possibilities of change-through-politics. I am tempted to paraphrase the commercial slogan of a great chemical company: Better things for better living through politics. The style of politics may be violent or legalistic, pragmatic or ideological, in any of many possible combinations. The style of African politics has on the whole been remarkably sound, when we compare it with the style of politics in most other developing countries or, as for that matter, in most developed or over-developed countries. Most African leaders, like the founders of political science two and a half millenia ago, though with much less theoretical self-consciousness, believe in the primacy of politics and, they believe in therefore, the primacy of the development of politics over the development of anything else. The military, whatever else they may contribute to a political system, are ill prepared by training, experience, and outlook, to contribute constructively to the development of politics, as both Daalder and Pye point out. In the context of Africa south of Sahara, because of their numerical insignificance and, in most cases, because of the youth of military establishments, they are even more poorly prepared than in Latin America, Asia or the Middle East.

Africa's greatest asset consists of its politicians who, unlike their counterparts in the other areas, face little competition from the military. However, if certain presently discernible tendencies in the African perspectives and policies of the United States persist, then this situation could be changed, and we might have nothing to blame but a self-fulfilling prophecy.

East Africa:
Latin America Revisited?

1964

JONATHON WISE POLIER

Unlike much of Latin America which forcefully freed itself from the colonial rule of Spain, most of Africa has gained independence without the need for wars of national liberation. Some optimists in the field of political science have prophesied that since Africa lacks a military tradition, the military will not become a dominant force in the political arena.

However, in the past year African military forces have played a part in the intraterritorial politics of Algeria, Congo-Brazzaville, Congo-Leopoldville, Liberia, Togo and now in Kenya, Tanganyika, Uganda, and Zanzibar. The bloody change of government in Zanzibar and the abortive troop revolts in Kenya, Tanganyika and Uganda have shown (if proof were needed) that the former African colonies of Britain, like those of France and Belgium, are not immune to the military as a pressure group.

The violent overthrow of the minority Arab elite in Zanzibar comes as no surprise except for the alleged foreign training of the revolutionary forces. The revolts on the mainland are in a certain sense far more significant for whereas the events in Zanzibar indicate a foreign influence, the January uprisings in Kenya, Tanganyika and Uganda appear to be internal affairs and therefore hold great portent for many other African states.

Reprinted by permission from The Activist *(Oberlin, Ohio)*, 4 *(1964)*, 98–100.

In East Africa (note: by East Africa is meant the three territories of Kenya, Tanganyika and Uganda) the governments hold a nominal preponderance of the force within the state but this power is dependent on other groups: the police, the military, (often) the former colonial power, and the mass political party (ies). All these, as well as other interest groups such as trade unions, make demands upon the political system which, if ignored, can become dangerous to the political leaders. The governments of a developing state obviously find it difficult to meet the demands of all groups and in the last analysis must gratify some demands at the expense of others.

The specific demands of the East African troops were for the removal of British officers and for higher pay. However, were it not for the rapid intervention of British forces, it seems highly probable that the three governments would have found themselves at the mercy of increasing demands from elements of the military. Thanks to the United Kingdom's intervention, the East African governments have an opportunity to dissolve disloyal units and a chance to try to evolve some way of keeping the military out of politics—of avoiding the "Latinamericanization" of East Africa. It is to this pressing problem and how it might be met that this article is addressed.

There seem to be at least five overlapping lines of action which the East African governments can be expected to consider.

First, the role of the police might be greatly expanded so that it could act as a balance to the military's monopoly of the coercive power of the state. The creation of a Kenyan or Tanganyikan (NKVD-KGB) of such proportions and power is not without danger (not to mention cost) and therefore, African governments which do not need large armies may seek a less dangerous solution.

A second line of action is for the military to be integrated and made subordinate to the ruling political party. This method has been used in the Soviet Union and to a lesser extent in Guinea. However, there would need to be definite limitations to the full applicability of such a system to East Africa. While both the CPSU and the PDG (*Partie Democratique de Guinee*) are largely totalitarian parties controlling the educative-communicative function, both Kenya and Uganda are multi-party states; to date Tanganyika has not achieved a monolithic one-party system. In the far more "open" society of East Africa, it will prove more difficult for one party to indoctrinate and absorb the military. Nevertheless, President Julius Nyerere, who has pushed for a one-party system in Tanganyika, has indicated his intention to have the disloyal units disbanded and to have the youth cadres of the Tanganyikan African National Union provide the base for future units. This program might prove to be a partial answer for Tanganyika but seems to hold little promise for either Kenya or Uganda.

A third answer, which has already been put into operation with British support, is to "buy off" the army with an 150 per cent pay increase at the recruit level. This would seem to be more a stopgap measure than a panacea for several reasons:

(1) Such increases can and will undoubtedly increase demands for higher salaries by the police and the civil service which the East African governments cannot afford. However, the governments may consider cutting the size of the military establishment and thereby attempt to provide a higher standard of living without diverting necessary development funds to an expanding military. There is a certain advantage to be gained from a system of higher pay to the army. Although the use of a small "professional" army, rather than a militia system, does involve potential dangers for the state, the provision of a better living standard and generous retirement benefits would tend to make the military identify with the government and not the people.

(2) Even if increased financial rewards were possible, it would not completely solve the problem of status gratification. This is by no means a minor question. On January 13, 1963, the military junta, which a few hours before had seized power in Togo, announced that two of its four reasons for the *coup d'état* were President Sylvanus Olympio's "sterile isolationism" in foreign policy and his "profound contempt for the military" (i.e., his refusal of suggested increases in the military budget). A more aggressive foreign policy calling for the "liberation" of Mozambique could be used but only at the risk of raising public expectations and placing the army in a position where it can force the

government to give it an evergrowing part of the budget. Since Tanganyika and Kenya cannot expect to quickly force Portugal out of Mozambique, the raising of the popular level of expectations without a chance of meeting new demands would be extremely dysfunctional.

Fourthly, the events of January can be expected to give new emphasis to the movement towards federation with greater and more stable economic cooperation within the East African Common Market. The aggregate benefits of the Common Services Organization and Common Market are clear. If East Africa is to meet the demands of rising expectations of the army and other groups, these governments can ill afford to ignore the benefit of such cooperation. However, economic cooperation is, needless to say, a political question, the problems are many (Raisman Report, Comnd 1279, 1961), and positive steps in that direction in the near future do not seem very likely.

Finally, in the future training of officers, NCO's and recruits, the government can attempt to instill a sense (if not a tradition) that the military has no business in politics and must, as a pressure group, limit itself to legitimate channels of expression. Such an increased emphasis is important but certainly not sufficient to solve the problem.

Assuming that there will be an East African military pressure group, despite reforms it seems likely that the East African governments will follow two broad programs. First, they will seek to satisfy the demands of many groups in the system through more rapid economic growth and a rising standard of living. A public (which includes the military) which feels that its government is honestly and boldly attempting to fulfill its expectation will tend to support that government. However, if the government fails to be efficacious, there will be pressure to change the government and the army is in one of the best positions to do so. Second, the government will seek to manipulate its propaganda, rewards, and punishments to hold the support of the military as a key interest group in East Africa.

The problem of the "Latinamericanization" of Africa will not be solved in this decade. As long as there continues to be a minimum sense of consensus and common values within the community, and as long as there are insufficient rewards for large sections of the population, there will be a significant danger that groups may appeal to force to influence the political and economic evolution.

The Role of the Army
in Contemporary Africa

1965

PIERRE L. VAN DEN BERGHE

Probably more than any other continent at any time in world history, Africa is led by pen-wielding intellectuals, rather than by the modern equivalent of saber-rattling men on horseback. In 1963, only seven of the 34 independent African states had armies of over 10,000 men and 10 had armed forces of 1,000 or less. The per capita annual military expenditure was less than $5 in 27 of the 33 states where data was available, and less than $1 in 11 cases. (See "The Armies of Africa," *Africa Report,* January 1964.) The continent as a whole (with a population of 270,000,000) spent slightly over $800,000,000 on defense, compared to over $50 billion for the United States, with a population of about 192,000,000. Well over half the African total was accounted for by only two states, the United Arab Republic and South Africa.

Despite these statistics, and the fact that one of the continent's two politico-military juntas was replaced by a civilian government in late 1964, the role of the military cannot be ignored in modern Africa. In the first place, it seems likely that present conditions are only temporary, and that Africa will become increasingly militarized. Colonial governments fought their battles largely in Europe, and maintained relatively small garrisons in their overseas outposts, mainly for internal security purposes.

Reprinted from Africa Report, 10 *(March 1965), 12–17, by permission of the* author *and the* publisher.

Independence reopened all of the conflicting territorial claims of the colonial period, and transferred the foci of these conflicts from London, Brussels, and Paris to Nairobi, Mogadiscio, Accra, Leopoldville, Rabat, and Algiers. Arms races, if not wars, are likely to result from regional disputes. Secondly, a number of special circumstances make African armies, however small, a particularly fascinating object of political analysis during this period of rapid transition from dependency to sovereignty.

Six Types of Armies

Six main types of armies may be distinguished on the continent, of which the last two are unique to Africa:

(1) *The Raiding Citizen Army*, characterized by non-professionalism and egalitarianism, has only ethnographic and historical significance. Many cattle-herding, stateless societies of eastern Africa, such as the Nuer and the Dinka, had armies of this type. That is, all able-bodied men (sometimes organized as age sets) fought together in periodic raids against their neighbors under the informal, spontaneous leadership of warriors who had no permanent military offices. The Boer commandos of South Africa up to the Anglo-Boer War could also be placed in this category. With the rise of centralized monarchies, the Raiding Citizen Army became more permanently organized, more rigidly structured, and more professional (as among the Zulu, Swazi, and Matabele), thus evolving into the second major type of African force.

(2) *The Palace Army*, characteristic of many traditional monarchies, is led by a corps of professional officers, often with a largely professional rank-and-file. Such an army constitutes the major instrument of power for the "Establishment"—king, nobility, and sometimes the clergy of the official state religion. The Palace Army is apolitical: though used as a tool to preserve the status quo, it is not an independent source of power or policy. Palace armies were common in pre-colonial states such as the Sudanic empires of Ghana, Mali, Songhai, Kanem, and Bornu, and in the Hausa, Nupe, and Fulani states. High officers were often aristocrats, while the soldiery were often low-status mercenaries, such as slaves or foreigners. Modernized versions of Palace

Armies still exist in Morocco, Libya, and Ethiopia. In the process of modernizing the technology of violence, and opening up the officer corps to commoners, the Palace Army can transform itself into a third type.

(3) *The Putsch Army* is characterized by a highly professionalized and politicized officer corps. This leads to the now-familiar pattern of military dictatorship, either of the *junta* form or the one-man *caudillo* type. Beginning as an instrument of power of a ruling class external to it, the army becomes synonymous with the government, and the army general staff with the ruling clique. Typically, military coups are led by young senior officers (often of colonel rank) from privileged units such as armored cavalry or paratroops. The political ideology of military dictatorships is usually poorly formulated, and may range from rigid conservatism to "authoritarianism of the left." When conservative, military dictatorships tend to ally themselves more with the moneyed bourgeoisie than with the feudal aristocracy, which they often supplant. Being *parvenu* technocrats of violence, however, putschists are more often "modernist" and anti-traditional in outlook. In Africa, the most clearcut examples of the putsch army are those of the Sudan until 1964 and the UAR.

(4) *The Revolutionary Citizen Army,* which traces its ancestry back to the eighteenth century armies of the First French Republic, is represented in Africa by the Algerian FLN and by the Angolan insurgents. This fourth type shares with the first a non-professional and relatively egalitarian character. Its distinctive elements are its high degree of political fervor and its revolutionary aims.

Such an army is not so much an organization of specialists in violence as the militant vanguard of the masses in the overthrow of the status quo. Both ideology and the necessity for guerrilla warfare based on small-scale and relatively autonomous units serve to maintain egalitarianism. After victory, revolutionary armies are likely to become the national armies of the newly independent country, especially if led by an articulate and modernist intelligentsia as in the case of Algeria. The Mau Mau of Kenya might conceivably be put in this category, but it was politically less sophisticated and retained more the character of a revivalist secret society than of a militant guerrilla force within a mass revolutionary movement.

The remaining types of African armies deserve a closer look, as they are special cases hitherto neglected in political analysis.

(5) *The Herrenvolk Army* is represented by South Africa and, on a smaller scale, Rhodesia. The Boers were the only European colonists in Africa who did not arm the indigenous population and who monopolized the use of firearms themselves; non-whites were enlisted in the South African Army during both World Wars, but only as unarmed, non-combatant auxiliaries. During the Anglo-Boer War, Britain used some African troops, but the conflict remained, for all practical purposes, a white man's war. The present South African Army is a white force dedicated to the maintenance of white supremacy.

The Herrenvolk army is characterized by a relatively low degree of professionalism and a rather high degree of internal democracy traceable to its origins in the Boer commandos of the seventeenth, eighteenth, and nineteenth centuries. It has career officers, of course, but it is apolitical in the sense that it is neither an important autonomous source of power, nor a threat to whatever white government is in power. Furthermore, it represents the entire white population, rather than simply being a tool of the government clique. The South African Army thus has a dual nature: it is at once an instrument of minority rule and an internally democratic citizen army.

Even though "Herrenvolk egalitarianism" has inevitably waned with the increasing modernization and expansion of the army, the South African and Rhodesian armies remain distinctly different from any of the other types represented on the continent. In a sense, the Herrenvolk Army is a modernized and stabilized version of a Raiding Citizen Army whose members have become a ruling caste in a wider society. This Herrenvolk or vigilante army is now being strengthened to meet the growing menace of a potential African Revolutionary Citizen Army. Between 1961 and 1964, the South African military budget increased from $112,000,000 to $291,000,000 and is now the largest on the continent.

(6) *The Colonial Army* is perhaps the most common kind

in Africa and also the most typically African. As the name implies, the Colonial Army is constituted of the former "native troops" of the European powers: the French *tirailleurs sénégalais,* German *Askaris,* Belgian *Force Publique,* British *King's African Rifles,* etc.

Unlike the palace variety, Colonial Armies began as the power instruments of "modernist" foreign conquerors, instead of traditional native aristocracies. The term "mercenary" does not really apply to such armies. Except for the British, who relied mostly on volunteers except in war, the colonial powers generally exacted quotas of men from various chiefs or used one form or another of involuntary conscription. Nor were colonial soldiers comparable to conscripts in a Citizen Army. They were armed and somewhat privileged helots, more or less compelled by circumstances to serve their foreign masters in conquering and subjugating fellow Africans.

Under these conditions, "native" troops, though cheap, were not always reliable. Mutinies were not uncommon, though they were fairly easily repressed with the help of other "native" troops from rival ethnic groups; in any case, the mutineers usually lacked leadership and scattered into small, undisciplined bands. To increase the tractability of colonial troops, garrisons of one ethnic group were often stationed far from home, among traditional enemies, or at least among people with whom they had nothing in common. Consequently, they were often regarded by the local population with deep distrust, as hated tools of the white conqueror. Within the armies themselves, the officer ranks were the preserve of whites, except for token racial integration by France and Portugal. (Even there, non-white officers were often West Indians or Asians rather than Africans.) African soldiers came increasingly to regard their white officers as symbols of foreign domination so that loyalty was further eroded in the latter years of colonialism.

The role of Colonial Armies in supporting or undermining the colonial system as a whole warrants special interest. Generally, "native troops" served European imperialism well. They conquered much of Europe's empire, "pacified" African peoples into outward submission, and fought colonial wars as far as Asia. Yet

the service of African troops in the two World Wars also contributed significantly to the demise of colonialism. Tens of thousands
of Africans came in contact with the outside world, associated
with whites on terms of equality and intimacy, discovered different racial and political attitudes from those held by the white
governors and settlers to whom they had been previously exposed, and occasionally witnessed the military defeat of their colonial masters. In short, war experience unveiled a new world
where whites could not keep up their pretence of being a master
race. Many returning African servicemen, disgruntled at being
demobilized and unable to readjust to civilian life, added their
weight to the postwar groundswell of discontent and unrest
against the colonial regime. Partly because of educational limitations, however, soldiers were seldom in the leadership ranks of independence movements, and Colonial Armies remained largely
apolitical.

Alienated from the civilian population and from their own
officer corps, the holdover Colonial Armies have posed a special
danger for the new states, as already evidenced by the mutinies in
the Congo in 1960 and in Kenya, Uganda, and Tanganyika in
1964. Because they are regarded with such suspicion by the general population and also because they lack a caste of African career officers, they cannot be used for putsches, or indeed for any
concerted social purposes. Their very existence often poses a constant threat to the governments they are supposed to serve. With
the crash program of training for African commissioned officers
and the purge of mutineering elements in the former Colonial Armies, this volatile phase is clearly transitory, however, and many
of these troops are already being converted into reliable national
armies.

Factors Affecting Reliability

There are, of course, some notable exceptions to these gener-
alizations about the Colonial Army as a liability to new African
states. In Rwanda, a country sandwiched in between two states
where mutinies did take place, the former Colonial Army supported the republican government in the violent overthrow of the
Tutsi aristocracy. In Senegal, the army has twice stood by Sen-
ghor at critical moments. . . .

Two crucial factors seem to affect the reliability and stability of these holdover forces. One is the extent to which the officer corps was Africanized before independence. Here the case of the Sudan is instructive. Between 1953 and 1956, some 400 junior officers were trained at the military academy in Khartoum, so that the Sudanese Defense Force was entirely commanded by Africans at independence. The former Colonial Army had developed such a highly professional officer corps that it was easily converted into a Putsch Army when the need arose in 1958.

A second important factor in determining the post-independence behavior of former Colonial Armies is the extent to which they acquire legitimacy and prestige as genuine African institutions. In most parts of Africa, as noted earlier, the people have regarded the army with fear or hostility, and as symbols of white domination. In some traditional societies (mostly in West Africa) the military profession was linked with low social status, and this attitude was carried over to Colonial Armies. Unless the military was given legitimacy by the political leaders of liberation movements in anticipation of independence, its role in the process of nation building was jeopardized and has tended to be marginal. In Ghana, the discipline and stability of the army was in no small measure a result of Nkrumah's favorable attitude, despite the fact that only 10 percent of the officer corps was Africanized by 1957. The former Belgian Congo, where the *Force Publique* was completely alienated from the civilian population and had no African commissioned officers at independence, is an extreme case on the other side.

Another factor influencing the role of former Colonial Armies has been their ethnic composition. Colonial powers generally recruited troops from illiterates, who made more pliable soldiers, and from groups with military traditions or a reputation for fierceness. These were not the groups from which the Western-educated elite was usually drawn. In Kenya, for example, the intelligentsia was mainly Kikuyu and the King's African Rifles almost entirely non-Kikuyu; in Ghana and Nigeria, army recruits were mostly illiterate northern Moslems and the elite predominantly Christian and southern. These different ethnic backgrounds account for much of the antipathy of the intelligentsia—often now the ruling class—for the military.

Ethnic composition of the armed forces has special political significance in large states such as Congo-Leopoldville and Nigeria, where stability and unity hinge on a delicate regional and ethnic balance. Under colonialism, the army was essentially an instrument of repression, an aim best secured by fostering ethnic rivalries and stationing troops among strangers or even traditional enemies. The army of an independent state has the antithetical aim of serving national unity against outside threats. The difficulty of converting a Colonial Army into a tool of national policy is not eased when the ethnic balance of the army becomes a political football—as in Nigeria, where the mass of the troops are still mostly northern while officers and technicians have recently been drawn from the south.

The educational functions of former Colonial Armies are also widely at variance with the aims of independent governments. Although the later colonial armies trained some African mechanics and petty technicians, and France conceived of military training as a method of assimilation to French culture, colonial powers generally favored uneducated, apolitical troops from rural and traditional environments. Independent states, on the other hand, seek to create literate citizen-soldiers imbued with the national ideology. In some African armies, national unity is now being furthered by combining short-time military conscription with basic education and political indoctrination. Another way of integrating the army with the general population and of creating goodwill toward the military is to use the armed forces for constructive purposes such as sanitation, rescue, transportation, and public works. The Guinean, Malian, and the post-mutiny Tanzanian armies are notable examples of both of these approaches.

The Tasks Ahead

This quick survey barely scratches the surface of military problems in Africa. The categories are meant to be suggestive rather than definitive; the reality is more complex. For example, several types of armies can, and indeed often have, co-existed in the same territories. Colonial Armies have fought against armies of the first and second types. The Herrenvolk Army of South Africa is changing in anticipation of guerrilla warfare by a type-four army. Sometimes there is an inverse relationship between the development of several types of armies: for example, since the outbreak of the Angolan war in 1961, the Portuguese have practically disarmed the Colonial Armies in their "overseas provinces."

A possible model for those states which must transform Colonial Armies into a politically reliable instrument of domestic and foreign policy is the draftee army, led by a professional cadre of apolitical officers and non-coms, supplemented by specialized elite units of volunteers. This model, however, is most amenable to a multi-party, Western type of democracy and seems destined to be rare among the new states. Perhaps more in keeping with the one-party structures of many African states is the conception of the army as a party militia, highly politicized, but under firm civilian control. This alternative, most clearly demonstrated in Guinea, was advocated by President Julius Nyerere in setting forth the role of the post-mutiny Tanganyika Army: "I do not want it to be an elite force, but an arm integrated with the national life and attuned to our own political system . . . the task is to insure that the officers and men are integrated into the government and party so that they become no more of a risk than, say, the civil service. . . ." Such an army is a more logical outgrowth of the Revolutionary Citizen Army than of a Colonial Army, but with proper reorganization, indoctrination, and infiltration of the officer corps by party cadres, the transition is conceivable.

A third alternative is the transformation of former Colonial Armies into Putsch Armies as soon as they acquire a cadre of indigenous career officers. Recent successful or abortive coups in Togo, Dahomey, Congo-Brazzaville, and Gabon may indicate an incipient trend in this direction, although the existence of a monolithic party organization reaching down to the grass roots hinders the emergence of the military to power in several states.

Some Predictions

Despite the great diversity of African states, some broad predictions may be attempted concerning the conversion of Colonial Armies to meet new requirements:

(1) While the former colonial troops were primarily in-

tended to maintain internal security, the new national armies will increasingly fulfill international functions in conflicts between African states, the training of guerrillas for the liberation of Southern Africa, etc.

not really

(2) The new armies will have to be increasingly used as instruments of economic development, education, and social reform.

(3) The trend toward indigenous rather than foreign control of African armed forces will continue. More and more states will attempt to "multilateralize" the sources of necessary foreign technical and financial assistance, so far as the need for standardization of weapons, military traditions, and language of instruction permit. Indeed, we may reasonably expect that broad considerations of foreign and domestic policy will tend to override technical contingencies. Another problem in the rapid Africanization of armed forces is the potential discontent when promotion opportunities are curtailed after a brief period of dramatic rises from non-commissioned to senior field officer ranks.

(4) Concerted attempts will be made to integrate the new citizen armies into the national life and to revise the popular image of the military as an "alien" force whose purpose is to control the civilian population. We can expect a broadening of ethnic representation and a tendency away from ethnically homogenous units, so as to make military service a factor in cultural homogenization and national unity.

(5) Apolitical Colonial Armies will be increasingly indoctrinated into the nationalist ideology of the ruling party so that both officers and men will see themselves as active agents in a process of nation-building. Aside from technical competence and leadership ability, the role of officers as ideologues will be emphasized.

The conversion of colonial-type armies into reliable instruments of national policy and organic parts of the emerging nation-states is only one aspect of the complex social revolution now taking place throughout Africa. But it is an aspect that deserves far more serious study than it has received to date.

And Now Nkrumah: The Generals & the Future of Africa

1966

J. KIRK SALE

The coup that toppled Kwame Nkrumah last month came as a surprise, but in fact it is very much of a piece with the revolutions that have continued to rock Africa in its years of independence—and especially in the last year. Since their independence, no fewer than twenty-eight of the thirty-seven African nations have faced attempted coups; thirteen have been successful (Egypt, Sudan, Togo, Zanzibar, Rwanda, both Congos, Algeria, Dahomey, Central African Republic, Upper Volta, Nigeria, Ghana), and seven of these occurred within the last eight months. Each successful take-over was achieved by the army, except that of Congo-Brazzaville, where the army gave tacit support.

Like the others, the Ghana coup depended in most part upon the army and police, stable and powerful factors in an otherwise fluid and powerless society. Like the others, it was born of a deep dissatisfaction with politicians and nurtured by the assumption that military men, and with them civil servants, could do what others could not. Like the others, it was based on the belief —only recently proved valid—that the former colonial powers would not intervene. And like the others, it occurred about five years after the promises of independence (real or imagined) were thought to have been betrayed and a large segment of the trained young men had been disillusioned.

Reprinted by permission from The Nation, 202, *No. 12* (*March 21, 1966*), *317–322.*

Ghana, then, is interesting not only in itself but for the light it sheds on the other recent revolutions. Why did it happen, what sort of army engineered it, and what should we expect of the future?

Accra radio gave the short explanation of the coup on the morning after: "This act has been made necessary by the economic and political situation in the country. The concentration of power in the hands of one man has led to the abuse of individual rights and liberties. . . . He has been running the country as if it were his own personal property. . . . He has brought Ghana to the brink of bankruptcy." This was no news to the Ghanaians.

Economically, Ghana had been going downhill for a number of years. Though it had put through some very valuable measures—the Volta Dam, the Tema harbor, vast school development, some diversification of the economy—the Nkrumah regime had dissipated an estimated $560 million worth of foreign exchange on worthless (or merely prestigious) projects and unrealizable schemes, had run up its external debt to close to $1 billion, and had bartered away its decreasingly valuable cocoa crop for Czechoslovakian suede shoes, Chinese canned goods and Russian Volga cars. What began as a brilliant demonstration of how an independent country goes about throwing off the shackles of colonialism ended up as a serious misuse of the handsome physical resources of the country and its human resources as well.

Inevitably, the failure hit directly at the people. Since 1963, the cost of living has gone up 56 per cent and has been accompanied by a series of agonizing shortages—of such vital goods to the average Ghanaian consumer as flour, tea, sugar, butter, cheese and matches, plus such semi-luxury goods as liquor, cars, refrigerators, stoves, etc.

(For five months last year Ghana was without matches. The government had banned foreign imports and then discovered its own factory wasn't producing any—because, it eventually turned out, the very old man who was the only person in the country who knew how to keep together the factory's one very old dipping machine had died. Such incidents were not rare.)

Rationing had been instituted recently to ease the recurrent shortages, but it served mostly to drive up the price of ration books, along with the price of scarcities, on the black market. Moreover, the contrast between the rich and poor in the larger cities was increasingly more obvious. The poor were in many ways better off than a decade ago—though unemployment kept mounting as the parade to the cities grew—but the rich grew more and more extravagant; as Agricultural Minister Krobo Edusi put it, "socialism doesn't mean that if you've made a lot of money you can't keep it." And among the rich, it was quickly noted, were not only the officials of Nkrumah's CPP but also his personal friends and family members (one cousin ran the capital's most opulent night club) and, toward the end, Kwame Nkrumah, man of the people, himself. Nkrumah's official residence, Christiansborg Castle, was rebuilt a few years ago at the cost of $1 million and stood in shining splendor over the surrounding township of Christiansborg—the most squalid slum in all of Accra.

And just at the time that the economic picture was bleakest last year—food in short supply, jobs scarce, luxuries nonexistent—up went a Palace of African Unity built for a one-week conference at a cost variously put between $10 million and $35 million.

Other countries have weathered economic hard times without revolutions—why not Ghana? The answer is politics, the other half of the revolutionary equation.

First, Nkrumah's growing dictatorship and arbitrary rule alienated those who would have been most valuable in guiding public opinion through the economic crisis and devising sensible ways to get out of it: the intellectuals, the civil servants, the considerable middle class. Ghana was not a police state by any means, but its "preventive detention" of any one at any time, without trial, created an aura of fear and suspicion in which only the very secure and very old could afford to offer advice.

Second, Nkrumah openly cut himself off from his original source of power, the masses, and retired behind the walls of Flagstaff House, where his feelings of loneliness and unreality grew day by day. A less megalomaniac leader, one less remote from reality, might have successfully asked the people to tighten their belts for the greater glory of Ghana. But Nkrumah seemed hardly to care about their plight and let the party newspapers listlessly make the admonitions. Nor did the party sycophants around him try to wake him up—how would you explain to a "messianic majesty" and "national fount of honor" that the economy was collapsing and that grumbling, not only of stomach but of mouth, was mounting?

Finally, Nkrumah blocked any possibility of peaceful change or remedy. He was President for life and his party had absolute control over the governmental system. You cannot vote down a leader in Nkrumah's position; he is impervious to votes. There was no legal way for the discontented elements of the society, including the army and the police, to express their unhappiness or hopes for change. As a result, frustration spread, and revolution took shape.

That, then, was the dry tinder: economic collapse, political stagnation, mounting discontent. The sparks to light it came from the army.

Nkrumah had always been worried about his army. He knew, as do all dictators, that it represented the one source of power strong enough to fell him. But he didn't want to do without it: armies are prestigious, good for ceremonies, useful to guard borders against invaders (or more likely smugglers), valuable to keep internal order, and not bad at building roads. So Nkrumah first tried to keep the army under British control, even after independence, knowing full well that no British general would lead his troops against the commander in chief; would, in fact, do everything to put down a rebellion against him if it arose. But during the Congo turmoil Nkrumah came under immense pressure to discharge his British officers (Britain was, after all, an obvious imperialist power in the Congo) and in September, 1961, was forced to replace reliable old General Alexander with a Ghanaian general, Steve Otu, a hail-fellow kind of officer and not much of a threat.

But behind Otu were a number of more hard-minded officers, one of whom, Joseph Arthur Ankrah, was made Army Chief of Staff when Otu became Defense Chief. Nkrumah was never quite happy about Ankrah, and even had doubts about

Otu; they were kept under close watch and forced to go through regular loyalty drills for four years, until last July Nkrumah dismissed them both and replaced them with men more "socialist-minded."

Apparently neither Otu nor Ankrah had done anything specifically hostile, though it had become fairly common knowledge around Accra that Ankrah was less than enchanted with Nkrumah and had the temperament to do something about it. Nkrumah was apparently acting only to forestall trouble from the army, but inevitably he created discontent among Ankrah's followers and uncertainty among the other officers.

Three months after sacking Ankrah and Otu, Nkrumah proposed the formation of a "people's militia," ostensibly to be trained for an invasion of Rhodesia. Whether or not Nkrumah really intended to set up a militia personally loyal to him as a counterforce to the army, the army must certainly have thought that was his plan, and armies traditionally resist such invasion of their provinces (cf., Sukarno and Indonesia). And the militia was to be added to the already extant threat of Nkrumah's personal guard, commanded by a Soviet-trained colonel, advised by a dozen Russian officers, entirely armed and trained by the Russians (Nkrumah even encouraged them to use the Russian goose step) and quite free of army control.

That threat was the first spark; at the turn of the year came the second and decisive one. Military take-overs had succeeded with remarkable ease in six other countries. The politicians had proved powerless, lacking either the arms or popular support even to attempt a counterrevolution; the general populace accepted the coups joyously, or at least indifferently.

And no European power had intervened to thwart the recent revolts, as France had admittedly done at least ten times between 1960 and 1964 (most notably in Gabon in February, 1964), and as Britain had moved into East Africa in January, 1964. This was a clear demonstration that the former colonial powers were unwilling to get entangled in repeated internal troubles in their former colonies. The army men noted this hands-off attitude with some satisfaction.

Just five weeks after Nigeria's successful coup, at a time when both Nkrumah and his army commander were out of the country, the army sprang its revolution. Resistance was slight, popular opinion and up-to-date arms were on its side, and within a day the army (in coalition with the police) was in power.

Who are these men who have come to power in Ghana? In broad terms they are very much like the men who have led the other African revolutions. The African officers are Western-trained and Western-educated. Their values and goals are strongly influenced by the West. They regard the army's role approximately as a Western general would—a nonpolitical, nonideological force subservient to civil control—and not, by contrast, as a Chinese would.

Unlike the usual Latin American officer, they are not men of rich families or of entrenched interests who tend to be ultraconservative. They come for the most part from the lower bourgeoisie or better than average peasantry, a background not markedly different in custom and training from that of the middle-level civil servants, small businessmen or secondary-school teachers. They are educated, but usually only through secondary school; a number have gone to Sandhurst or St. Cyr, but most have had no more than a six-month course at metropolitan cadet schools plus wide experience in the army itself.

Almost all the older officers fought with the colonial powers in World War II and after; Generals Soglo (Dahomey), Bokassa (Central African Republic) and Lamizana (Upper Volta) served under the French in Indo-China; Ironsi (Nigeria) and Ankrah were in the West African army during the war and led troops in the Congo.

But they are not to be thought of as capitalist lackeys or bourgeois conservatives. They have no ideology to speak of, but they are—as military men often seem to be—dedicated nationalists. They have delighted, especially in Ghana, Algeria and the Congo, to display outwardly the vanities of independence (with new uniforms and equipment, ceremonial duties and international service). They have known race prejudice and ill treatment under colonial masters (it is only recently that they were *allowed* to be officers) and feel as strongly as any politician that the African nations must stand on their own feet, often with a thumb to the nose. If they do not like Nkrumah's socialism or Abubakar's capitalism—and they do not—they have no clear system to offer instead. They are not ideologues but military men.

And their strong point is getting things done. They have rebelled not because they want to replace socialism with capitalism or vice versa, but because they want to replace corruption with honesty, mismanagement with military efficiency, chaos with order, stagnation with progress. Whether they succeed or not, they have acted to make something better of their nations in the only way they know.

Ghana itself has perhaps the best army in all of black Africa. It has had a budget of about $35 million a year—roughly 12 per cent of the total—a military allocation larger than that of any other tropical African nation except the Congo; and it is generally thought to have the best training, men and equipment south of North Africa.

It has about 9,000 men (making it the fifth largest after Egypt, Ethiopia, Congo and the Sudan), some 60 per cent from the backward northern regions. Its officers, however, are almost all southern men, most of them in their 30s and none older than 50, all commissioned since 1950. Since independence, rapid promotion has created an officer strength of about 300, but more recently an inevitable "promotional freeze" has lessened the chances of advancement and caused some unhappiness in the ranks.

Major General Ankrah, now head of Ghana's National Liberation Council, is typical of the Ghanaian—and African—pattern. He was born in 1915 in Accra, his parents being members of the Ga tribe which originally settled the area. He went through secondary school in Accra, then joined the civil service as a teacher (1938), and was immediately seconded to the Education Corps of the Royal West African Frontier Force.

He was a private in this force when the war broke out in 1939 and rose to Warrant Officer II, in the meantime making a name for himself as a boxing champion and a fine soccer forward. Two years after the end of the war he was commissioned, only the second African to be made an officer by the British.

In 1960, he went to the Congo as commander of the 1st Battalion of the Ghana Infantry under the United Nations. The unit did a very impressive job in Kasai province under very difficult conditions (conditions so difficult, in fact, that one battalion mutinied). Ankrah is described by his then commander, General Alexander, as "probably the toughest fighting soldier in Ghana. He is incredibly ruthless in situations which demand violent action."

On the New Year's List of 1961, Ankrah was awarded the first Ghana Military Cross for his Congo service. Later that year he was appointed a Brigadier General and then in November, 1961, partly at Otu's insistence, was made Army Chief of Staff, a post he held until last July.

He says his hobbies are "football, fishing and reading"; his intellect is not thought to be remarkable, but he has a distinct way with his men, a blend of paternalism and autocracy that one finds in the best of Ghana's chiefs. He is reported to have three wives and twenty-two children, also in the fine chiefly tradition.

Little is known—even by the Ghanaians themselves—of the men around Ankrah, except J. W. K. Harley, the Commissioner of Police, who was appointed by Nkrumah in January, 1964, to replace a man suspected of having had a hand in the assassination attempt on the President earlier that month. Harley came in with many protestations of loyalty to Nkrumah and to the wonders of socialism. He allowed the police to play an active part in a much publicized drive to stamp out prostitution, close up European- and Lebanese-run night clubs, and in general to force on Ghana a socialist puritanism. But in time he became of the same mind as the army leaders, and his 8,000-man force was a vital element in supporting the coup.

What is the Westerner to make of this emergence to power of military men in Africa? In most quarters recently the opinion has been that it is all to the good—I've even heard one Ford Foundation official claim that "the army is the most democratic force in Africa" and argue, as many have done, that its efficiency and drive is the happy answer to Africa's problems.

In one sense, it *is* salutary to have the army in power. The old order—whether the dictatorship of Nkrumah, the corruption of Balewa (Nigeria), the bumbling of Dacko (Central African Republic) or the self-interest of Kasavubu (Congo) —is out, and the new cannot be any worse, at least at the beginning. Indeed, it is likely that in many immediate ways it will be better: it has aligned with the civil service to proclaim honesty and efficiency over politics and corruption, and by habit and training expects to get things done. The job won't be as easy as all that, as Mobutu in the Congo has now found out. Efficiency on Western patterns is simply not highly prized by the African populace, and honesty is only relative in cultures where nepotism and favor granting are traditionally effective instruments. But at least the drive is there.

In addition, the very fact that so many armies have taken over is a constant threat and reminder to politicians in power not to take things too easily—a lesson not lost on Uganda's Obote.

But a general is, after all, a general. The military mind that we know in the West is not so different from the military mind in Africa (the one, be it remembered, trained the other), and it is not, as we know, an especially open mind. Not that the generals will want to launch invasions or oppose fluoridation; but their patterns of thought are routinized and closed to novelty, their conception of jobs to be done is narrow, their notion of options is small. It would be impossible, for example, to think of Arthur Ankrah appreciating the distant but profound importance of the Volta River scheme; Nkrumah, for all his faults, understood it. Nor can one imagine General Ironsi sitting down to persuade a political opponent to subdue his personal designs for the good of the nation, as Balewa, for all his faults, did. We cannot expect from the military mind the grand designs and visions that Africa will need.

And this mind inevitably thinks in terms of force rather than persuasion, rigidity rather than fluidity; if politics is the art of the possible, soldiering is the science of the unreasonable. Suppose the army cannot get the efficiency it wants—does it cajole or does it force? Suppose directing a country is not quite as easy as directing a regiment—is the response orders and discipline, or is it rethinking and retooling? Nasser, it is now thought, had notions of turning the country back to the civilians (Latin Ameri-

can generals have occasionally had the same idea) but he came
around, not surprisingly, to believe that the civilians were inept
and that the military was the only force fit for the job. It is the
military mind at work.

This mind, at least in Africa, also has a very limited notion
of foreign affairs, and in fact the British-trained officers are
imbued with the idea that military men should keep so far out of
politics as not even to know East from West. The result of this
has been, as we have seen, a naïveté about the cold war and, as a
concomitant, an easy assumption that Russians and Chinese are
up to no good. The generals of Dahomey, Central African Republic and Burundi simply kicked out the Chinese; the Nige-
rians, Congolese and Upper Voltaians have pledged to keep out
or severely limit Communist delegations; and the Ghanaians are
now sending hundreds of Communists packing, including some
who were apparently performing much needed technical services.

This has all been greeted with much praise in the West, and
you could hear the editorial writers heave a sigh of relief that the
military men had brought the continent back to its senses and
put it in the Western camp. But it would be absolute folly for Africa to make of its neutralism a wall from which the Eastern blocs
were excluded. It would be folly because it would cut off a very
real source of aid; because it would tend to make these nations
client states of the West; and, most important, because it would
lessen, rather than increase, the amount of Western and especially
American aid, since our obvious and stated policy is to send in
money where there is a "Communist threat" and to be indifferent
where there is none. (On this last point, it is apparent that our
interest in Africa has sharply declined since about 1962, when the
Russians decided that their full-scale thrust into Africa was pre-
mature and began limiting their support. In fact, State Department policy makers cheerfully acknowledge that sub-Saharan Africa, of all areas in the world, has the lowest priority because it is
in least danger of Communist subversion.)

I see no reason, therefore, to greet the military take-overs
with an enthusiasm stripped of previous distaste for military regimes. It is proper to argue that the military has recently per-
formed some very real services to Africa; but to say then that they

are therefore champions of democracy, the panacea for economic ills and, especially, a bulwark of Western support, is dangerous and absurd. Indeed, whatever their short-term value, it will be the better for Africa—and for America—to see them safely back in their barracks.

And so what of the future? First, it is obvious that Nkrumah does not want to take all this lying down, but he really has no very good way of standing up to it. It is possible that from a base in Guinea he could use whatever money he has stashed away (and his opponents say it runs to the millions) to form a guerrilla army to invade Ghana through the "back door," the unguarded wastelands of the north. But the logistics problem is immense —none of the nations bordering Ghana has the slightest affection for the ex-"champion of Africa"—and neither Touré nor the other Nkrumah supporters can have much taste for getting their armies into an all-out war with Ghana's. It is much more likely that we shall see Nkrumah as professor of Neo-Colonialism at Conakry University than as General of a Liberation Brigade.

Nonetheless, we must not forget Nkrumah's very real and very emotional appeal in potent quarters throughout the continent. He has built up a tremendous reservoir of adulation among the politically awakened, especially in the southern nations where he often seemed to be the only leader prepared to do anything about helping them, the only one to cut through the cant about "liberating the south" with guns, money and refuge.

It is unlikely that this good will can be translated into action to put Nkrumah back on his throne, but it will remain an important ideological force for many years. The Ghanaian leaders should not ignore the influence of this "Nkrumahism," for, like Bonapartism, it has come to stand for certain noble aims and practical victories and, like Bonapartism, may become an idealized dream from which the horrors are left out. It will linger in the minds of the peasants if subsequent regimes do not live up to their promises.

Beyond the issue of Nkrumah himself, there is the question of what the military men can actually accomplish. At least for the

next year we can expect considerable progress on the econom
side: the closing of useless government bureaus, embassies, corp¢
rations and industries, and the efficient management of others.
The money saved by eliminating Ghana's silly show places, ration-
alizing Nigeria's regional industry, working instead of fighting in
the Congo, and cutting corruption in Dahomey and Upper Volta,
can bolster the faltering economies.

Also, the dedication and eagerness that a new regime brings
will increase efficiency and production. And with the cooperation
of now unfettered civil servants, overall economic plans can be
drawn up to chart progress on realistic rather than political
grounds, spur capital investment at home and from overseas, and
spell out the necessary but unpleasant tasks of relocation, re-
trenchment and reorganization. The military will do everything
it can to improve the lot of the common man—at least at the
start.

But will the civilians be back? The new regimes have all said
so (even Mobutu, though he is setting the rather comfortable
deadline of five years) , but these pledges have a way of getting
pushed off year after year as new crises develop (as they will) .
Not that the generals necessarily want to stay on—in fact Soglo in
Dahomey has tried twice to step down—but they'll think they
must. We can say, with the cynicism of experience, that the pros-
pects are not good for civilian rule (Pakistan and the Sudan are
exceptional) and that it will take all the pressure of liberal opinion, both there and outside, to make it come about.

Finally, what about the shock waves from the recent coups
reverberating in other countries? It is almost certain that other
nations will follow the pattern. Gabon, Tunisia, Liberia, Guinea,
Cameroun, Uganda, Kenya and Tanganyika have all already
faced threats from their armies, and there is no reason to think
that attempts will not be made again—especially in Liberia,
Uganda and Guinea. The military in Guinea, Mali, Egypt, Congo-
Brazzaville and Tanganyika is much more conservative, to the extent that it is political at all, than the politicians in power, and
this suggests a potential tinderbox, especially if the economic life
worsens. Only little Gambia seems relatively safe from a military
take-over—it has no army.

The problem, of course, is a difficult one for the civilian ruler. Does he build up the army, both to keep it quiet (soldiers love promotions and power) and to aid the economy (armies siphon off the unemployed and are very helpful in infrastructural development)? Or does he try to keep it small and forget about guarding his borders, keeping internal order, building national prestige and fulfilling international obligations? And if he builds the army, what does he use as a counterforce to keep it down on the base—a personal guard, or a people's militia (both anathema to the professional soldiers), places in the cabinet (the pattern in Latin America), occasional wars (as in Egypt), political control and indoctrination (as in Russia and China)?

It is a difficult tightrope to walk, and African leaders will have to use all their considerable skills to keep from tumbling. It is up to the rest of the world to do everything to help them. The threat is always there. Kwame Nkrumah knew of it: "When a social system . . . becomes . . . diseased," he wrote a few weeks ago, "a point is reached where the only alternative to constitutional change is a violent revolution." As it was, so it shall be.

Summation

The Developing Nations and International Order

The Developing Nations and International Order

WILSON C. McWILLIAMS

Toward a Definition of "Developing Nations"

Few political leaders in our time would question the importance of the developing nations in world politics. That importance has little to do with the present resources of the new nations. New states do control some raw materials which contribute, without being essential, to the strength of the great powers. Yet the most intense conflicts have been waged over states which count for little in raw materials; the resources of Cuba, for example, exist largely in the romantic visions of her chief of state.

The psychology of the publics of the great powers, rather than the strength of new nations, is responsible for the importance of the latter in world politics. At least in the United States, American-Soviet rivalry is conceived as an international football game, in which success is measured by the yardage occupied on a world map. We disliked "losing" China and we fear to "lose" South Viet Nam. These sentiments must receive their due. If important elements of opinion in either of the great powers become convinced that they are "losing" and that "time is against us," they may seek to employ violence in a desperate effort to avert disaster.[1]

[1] Charles Wolf, "Some Aspects of the 'Value' of Less Developed Countries to the United States," *World Politics, 15* (1963) , 623–635.

Adapted from a paper presented to the Conference on the Military in Developing Nations, sponsored by the Oberlin College student International Affairs Committee, March 1965.

The political significance of the developing nations, at the moment, is that they serve as an arena for conducting contests between the great powers at a time when a direct contest is too perilous to contemplate. That function is an old one: it is directly analogous to the "importance" of the non-Western areas in the age of imperialism. In fact, the bargaining of neutralist leaders is not entirely dissimilar to the efforts of traditional rulers in the nineteenth century, who sought to gain the greatest possible advantage from various willing European "protectors." If leaders in new states today find themselves in a stronger bargaining position, that position is the result not of increased relative strength in the new states themselves, but of the sharper conflicts of our own period. There is less agreement among the great powers to "fix prices" in the more competitive market of the Cold War.

Nevertheless, any approach to international politics based on the present alone is a very dangerous one. Too often diplomats and experts have conceived the world in terms of a static image fixed by their own expertise. That tendency may be greater in our times, when the pressure of events makes grand conceptions of the future a luxury and the future is darkened by the rapidity of change itself. Certainly, statesmen in the great states must beware of the parochial vision which would perceive international politics solely in terms of present realities, and any study of world politics in an age of change must consider the dynamic forces at work to revise the existing scheme of things. In that sense, the developing nations—states which we conceive of in dynamic images—may hold much that is important to the future of international politics.

To speak of "the developing nations" is, of course, to oversimplify. Great differences exist between particular states in terms of traditional culture and institutions, the character of their contact with the West, and the resources available for the tasks of development. There are similarities as well as differences—common problems and processes which may be more important to international politics than are the disparities between particular states.

Not the least of the common elements is the process of "development" itself. The term has ambiguities, but its central meaning is clear. It refers to that process which has given unity to the last four and a half centuries of international political history: the expansion of modern political organization, based on an equally dynamic expansion of industrialism and technology. That one may speak of *an* international politics, and not merely the politics of states within some limited (ecumene,) is a result of those dynamic forces which have expanded the European state system until it includes the world.[2]

In our times, the process of technological change and the expansion of man's power over nature has become almost divorced from the decisions of states and men. It is, as Arnold Gehlen has termed it, a "meta-human" process to which men and states adapt themselves or perish. This is not an age when men are confident of the future, nor one which is charmed by visions of utopia. Power over nature involves power over man, and the early hope that this might make possible a transformation of human life has been fulfilled only too well. If technology has greatly lightened the burdens of men, it has also proved to be subject to the most horrifying abuses and productive of the greatest perils in human history. Man in nature can be commanded by reducing him to an object in nature: by threatening him with violence and terror; by controlling his emotions and perceptions; by the insecurity which results when he sees himself—accurately enough—as a small unit in an incomprehensible world, and is compelled to combine that perception of finitude with the despair of loneliness and isolation.[3]

The expansion of power over men has come to seem the only security in a world in which power grows by what appear to be its own laws. To be safe is to command; to control provides the only sense of being free. It is easy to criticize the thesis of Professor Hans Morgenthau, that all states are moved by the *animus dominandi,* but it is impossible to deny its persuasiveness as a description of the political life of the modern world. Softer language

[2] F. H. Hinsley, *Power and the Pursuit of Peace* (London: Cambridge University Press, 1963).

[3] Arnold Gehlen, "L'Avenir de la Culture," *Bulletin SEDEIS*, Futuribles No. 50 (March 10, 1963). Bertrand de Jouvenel, *On Power* (New York: Viking, 1949). Hannah Arendt, *The Origins of Totalitarianism* (New York: Harcourt, Brace, 1952).

conceals the same creed: the belief of many that the Cold War is a "struggle for the minds of men" has implications which are grim enough, seen in its proper light. We are far removed from that springtime creed which pronounced that the expansion of power over nature was safe because only the civilized could possess that power and the civilized would never employ it. And we are only slightly less distant from that axiom of Spinoza's that the mind, unlike the body, cannot be chained.[4]

For the West, this foreboding is new enough. The process of expansion began in Western Europe, where, as a result, change was a matter of choice and a decision which seemed the result of individual will. The West has, for the most part, retained the lead which it won by that early advantage, and the sense of initiative has remained high. Indeed, the West has been prone to the great illusion of the initiators: He who acts first controls, and he who wins the race commands. Only recently have we been forced to realize that the race and the contest command the contestants, whoever emerges with the laurel. Not for nothing have the Western nations conceived of nationality and politics in terms of the choices of individuals, or spoken of the nation, as Renan did, as a "daily plebiscite." In fact, a persistent problem of American foreign policy arises from the widespread belief that a firm will is all that is required in order to shape the international order according to our desires.

Indeed, the least suggestion that our lead has been lost has proved capable of galvanizing the United States as few other political facts have sufficed to do. The missile gap by becoming rumor became fact; the Russian sputnik sparked a demand for a revolution in American education. In a world in which the fragile security of men has been stripped of most of its insulating myths, and insecurity has become the ubiquitous fact of the time, the ability to make others "dance to our tune" has become the last of the myths available to nations and men.

---

[4] Hans Speier, "Risk, Security and Modern Hero-Worship," in Speier, *The Social Order and the Risks of War* (New York: George Stewart, 1952), pp. 112–128. J. F. Wolpert, "The Myth of Revolution," *Ethics, 58* (1948), 245–255. Bertrand de Jouvenel, *Sovereignty* (Chicago: University of Chicago Press, 1957). H. J. Morgenthau, *Politics Among Nations* (New York: Knopf, 1952).

For the developing nations of Africa, Asia, and Latin America, there have been few comforting myths, and least of all the myth of control. These are the passive lands whose only choice has been that between changing and being changed, between internal transformation as the price of survival or transformation imposed by direct imperialism or the more indirect methods of commercial penetration. The myth of exploitation, whatever its reality, gained strength because of the obvious fact that the developing nations would not have been able to prevent exploitation had it been the policy of the West.

Trust does not exist where one acts with impunity and the other must obey. Even charity, in such circumstances, is condescending and degrading to him who receives it, and becomes a source of hostility. The smug assumptions of Western nations that our culture was superior, if not our race, has only added to what, in any case, would have been a history of indignity.[5]

The developing nations are, in fact, the "undignified nations," the states which have had to dance to the tune of others. To recognize that fact is to penetrate much of the obscurity that surrounds the term "developing." The phrase "emerging nations" was closer to the truth—embarrassingly close, in fact, because it suggested states emerging from darkness into light. Does the term "developing" imply that the United States or Western Europe is static? More to the point, why are Spain and Portugal not included among the developing nations? The Iberian powers are no less poor than many new nations; they are no less static and feudal than Ethiopia or Yemen. Yet there is something about Iberia: Spain and Portugal were *once* part of the league of initiators, once elements of the international community, and once possessed of dignity. In short, they have a past if not a present, and, in fact, they might be called the *déclassé*, as opposed to the developing, nations.

The index of political development is not a particular political system like "democracy" or "the rule of law": it is the *capacity to command dignity*, to escape the "cultural shame" of a people forced to change regardless of their own will. The ability to com-

<hr>

[5] L. Solomon, "Power, Game Strategies and Interpersonal Trust," *Journal of Abnormal and Social Psychology, 61* (1960), 223–230.

mand dignity is not simply the ability to command attention: a child can do as much without acquiring dignity, though his cries are doubtless a protest against the indignity of his lot. *Dignitas,* as the Romans knew, implies the ability to control in part the actions of others.[6]

Of course, one may speak of the "dignity of the individual." The indignity suffered by the developing nations has, for the most part, been collective and cultural. The individual lacks the means of acquiring dignity for himself; that much has been the universal experience of those "Westernized" intellectuals who have found themselves second-class members, at best, of the culture of the West. The reaction of those intellectuals has been the same the world over: to seek to develop or discover in one's own people a dignity equal to that offered by the culture of the West. The ideologies of nationalism outside Western Europe have a common structure and content. They begin by postulating certain beliefs and institutions as "Western," normally those negative qualities which have been subjected to the critique of Western romantics. The opposing qualities, valued by the disenchanted intellectuals of the West, are postulated as the "traits" of one's own people. "They," the argument goes, "are rationalized, individualized, materialistic, segmental personalities which have lost wholeness in an urban civilization. We, by contrast, are close to the emotions, to the spirit, to nature and the soil; our genius is collective and conducive to wholeness of personality and the integration of man." The theme is much the same, whether those who voice it speak of a *Volksgeist,* a Slavic soul, Eastern wisdom, or *négritude.*[7]

[6] On the concept of dignity, see R. E. Gahringer, "On the Moral Importance of Status and Position," *Ethics,* 67 (1957), 200–202. With respect to the new states, see Rupert Emerson, "Nationalism and Political Development," *Journal of Politics,* 22 (1960), 3–28; and James Coleman, "Economic Development and Political Reorientation," in M. J. Herskovits and Mitchell Harwitz, eds., *Economic Transition in Africa* (Evanston, Ill.: Northwestern University Press, 1963), p. 381. On the concept of cultural shame, see Pierre van den Berghe, *Caneville: The Social Structure of a South African Town* (Middletown, Conn.: Wesleyan University Press, 1963), pp. 46–59.

[7] C. J. H. Hayes, *The Historical Evolution of Modern Nationalism* (New York: Macmillan, 1931). P. Padhye, "The Intellectual in Modern Asia," in H. Passen, ed., *Cultural Freedom in Asia* (New York: Tuttle, 1956), pp. 68–81.

It has seemed paradoxical to those Westerners who admired these doctrines that the states professing them should seek to acquire those Western techniques and institutions which the ideology denounces. Yet the same thread unites the doctrine (with its accents of Rousseau) and the policy of seeking technological and industrial growth: the search for the collective dignity of people.

Those who admired the romantic nationalism of the nineteenth century learned, to their cost, that it contains an element of implicit imperialism. Indeed, Richard Koebner identified one meaning of imperialism *with* the sense of "collective dignity." In this sense, imperialism need not be expansionistic: one may feel dignity in one's own country. Still, dignity always involves the sense of control. Secure men may refrain from exercising their powers, confident of their ability to appeal to power should the need arise. New states and new nations, however, are neither confident nor secure, and even the confidence of the greatest powers may be shattered in an age like our own. The new nations have reminded us of our own desire for collective dignity, the "neocolonialism" which expresses itself softly in the demand for gratitude from those we aid and, as often, in stronger measures and techniques. It is only just that we should not hesitate to observe the same temptations in the new nations, temptations made only greater by the resentment which is the heritage of the past. The process of technological change is the heritage of all men, and increasingly the indignities that it inflicts and the resentments against them are suffered by all nations alike.[8]

Assimilation and Mobilization to the International Order

Although Karl Deutsch's *Nationalism and Social Communication* was designed to apply to the analysis of internal politics, his concepts may be employed in the analysis of the international order. Deutsch argues that nationalism arises where groups are "mobilized" to a central political system of decision without

---

Boyd Shafer, *Nationalism: Myth and Reality* (New York: Harcourt, Brace, 1955), Chap. 7. B. Malinowski, *The Dynamics of Cultural Change* (New Haven, Conn.: Yale University Press, 1945).

[8] Richard Koebner, *Empire* (New York: Grosset and Dunlap, 1956).

being "assimilated" to it, provided that the barriers which prevent assimilation are perceived as based on the "nationality" of the mobilized (rather than, for example, on their class or race).[9]

Obviously, within the developing nations, such a process of mobilization is proceeding apace, and such states face a race to "assimilate" traditional ethnic and tribal groups to the "nation." Where such assimilation falls short, particularistic and secessionistic "national" movements are likely to develop around the symbols of tribe and ethnicity. In this sense, Gonzalez Casanova has argued, the developing nations are engaged in a task of "internal colonialism." [10]

Yet the developing nation as a whole has also been "mobilized" to the international order without being "assimilated" to it. That African, Asian, and Latin American nations have been admitted to the United Nations only symbolizes the extent to which the U.N. is not the arena in which the great decisions of international politics are made. Were the United States or the Soviet Union to consult a developing nation on the great issues of the time, it would be a gracious, but condescending, gesture.[11]

The two processes of mobilization—internal and international—are distinct; yet the internal mobilization of traditional groups is a part of, and contained within, the mobilization of the state as a whole to the international order. There are few enough common standards of value within a new state, and it is understandable if political leaders appeal for unity on the basis of the one political attitude shared by traditional and modern sectors of the economy and society of new states: hostility to the foreign powers which have imposed indignity on all the citizens of a new nation. Few states in the present age are entirely free from the need for an object of hostility to justify sacrifices and to serve as an outlet for aggression for citizens who sense their personal importance in the state as too miniscule to serve as the basis for pos-

[9] Karl W. Deutsch, *Nationalism and Social Communication* (New York: Wiley, 1953).

[10] Pablo Gonzalez Casanova, "Sociedad Plural, Colonialismo Interno, y Desarrollo," *America Latina, 6* (1963), 15–32.

[11] Ali A. Mazrui, "On the Concept 'We are all Africans,'" *American Political Science Review, 58* (1963), 88–97. Kenneth Grundy, "Nkrumah's Theory of Underdevelopment," *World Politics, 15* (1963), 438–454.

itive loyalties. The "movement states" find that object of hostility almost entirely essential.[12]

Acquiring the economic and technical sinews of the modern state is a deeply frustrating process. Traditional values must be set aside and traditional institutions cast into discard. Immediate satisfactions, and the immediate relations between men, must be repressed when they are contrary to hopes for economic growth in the "long term." Even a developed state like the Soviet Union restricts economic consumption in ways Americans would find intolerable. As social theorists have always realized, "civilization" demands that much of the expression of emotion in interpersonal relations be suppressed, and that men govern themselves not by their immediate judgment but by institutional processes thought to be "functional" for the state as a whole.[13]

Obviously, emotional repression accounts for much of the fascination with romance which has been the undertow of modern culture. Yet any state must allow some minimal expression of affection and emotion, and most states can afford to do so. It is essential, however, that the state exclude the expression of violence or aggression in interpersonal relations—that, in the sociological dictum, the state acquire a "monopoly of the legitimate use of violence." Romance may find some outlet inside the state; aggression can seek expression only outside it.[14]

The frustrations of development, difficult enough in a comparatively affluent state, are magnified greatly in a new state, which, if it hopes to close the gap separating it from the industrial powers, must demand massive austerities precisely at the point in time characterized by a "revolution of rising expecta-

[12] Robert Tucker, "Toward a Comparative Politics of Movement Regimes," *American Political Science Review, 55* (1961), 281–289.

[13] Sigmund Freud, *Civilization and its Discontents* (London: Hogarth, 1955; orig. pub. 1929). K. H. Silvert, "National Values, Development, and Leaders and Followers," *International Social Science Journal, 5* (1963), 560–570. Wilson C. McWilliams and Jonathon W. Polier, "Pan Africanism and the Dilemmas of National Development," *Phylon, 25* (1964), 47–49. F. Deyrup, "The Limits of Governmental Activity," *Social Research, 24* (1957), 191–201.

[14] Friederich von Wieser, *Das Gesetz der Macht* (Vienna: Springer, 1926). K. F. Helleiner, "Moral Conditions of Economic Growth," *Journal of Economic History, 12* (1951), 112–113.

tions" among its people. Frustrations and resentments rise accordingly, and states fear to tolerate even that verbal aggression which characterizes opposing political parties. Opposition is too divisive of the strength of a people, the argument goes, who must channel as much as possible of their emotions and energies into the quest for the future and the search for dignity.

The solution of the internal crisis of new states only *raises* the problem posed for the international order. *Assimilating* the vast majority of citizens to the "nation state" only has the effect of *mobilizing* them to the international political system. Indeed, it is not among the traditionalistic and tribal that the greatest hostility to the great powers is found; it is encountered among those who have learned "cultural shame," the sense that traditional cultures are inferior without having developed a new culture that can command international dignity.[15]

One may, in fact, notice a marked distinction between the first and second generations in the history of "developing states" in the past. The first generation of nationalist leaders is inclined to accept the international system as a given to which the nation must "adapt itself." The leaders of the first generation are forced to accept technical and economic inferiority as a *fact*. In their efforts to obtain independence or to protect it, they are inclined to rely on political weapons—on the doctrines of democracy and self-determination and on the maneuvers of what is often a very subtle diplomacy. Indeed, even if they originally conceived of the practices of diplomacy and the doctrines of democratic rule as tools to be employed in the quest for national dignity, they may develop a deep identification with those symbols as such. The first generation is, moreover, preoccupied with the problems of *internal* development and change, inclined to offer broad promises for the future and to invite sacrifice in the interests of gains to be won.

Second generations—the designation is, of course, a loose one—may very well differ. The first generation of leaders may

[15] Emerson, *loc. cit.* T. C. Smith, "The Discontented," *Journal of Asian Studies, 22* (1962), 215–219. David Riesman, "Las Personas Particulares, La Política Pública," *Ciencias Sociales, 4* (1960), 541–560.

feel that it has acquired sufficient *dignitas* in the establishment of a nation-state. The second generation of nationalists, a vastly larger group than the first, takes the state as a given, not as their own achievement. Indeed, the accomplishments of the state may seem tawdry in the light of the promises of early leaders. Prudent consideration of the state's weakness may appear pusillanimous and unworthy. Moreover, the second generation may feel more at home with the instruments of technology, more adept in manipulating violence, than was possible for the "symbol wielders" of the first. Indeed, the older generation will increasingly come to appear bombastic, uneducated, crude, incompetent, and—worse—traitors to the national destiny, "white Africans" over-awed by their former superiors.[16]

Benjamin Franklin observed long ago that, to become free of alien rule, it is not sufficient to win a war of rebellion. Political independence and internal consolidation do not—Dr. Nkrumah aside—"grant all things" to a new state, international dignity least of all. Our own history provides many illustrations: the passing of the Constitutional generation opened the door, gradually, to the "war hawks" of 1812 and, eventually, to those second-generation leaders who felt assured that the dignity of the United States required that she demonstrate her "manifest destiny."

In the modern world it is impossible to attain "freedom from alien rule." The lesson which the leaders of the great states—and many of the first generation of leaders in the new nations—have learned (and their publics have not) is that "alien rule" can be avoided in modern life only when all men cease to regard one another as aliens. Short of that ideal, we must all become accus-

[16] Georges Blond, *Admiral Togo* (New York: Macmillan, 1960), pp. 22–23, 127–128. H. Feith, "Indonesia's Political Symbols and Their Wielders," *World Politics, 16* (1964), 79–97. T. Yoshihashi, *Conspiracy at Mukden* (New Haven, Conn.: Yale University Press, 1963). Richard Hughes, "Red Army out of Step," *New Republic, 147* (September 17, 1962), 9–11. Martin Kilson, "Nationalism and Classes in British West Africa," *Journal of Politics, 20* (1958), 368–387. S. D. Brown, "Okubo Toshimichi," *Journal of Asian Studies, 21* (1962), 183–197. L. Berkowitz, "Repeated Frustrations and Expectations in Hostility Arousal," *Journal of Abnormal and Social Psychology, 60* (1960), 422–429.

tomed to the fact that many of the decisions which shape and structure our lives will be made by persons and groups abroad.[17]

The Military at Home and Abroad

Few states indeed have avoided a period of aggressive and truculent behavior in international affairs. Yet, just as the object of aggression is the international order which is thought to deny a given state its "place in the sun," so the limits and the forms of aggression are set by the nature of the international order in which the state finds itself. The very fact that total freedom from alien rule is impossible suggests that supranational forces *govern* and that national forces are expressed within the context established by those larger forces. The structure of international politics can act to mitigate, as it can encourage, aggressive behavior in the relations of nations.[18]

Certainly, it has been difficult for most political scientists (especially for liberal political scientists) to imagine the new nations in an aggressive role in the international order. The circumstances of new states have encouraged the development of an ideology, common to most of their governmental elites, which is almost aggressively nonviolent, or even pacifistic. Such doctrines have two advantages: (1) They are immensely fashionable; and (2) they express the hostility of new states toward the massive armaments of the great powers, the symptom of their ascendancy over new states in the international order. Yet, as has been suggested, such doctrines may be more characteristic of the first, rather than the second, generation of leaders of new states.

Even in the first generation, the ideologies of nonviolence tend, at best, to be a feeble reed on which to rest hope. India's Gandhism has not prevented her successive conflicts with Hyderabad, with Pakistan, with Portugal, and with China; the "spiritual atom bomb" of Peking has acquired a most unspiritual form. When Obafemi Awolowo sought to gain the endorsement of his own nonviolent views from his Action Group in Nigeria, his

[17] William Kornhauser, "Rebellion and Political Development," in Harry Ekstein, ed., *Internal War* (New York: Free Press, 1964), pp. 142–156.

[18] Simon Kuznets, "The State as a Unit in the Study of Economic Growth," *Journal of Economic History, 11* (1951), 34–35.

proposal was rejected. (And, paradoxically, Awolowo was subsequently indicted by the Nigerian government for planning violent revolution against the regime.) [19]

The ideologies of nonviolence and pacifism represent, at best, the commitment of individual leaders and groups within new states. They do not represent the basic commitment of the state as a political order. As Ali A. Mazrui has argued, the highest value in the ethical hierarchy of the new states is not peace but dignity, which is felt to justify violations of the peace. The new state is likely to excuse China's atomic testing, while it could not exculpate the great powers of France for the same offense; China's expansionism appears less reprehensible than the policy of the Republic of South Africa, admittedly peaceful but offensive to human dignity. This, in fact, is only to restate the obvious: that a concern for the dignity of men or groups of men is not always conducive to the peace, an end better attained by humility than pride. Hitler, after all, could speak of a "higher humanity" as the chief aim of Nazi policy. As Thomas Hobbes knew better than many philosophers of our own time, "vainglory" ranks high among the causes of conflict between men. [20]

The quest for dignity is normally expressed in the rhetoric of "national self-determination." That doctrine has always been ambiguous, and self-determination has, in the literal sense, become impossible in the modern world. (Logically, self-determination in conditions of interdependence can only imply the right to control others.) As the theorists of the social contract knew, the rational solution in such a situation is a "contract" based on mutual limitation and control. Modern theorists who have hoped that "technical interdependence" or a "world balance of power" would lead, gradually, to expanded international government often tend to forget what the social-contract theorist

[19] McWilliams and Polier, *loc. cit.*, pp. 62–63. Coleman, *op. cit.*, p. 389. Richard Sklar, *Nigerian Political Parties: Power in an Emergent African Nation* (Princeton, N.J.: Princeton University Press, 1963).

[20] A. A. Mazrui, "The United Nations and Some African Political Attitudes," *International Organization, 18* (1964), 499–520. T. A. Sumberg, "After Imperialism," *American Journal of Economics and Sociology, 22* (1963), 527–532. Adolf Hitler, *Mein Kampf* (New York: Reynal and Hitchcock, 1938), pp. 592–595.

knew only too well: men tend to accept the necessity for such a contract only after they have passed through a "state of war." [21]

In the eyes of the new nations, international law is not the result of a "natural law," nor even of a very exalted standard of human values. (Latin American nations, inheritors of traditional reverence for international law, tend to regard that law as hopelessly perverted in the present time.) The most "realistic" of nations, they incline to regard international law as the handmaiden of force. Thrasymachus, and not Socrates, forms the basis of their conception of international justice.

The rejection of the "law of dominion" and the conception that colonialism represents "permanent aggression," stripped of its high-flown language, comes down to the argument that established international rights have no value, if in the judgment of a given state those rights violate the "self-determination" of the people concerned. What upholds the rights of South Africa, or Portugal, or of regimes thought to be "instruments" of the United States or some other "colonial" power is not right but force. Nor can one argue that there is no justification for this position: those who live by the sword may well expect to perish by it. The argument of the new nations is irrefutable: The rights of colonial powers were established by force, and the current dominion of the Big Two is a result of force. When the great powers before World War II solemnly signed treaties with the Nazi regime, they hardly established respect for the rules of international law beyond what force will maintain.[22]

The expansion of the international community since 1856 has not resulted from a sense of international justice. Rather, it has resulted from the increasing value attached *by the great powers to peace* over claims to dignity and justice. Indeed, that value is the great weapon which lies in the hands of the new states. As commitment to peace rises, men lose the capacity to attach conditions to it, to specify the *kind* of peace which they will accept. If

[21] Hinsley, *op. cit.* A. Etzioni, "The Dialectics of Supra-National Unification," *American Political Science Review, 56* (1962), 927–935.

[22] A. A. Mazrui, "Consent, Colonialism and Sovereignty," *Political Studies, 11* (1963), 36–55. C. W. Jenks, *The Common Law of Mankind* (New York: Praeger, 1958). R. Aron, "The Diffusion of Atomic Weapons," *Atlantic, 215* (January 1965), 50.

"peace at any price" is not yet the rule, the price is clearly higher than any which a nineteenth-century state would have accepted. Entrance into the international community, as Rolling has indicated, ceased to be based on "Christianity" by 1856 (if not before) ; by 1933, "civilization" ceased to be its basis either. The limitation in the Charter of the United Nations, that members must be "peace-loving," reduced the conditions for membership to the sole condition that a state should *prefer* peace to war as a condition for gaining its ends; the importance assigned to force in the Charter was designed to strengthen that preference by the *fear* of violence.[23] Yet it is possible to argue that today, the condition of membership has declined from peace-loving to peace-accepting. Any state which can *threaten* the peace becomes less an object of potential sanctions by the United Nations or the international community than an object to be wooed with the aim of inducing her to accept the peace by concessions. Few would be so bold as to argue that the Chinese regime "loves" peace, yet the argument of many is that *because* the Chinese do not love peace, we must admit them into the international community in the hope that they will learn to do so—an argument with great validity in the age of nuclear weapons.

It is hardly to be expected that the new nations will fail to learn the lesson: International dignity and consideration can be won as readily, if not more readily, by those who set their honor and prestige at a higher price than they do peace. Not for nothing did the Casablanca powers at Addis Ababa direct their policy toward the establishment of an African military command, or make the gesture of a $700,000 fund for a combined force for an African "Common Market."[24]

What limits the aggressiveness of new nations is not doctrine nor a commitment to international law, but the wisdom of their leaders and the perception of their own weakness. The "fund" of the African nations is ludicrous on the international scale, and the new nations confront a military inferiority far greater than

[23] B. V. Rolling, *International Law in an Expanded World* (Amsterdam: Djambattan, 1960) .

[24] McWilliams and Polier, *loc. cit.*, p. 51. V. McKay, *Africa in World Politics* (New York: Harper, 1963) , pp. 400–401.

that which inhibited such early "new nations" as Japan, Italy, or the Soviet Union.

Military historians have demarcated at least six distinct stages of military technology since 1800, and these stages have succeeded one another with increasing rapidity. The emergent nation which would play a military role in international politics has confronted an increasingly difficult task. States which began the process of development in the period from 1850 to 1890 had only to develop a military technology adequate for the second stage: a military system dominated by the breech-loading rifle, light rifled field guns, and comparatively small ironclad steam vessels. Virtually all of the new states which developed as great powers in a military sense acquired national independence or began industrial development during this period: Germany, Italy, Japan, and Russia. For the states which began the process after 1890, the technological level which must be reached as a condition of great-power status is increasingly high. Indeed, Italy found herself unable to keep pace by 1939, if not earlier.[25]

Technological change in the military sphere implied very early that small states would cease to be vital units in the international military system. "In former times," Cyril Falls comments, "the small nations suffered only from the disadvantage of being small, not from that of being proportionately worse armed." [26] In recent times, by contrast, a vast gap has opened between the military *equipment* as well as the resources of small and large states. Indeed, what constitutes a "small power" in our time is not so much its *size* in territory or population—or even in resources (though these factors remain important)—as its ability to maintain the *pace of development and obsolescence*. In other words, the test of military power in the contemporary period has become the command of (1) sufficient technological and scientific skills to develop new weapons systems and (2) sufficient economic resources to produce such weapons rapidly and to enable the state to afford the cost of discarding and replacing obsolete weapons.

[25] Cyril Falls, *A Hundred Years of War, 1850–1950* (London: Duckworth, 1953). On technological rates of change, see Charles Beard and G. Smith, *The Old Deal and the New* (New York: Macmillan, 1940), p. 7.

[26] Falls, *op. cit.,* p. 16.

Many developed nations have the first, but lack the second; Sweden and, in recent years, Great Britain fall into this category. Such states are the small powers of the present world. In both areas, the preeminence of the United States and the Soviet Union is too great to brook competition.[27]

This statement is not meant to imply that the traditional distinction between *resources* and the *intensity* with which those resources are used has been abolished. Far from it: the resources of the Soviet Union are probably considerably less than those of the United States, but they are employed in a military effort of comparatively greater intensity. In two senses, the importance of resources relative to intensity has grown: (1) The distinction between military and civilian uses of technology has decreased markedly, so that any resource can with comparative ease become a military resource; and (2) the arms race and the Cold War have raised the *intensity* with which the inherent resources of the great powers are used, thus decreasing the ability of lesser states to compensate for weakness by increased sacrifices.

Although France's *force de frappe* is not intended as a direct challenge to the great powers, she has found the cost of such a force to be very high indeed. At the cost of great economic sacrifices, China has managed to develop an atomic weapon. It must be emphasized, however, that China's sacrifice has purchased her a weapon already obsolete. Even if China developed the technology to produce the hydrogen bomb and the missile systems which are the symbols of *current* weapons technology, and if she concentrated a high percentage of her resources in producing them in quantities sufficient to make them effective, she would almost certainly find those weapons obsolete by the time they were developed.[28] Moreover, China is, in a certain sense, *sui generis*. Few developing states have anything approaching her capacity for central control and decision; fewer still have anything vaguely approximating her great inherent resources.

Indeed, for most developing nations, the cost of military

---

[27] *Ibid.*, pp. 18–19. Kenneth Waltz, "The Stability of a Bipolar World," *Daedalus, 93* (1964), 894–895.

[28] Waltz, *loc. cit.* Cf. *The New York Times,* February 4, 1964, p. 2, and April 17, 1964, p. 3.

forces on even a modest scale is too high to bear. Nigeria, one of the most inherently powerful states of Africa, expended 17.9 per cent of her budget in 1961 for defense—and obtained a military force of 8,000 troops and 12,000 police. Guinea has thought of herself as a nation in arms and of her army as a vehicle for civic education. Yet, in 1961, with 25 per cent of her budget devoted to the military, Guinean forces totaled only 5,500 troops and 2,100 police.[29]

Internal violence and guerrilla war may take place in the developing nations, but such violence exists well within the limits established by the system of relations established by the great powers. The rise of guerrilla war in prominence in recent years should not delude international analysts; it is an old weapon, and a characteristic weapon of developing states. Always restricted to areas of rough or dense terrain, isolated or rural settlement, the classic problem of guerrilla war was the inability to coordinate the activities of widely scattered guerrilla bands. Modern flexible and mobile communication has made guerrilla war marvelously more effective, but it has not changed its nature. Guerrilla war is an index of the *weakness* of a state or a colony in the international system. Industrial organization and modern police establishments make it virtually impossible; the famous *résistance* of World War II was little more than an annoyance to the Germans. A disorganized or highly decentralized social organization makes a state difficult to control, but it is also a measure of its weakness in the international order. Machiavelli commented that the France of his times was "hard to keep," which was only the corollary of the fact that she was "easy to conquer." [30]

A guerrilla war may overthrow a weak domestic regime; it cannot militarily defeat a great power. The aim of guerrilla armies, like those in Algeria or the successive forces in Viet Nam, which find themselves ranged against a comparatively powerful state, is to create such annoyance as to make the area *not worth fighting for* in the eyes of the great power itself. Weakness,

[29] McKay, *loc. cit.* Cf. V. du Bois, "The Role of the Military in Guinea," *Africa Report, 8* (January 1963) , 3–5.

[30] Machiavelli, *The Prince* (New York: Modern Library, 1950; orig. pub. 1532) , Chap. 4. Waltz, *loc. cit.*, p. 887.

George Orwell might have commented, is strength: the unimportance of the area is an indication of the likelihood that guerrilla war will succeed against a great power. The true strength of a guerrilla movement is in that variety of irrationality known as "zeal" and "patriotism": in the eyes of the patriot, the value of his country is magnified beyond any standard that its resources might suggest to any state which employed a purely utilitarian calculus.

It is likely enough that there will be conflicts *among* the developing nations. The first assaults of a new state have normally been directed at its "traditional" rivals, not at the great powers themselves. (The Sino-Japanese war of the 1890's and the "War of the Pacific" in Latin America are illustrations.) The risks of adventurism are minimal; the internal political gains in solidarity may be great. Indeed, the world of the new nations has proliferated a series of irredentist conflicts which—in the case of the Arab-Israeli conflict—almost reach the stage of total war. The Arab-Israeli conflict is illustrative. The war, as perceived by the Arabs, is a war against a *Western* state; it is the analogue of African hostility to the remnants of colonial powers. Such wars—as the African conflict with South Africa may become—tend to be total because the object of enmity symbolizes all the resentment and felt inferiority of the new state itself; it is not a case of hostility diverted from its "natural" object to a convenient foe (as, say, the Moroccan-Algerian conflict appears to be). Thus, at least two forms of international conflict seem likely to take place in non-Western areas: (1) conflicts between non-Western nations, normally waged in support of irredentist claims, or against governments thought to be pro-Western and betrayers of the "solidarity" of new nations, and (2) conflicts between non-Western nations and weak or peripheral Western states—Portugal, Israel, or the South African Republic.[31]

[31] I. M. Lewis, "Pan Africanism and Pan Somalism," *Journal of Modern African Studies, 1* (1963), 147–162. Dennis Austin, "The Uncertain Frontier: Ghana Togo," *Journal of Modern African Studies, 1* (1963), 139–145. Douglas Ashford, "The Irredentist Appeal in Morocco and Mauretania," *Western Political Quarterly, 15* (1962), 641–645; and "Politics and Violence in Morocco," *Middle East Journal, 13* (1954), 11–25. Jean Ziegler, *La Contre Révolution en Afrique* (Paris: Payot, 1963).

Such conflicts, it must be noted, will take place only within the context established by the international system at large. To the extent that such conflicts are felt to be dangerous to the great powers, the great states are likely to intervene to prevent such conflicts from taking place. The United States has consistently prevented conflict in the Caribbean area and, with less uniformity, in Latin America in general. The perennial Romanian and Hungarian dispute over Transylvania is not likely to result in violence. Similar, if not identical, limitations restrict the conflict of Israel with her neighbors, and of India with Pakistan.

The military and political weakness of the new nations makes it less likely that they will adopt the policy of the nation in arms, at least at the moment. Although such a policy permits a state to demand great sacrifices, it must make those sacrifices proportional to some hoped-for gain or to the danger of some proximate threat. Threats may exist (Cuba is the obvious example), but these are comparatively rare. It does not pay a great state to threaten a weaker one which can be allowed the expense of independence without much loss to the great power itself. Very few potential gains are open to new states which might make sacrifice seem worth the effort. Even the citizens of a small state, David Rapoport has observed, may regard their government as too unimportant in the international system to be worthy of great sacrifices. The revolution of expectations only makes it more difficult to extract sacrifice: the gains must seem greater, the threats more menacing with the passage of time. Indeed, without potential foreign threats or gains, a national militia is a perilous thing for a regime to establish, for it can easily turn on the regime itself. It was with some irony that the republican Machiavelli advised the prince to seek a civil militia because "where there are good arms, there must be good laws." [32]

Crisis does not always draw the people of a nation together.[33] A crisis must have some apparent solution which group action

---

[32] *The Prince,* Chap. 12. David Rapoport, "A Comparative Theory of Political and Military Types," in Samuel Huntington, ed., *Changing Patterns of Military Politics* (New York: Free Press, 1962), pp. 99–101.

[33] R. Hamblen, "Group Integration during a Crisis," *Human Relations,* *11* (1958), 67–76.

can obtain. To concentrate too much attention on foreign dangers which *cannot* be eliminated is to divide, rather than unite, the community. In the extreme case, such irremediable menace leads to a *sauve qui peut* akin to that in South Viet Nam. In less extreme cases, it tends to lead to declining confidence in a regime which has proved unable to eliminate the danger to the nation.

Since hostility to foreign powers is the common denominator of consensus in the new nations, and since the opportunity to express such aggression overtly is limited, internal divisions and crises are likely to persist in the new states. Where such crisis becomes extreme, the military may attempt to impose order by force, or a civil government may seek to use the military for that purpose. In the Middle East, it has long been observed that military regimes have followed defeat in foreign wars. (The rise of a politicized military in Germany after World War I and in France from 1940 to 1958 is an example.) Yet equally, military dominance may arise in a period of enforced peace, when national hostilities cannot be expressed in open conflict (in Japan in the 1920's, the Balkan states in the same period, or, for that matter, in the United States today). Indeed, the aggressive behavior of more than one new state may be an effort to keep the military employed in activities abroad so that it cannot seek a domestic political role.[34]

Military rule has its advantages, but it demands that the military be strong enough to impose order on dissident opponents. Most non-Western nations, especially in Africa, are militarily weak enough that an effort to establish order by force is very difficult if not impossible.[35] Yet, if states cannot rule by force nor act forcefully abroad, they confront a future which must seem melancholy: internal social crisis finding expression in internal disorder or in guerrilla war. The leaders of the new states are likely to feel an increasing pressure to expand their military establishment, for order at home if not for adventures abroad.

Nor can the great powers rest complacent in their overawing

---

[34] D. A. Rustow, "The Military in Middle Eastern Society and Politics," in S. Fisher, ed., *The Military in the Middle East* (Columbus: Ohio State University Press, 1963).

[35] McWilliams and Polier, *loc. cit.*, p. 49.

superiority. The conflict between the Big Two limits the degree to which either can employ its massive arsenal of weapons. So long as new states restrict themselves to military violence which is not "worth" the cost of total war, the "atomic shield" of one of the opposing powers is likely to protect it. Moreover, of course, new states will increasingly be able to acquire nuclear weapons of their own, as the cost of such weapons falls and the technology for manufacturing them becomes more widely known. This appraisal is not meant to suggest that nuclear weapons are the "great equalizers" in international affairs and that new states will rival the supremacy of the great states in absolute terms. Two effects, however, seem likely to result.

First, the absolute destructiveness of nuclear weapons renders the resources of a state less relevant than the forces existing at the time combat begins. If a great state relaxes its military efforts, a small power may hope to compensate for its inherent inferiority by a greater intensity and a greater state of military mobilization. It may, moreover, hope to obtain a "technological surprise" by being the first to develop a new weapons system, if the great state relaxes its research. Neither of these developments is likely to occur. Yet either possibility makes it less likely that there can be any abatement of the arms race. Indeed, only the great powers have any clear interest in atomic disarmament, for then their inherent resources would weigh even more heavily in the international system.[36]

Second, new states may be tempted to combine the atomic shield and the conventional sword. A comparatively small nuclear force may serve to *deter* a great power which, if war broke out, it could not hope to *defeat*. The superstates, after all, have more to lose by any conflict which reached nuclear proportions. The risks of atomic war can be judged tolerable or intolerable only in relation to the gains a state hopes for and the losses it fears to suffer from such a war. Highly adventuristic policies are unlikely so long as new states feel that time is on their side; yet many may be tempted to use conventional violence, confident that a great power will not intervene if threatened with even a

[36] A. L. Burns, "International Consequences of Expecting Surprise," *World Politics, 10* (1958) , 512–536.

small-scale nuclear war and the risks of escalation. Again, such policies are unlikely to change the structure of international politics, but they are likely to encourage the great powers to increase their conventional forces so that they can respond to local threats. The result is, again, likely to be a stepped-up pace in the arms race, overriding those tendencies which have worked to limit it.[37]

Of course, it is possible that the great powers, concerned with increasing the economic and social comfort of their peoples, will refuse to follow the military logic of affairs. Yet that too is unlikely, given (1) the immense productive potential of the United States, which allows military effort without much domestic sacrifice, and (2) the comparative weakness of public opinion in influencing the government of the Soviet Union. Even if such military self-abnegation prevailed, the result would be more perilous than promising: in a world of atomic powers, "flexibility" is not to be valued over stability in international affairs.

Toward a Policy vis-à-vis the Developing Nations

Any prescriptions for policy which may be drawn from this analysis will be far from startling. In the main, they constitute the three major lines of American foreign policy to date.

1. The primary aim of a policy for the developing nations must be the assimilation of the new nations in the international order, providing *within* its institutions the sense of dignity which will otherwise be sought outside it. It is part of that task to recognize the achievements of new states which have been reached by the path of peace. It is equally necessary, when we provide assistance to new and sensitive nations, that we *ask* for something in return: He who only receives, resents. In Europe, the counterpart funds of the Marshall Plan seem to have created a sense of participation in a collective enterprise which eased feelings of dependence. Similar reciprocal elements of assistance ought to be applied to the new nations, taking due account of their resources and their attitudes. The easiest aspect of the problem is the at-

[37] Aron, *loc. cit.*, pp. 47, 50. S. F. Giffin, "Tomorrow's Military Matrix," *World Politics, 14* (1962), 433–438. M. H. Halperin, "Nuclear Weapons and Limited War," *Journal of Conflict Resolution, 5* (1961), 146–166.

tempt to ease the burdens of economic development through foreign assistance, which can serve to make the need for sacrifice less extreme and the burden of frustration less heavy. Our greatest asset, as Rapoport remarks, is the unwillingness of men to sacrifice, if we make it comparatively unnecessary to do so. Of course, it must be emphasized that economic assistance alone is not enough for states which seek dignity.

2. Second, we must bear in mind that there is a negative side to the rewards for a state which accepts the path of peace and the rule of law. There must be sanctions and penalties for those who do not. Neither we nor the Soviet Union can afford to relax our state of military preparedness, unless we can agree to impose some form of arms limitation on the developing nations *with or without their consent*. Barring such cooperation, it is important that the United States avoid taking any measure which may seem to encourage violence in the international order. This contention does not imply that we must always take a "hard line": indeed, it suggests that we must often yield without fighting what we are not prepared to defend strongly. It does suggest, however, that once fighting has begun, we must not yield to violence alone nor give the appearance of so doing.

3. We must avoid the American propensity for hostility toward regimes which do not conform to our ideal of democracy, if they seem inclined to accept the peace. Nor should we hesitate to be hostile toward any state—however liberal and democratic, popular in base, or "self-determined" in nature—whose policies and internal dynamics seem to menace the peace. Indeed, we must overcome what remains of our "contest" mentality vis-à-vis the Soviet Union, while not forgetting our very real differences with her. The future of the world depends on the great powers, who must govern and order the world if any are to do so. Perhaps the ultimate ideal is simply that the great powers should come to regard peace so highly and their own ideologies so little that they will cooperate against any state, however "aligned," which threatens that peace.

It is often asked where we acquired the right to concern ourselves with the affairs of others and to pass judgment on their regimes. It is not at all certain that we have any right, nor indeed that it is right for man to possess the powers of destruction and construction that he has arrogated to himself. Yet the demon is let loose and will not be exorcised. It belongs to the great nations to use responsibly the powers that no nation has a clear right to hold. Perhaps the greatest lesson for contemporary international politics, for ourselves, and for the developing nations is that the language of rights and of national freedoms has become outdated. The "right to rule yourself badly," which Gandhi proclaimed, is not only absurd in the modern world; it is an ideal which was never more than tawdry, a doctrine appropriate only to the international adherents of the *Triumph des Willens*. Better in fact that we ourselves seek, and encourage the developing nations to seek, a policy which begins with the understanding that in our time no nation is free and that all nations bear some measure of responsibility for the future and the destiny of man.

SELECTED
BIBLIOGRAPHY

Andrzejewski, S. *Military Organization and Society*. London: Routledge and Kegan Paul, 1954.

Chorley, Katharine. *Armies and the Art of Revolution*. London: Faber and Faber, 1943.

de la Gorce, Paul-Marie. *The French Army: A Military-Political History*. New York: Braziller, 1963.

Finer, S. E. *The Man on Horseback: The Role of the Military in Politics*. New York: Praeger, 1962.

Fischer, Sidney N., ed. *The Military in the Middle East*. Columbus: Ohio State University Press, 1963.

Goerlitz, Walter. *History of the German General Staff*. New York: Praeger, 1953.

Gutteridge, William F. *Armed Forces in New States*. London: Oxford University Press, 1962.

———. *Military Institutions and Power in the New States*. New York: Praeger, 1965.

Howard, M., ed. *Soldiers and Governments: Nine Case Studies in Civil-Military Relations*. London: Eyre and Spottiswoode, 1957.

Huntington, Samuel P. *The Soldier and the State: Theory and Politics of Civil-Military Relations*. Cambridge, Mass.: Harvard University Press, 1957.

———, ed. *Changing Patterns of Military Politics*. New York: Free Press, 1962.

Janowitz, Morris. *The Military in the Political Development of New Nations*. Chicago: University of Chicago Press, 1964.

———. *The Professional Soldier*. New York: Free Press, 1960.

———, ed. *The New Military*. New York: Russell Sage Foundation, 1964.

Johnson, John J. *The Military and Society in Latin America*. Stanford, Calif.: Stanford University Press, 1964.

————, ed. *The Role of the Military in Underdeveloped Countries*. Princeton, N.J.: Princeton University Press, 1962.

Lieuwen, Edwin. *Arms and Politics in Latin America*. New York: Praeger, 1961.

————. *Generals vs. Presidents: The New Military in Latin America*. New York: Praeger, 1964.

Millis, Walter. *Arms and Men*. New York: Putnam, 1956.

Nef, John U. *War and Human Progress*. Cambridge, Mass.: Harvard University Press, 1950.

Speier, Hans. *The Social Order and the Risks of War*. New York: George Stewart, 1952.

Stouffer, Samuel A., *et al*. *The American Soldier: Studies in Social Psychology in World War II*. 2 vols.; Princeton, N.J.: Princeton University Press, 1949.

Vatikiotis, P. J. *The Egyptian Army in Politics: Pattern for New Nations?* Bloomington: University of Indiana Press, 1961.

INDEX